£12·99

FROM REVIEWS OF THE FIRST EDITION OF *THE GREEN TRAVEL GUIDE*

'Greg Neale ... makes practical suggestions for greener tourism that go beyond giving up smoking and sticking to veg... this guide for "low-impact" tourists [is] indispensable'
The Sunday Times

'Excellent guide to being a green traveller... Tips on making conventional holidays more eco-responsible, listings for tourism organisations and embassies, and information on every area of the world'
Time Out

'With an excellent overview of the many "green holidays" on offer, *The Green Travel Guide* has its rather large heart firmly in the right place'
The Independent on Sunday

'An incredible piece of work. A guide to "green" tourism. It is certainly comprehensive. It is definitely witty, authoritative and packed with information'
Environmental Education

'*The Green Travel Guide* by Greg Neale is for you. With plenty of practical information for the concerned traveller it offers a detailed place by place guide to green holidays worldwide and highlights initiatives by NGOs and conservation groups to make tourism environmentally friendly'
Geographical

'Neale offers much practical guidance, while making an excellent contribution to the debate about the ethics of tourism'
The Guardian

"SEE KENYA - SEE AFRICA"

No other country contains a greater variety and concentration of wild animals and birds than Kenya, home of the safari - which actually means 'journey' in Swahili. There are many different types of safari and visitors are spoilt for choice when deciding how to take their safari, available on foot, by bicycle, by four-wheel drive, by camel, by horse, by ox wagon, by balloon or by classical aerial safari. Safaris can be focused on a variety of activities including the most traditional, the wildlife safari, a must for all travellers. Kenya is the ideal spot from which to catch a glimpse of the spectacular range of animals including the big five (lion, elephant, rhino, buffalo and leopard) graceful giraffe, herds of zebra, gazelle and wildebeest. Many other exciting safaris are also to be found in Kenya including bird watching, bird-shooting, fishing, photography and mountain climbing. Kenya has an amazing variety of accommodation types for the visitor on safari from basic tented camps to hotels, lodges and well known glamour spots such as the Mount Kenya Safari club, or the more spartan, but equally famous Treetops, where Princess Elisabeth learned that she had become Queen.

SAFARIS WITH A DIFFERENCE
Camel Safaris
Several different camel safaris are offered in the drier northern parts of Kenya, and are generally suspended during the rainy season. Typically the camels are led through dramatic unspoiled scenery where the visitor encounters wild animals or occasionally Samburu herdsmen or small tribal settlements. Visitors do not have to be particularly fit for these safaris. The pace and amount of riding/walking will be geared up to the group. Each evening a tented camp is set up, dinner prepared, a camp fire lit and water warmed for a bucket shower.

Hot Air Balloon Safaris
For a wonderful perspective on the wilderness we recommend visitors take an early-morning hot air balloon across the wide savannah.

Private Camping Safaris
Girl guide summer camps spring to mind when camping-and-tents are mentioned. This is not the case with Kenya's luxury private camping safaris. Tents come equipped with dressing tables and en suite bathrooms and campfire dinners are more of the candlelight soufflé variety.

THE GREEN TRAVEL GUIDE

Quality Escorted Tours Worldwide

Discover why more and more discerning travellers
are choosing Titan for their worldwide travel.

- **VIP Local Departure Service™**
  available from over 1200 UK points on
  every date - when you go is up to you.

- Best international coaching - with
  courteous and informed drivers.

- Pleasantly comfortable accommodation
  - including many top range hotels.

- Exciting itineraries expertly planned -
  we really know the countries we
  take you to.

- Highly professional tour managers -
  24 hour service and assistance.

- Absolutely NO surcharges - our
  22 years unbroken guarantee.

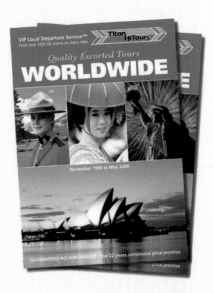

DISCOVER OUR RANGE OF COACH TOURING AND CRUISE & TOUR™ HOLIDAYS

USA • Canada • Latin America
Australia • New Zealand • Africa
Far East • Middle East • Europe

Prices from £595 - £4075

*"Thank you for a wonderful holiday.
Your reputation goes before you, but your
organisation, quality of hotels, tour manager and
driver were even better than we anticipated."*
Mr and Mrs Drummond, Newcastle.

To receive your brochure and details of how to book, please call us on 01737 760033
quoting reference *TG0199* or write to us at: Titan Travel Ltd., HiTours House,
Dept. *TG0199*, 26-30 Holmethorpe Ave, Redhill, Surrey. RH1 2NL.

Our Service Makes a World of Difference!®

THE GREEN TRAVEL GUIDE

SECOND EDITION

Greg Neale

With Trish Nicholson

  BRITISH AIRWAYS

Published in association with *The Sunday Telegraph*, British Airways
and the World Wide Fund For Nature (UK)

EARTHSCAN

Earthscan Publications Ltd, London

Second edition first published in the UK in 1999
by Earthscan Publications Ltd

First edition 1998

A catalogue record for this book is available from the British Library

ISBN: 1 85383 596 X

Every attempt has been made to ensure that the information given in this guide is accurate. Neither the author nor the publishers accept responsibility, legal or otherwise, for any inaccuracy, nor any loss arising.

Typesetting by PCS Mapping & DTP
Printed and bound by Thanet Press Ltd, Margate, Kent
Cover design by Declan Buckley

WWF-UK is a Registered Charity, No 201707
Panda logo © 1986 World Wide Fund For Nature
In the US and Canada, WWF is known as World Wildlife Fund

For a full list of publications please contact:

Earthscan Publications Ltd
120 Pentonville Road
London, N1 9JN, UK
Tel: +44 (0)171 278 0433
Fax: +44 (0)171 278 1142
Email: earthinfo@earthscan.co.uk
http://www.earthscan.co.uk

Earthscan is an editorially independent subsidiary of Kogan Page Ltd and publishes in association with WWF-UK and the International Institute for Environment and Development

This book is printed on elemental chlorine free paper

Earthscan is grateful to the following organisations and individuals for providing photographs:

Julia Bayne
British Horse Society
British Marine Industries Federation
British Trust for Conservation Volunteers
Mike Collins
Earthwatch Institute
Field Studies Council
Ed Gibbons
Nichola Gregory
Anna Hemy
Isle of Man Tourism
Rosemary Lynch
Robert Morris

The National Trust
Trish Nicholson
James Niven
Charlotte Prager
Cathy Preston
The Ramblers' Association
Sue Randall
Jenny Rawlinson
Rebecca Rogers
Sustrans
Theresa Thompson
Voluntary Service Overseas
World Wide Fund For Nature

WWF-UK Photographs
Page 1: pinnate leaf © Mattias Klum/WWF-UK
Page 3: humpback whale tail © D Murrell/WWF-UK
Page 35: circular spadefish (*Platax orbicularis*) © Jack Jackson/WWF-UK
Page 105: orange orchid (*Epidendrum radicans*) © M Rautkari/WWF-UK
Page 107: straw bales, Suffolk © Ann Simpson/WWF-UK
Page 126: pearl-bordered fritillary (*Clossiana eurphrosyne*) © J Plant/WWF-UK
Page 143: red coral trout © Charles Hood/WWF-UK
Page 148: black rhinoceros © Chris Harvey/WWF-UK
Page 160: clownfish (*Amphiprion bicinctus*) © Charles Hood/WWF-UK
Page 170: oxeye daisy © Micky White/WWF-UK
Page 181: snakelock anemone © J Archer-Thompson/WWF-UK
Page 185: scarlet macaws (*Ara macao*) © David Lawson/WWF-UK
Page 192: Indian tiger © David Lawson/WWF-UK
Page 198: pink orchid (*Phalenopsis*) © E Parker/WWF-UK
Page 202: native plant of Irian Jaya, Indonesia © Ian Craven/WWF-UK
Page 212: beach © Paul C Beetham/WWF-UK
Page 216: jewel anemone (*Corynactis viridis*) © Charles Hood/WWF-UK
Page 225: Pointe Geologie, Antarctica © J Martin Jones/WWF-UK

CONTENTS

THE TRAVELLER'S DILEMMA...

A FASHIONABLE HOTEL IN BARBADOS OR A JUNGLE RETREAT IN MALAYSIA? A COUNTRY HIDEAWAY IN SPAIN OR A CHARMING CHATEAU IN FRANCE? A GLAMOROUS RESORT IN MAURITIUS OR A TROPICAL ESCAPE IN FIJI? MAYBE EVEN A PRIVATE YACHT OR A LUXURY VILLA? CALL FOR ONE OF OUR BEAUTIFUL BROCHURES — EUROPE, WORLDWIDE, OR CARIBBEAN — AND LET ELEGANT RESORTS BE YOUR GUIDE TO THE WORLD'S MOST SOUGHT-AFTER AND ROMANTIC HOLIDAY DESTINATIONS...

LUXURY HOLIDAYS WORLDWIDE

A COLLECTION OF THE FINEST HOTELS, EACH SELECTED FOR ITS INDIVIDUAL CHARACTER AND ALL UNITED BY THEIR IMPECCABLE STANDARDS. TO DISCUSS YOUR PERSONAL REQUIREMENTS, PLEASE CALL OUR TRAVEL DESK. EUROPE: 01244 897 777. WORLDWIDE: 01244 897 888. CARIBBEAN: 01244 897 111.

ELEGANT RESORTS LTD., THE OLD PALACE, CHESTER CH1 1RB.

FROM NOW ON, WE'LL
revolutionise
THE WAY YOU BOOK
your holiday.

The TV Travel Shop is the way to check out and buy your holiday.

There are thousands of competitively-priced holidays and special offers from all the major tour operators, including Airtours, Virgin Holidays, Sunworld and First Choice, with discounts available on every single overseas holiday.

Once you've seen the holiday you want on TV, you can just call up and book it over the phone, 24 hours-a-day, seven days-a-week.

TV Travel Shop is live on satellite and cable, 6am – 5pm (before Challenge TV), then switches to transponder 56 from 6pm – 5am.

Cable viewers, contact your local operator.

To book your holiday now, call:
0870 606 0747

www.tvtravelshop.co.uk

Careful. After Kerala, you may want to drift through life forever.

Years ago, people came to Kerala in search of rare spices. Now they seek its blue seas, golden beaches and relaxing way of life.

Most visitors arrive in the state capital, Trivandrum, by air. Many then make the short journey south to find Kovalam, one of the most famous beaches in India.

Perhaps you'd prefer to make your way inland, to see hill stations, temples and acres and acres of fragrant tea at Munnar. Or to Thekkadi, an extensive sanctuary set around a huge lake, to see elephants, bison, wild boar and a host of rare birds. Even big cats if you're lucky.

No visit to Kerala is complete without taking the time to investigate Cochin with its winding streets, 500-year-old Portuguese houses, cantilevered Chinese fishing nets, a 16th century synagogue, a Dutch Palace, a museum, a fort and a port.

But it is the calm, peaceful backwater tours, drifting along mile upon mile of verdant waterways, that will beguile you. Beware, you could lose track of time altogether.

For your free colour brochure, call our brochure hotline 01233 211999 or clip the coupon below.

For a free brochure call 01233 211999 or post this coupon to, India Tourist Office, 7 Cork Street, London W1X 2LN.

Name

Address

TGT99

india
changes you

FOREWORD

Travel and tourism has an enormous capacity, both actual and potential, for much-needed economic development in every part of the world. By its very nature, however, it also has the potential for inflicting damage on fragile environments.

The industry and its customers have a deep obligation to promote the best aspects of travel and tourism and to eliminate its worst effects on the world at large.

This means an absolute commitment to sustainable development at every level – from the construction of an airport at a major city, to the creation of resort facilities on some far-flung atoll. The physical environment, both built and natural, is after all the industry's stock in trade. Damage or careless development inflicted now will not only inhibit future growth prospects, it will also devalue the travel and tourism legacy handed down to future generations.

The British Airways Tourism for Tomorrow Awards, now in their tenth year, are designed to acclaim the world's finest examples of environmental care and sustainable development, as a means of raising standards throughout the industry, across the world. They stand as a pledge of care for the future of this planet.

The Green Travel Guide, as a valuable reference work for the increasing numbers of environmentally-conscious tourists – and as a critical assessor of the industry – shares this commitment. I welcome the second edition.

Lord Marshall of Knightsbridge
Chairman, British Airways

See the World

through different eyes

Hayes and Jarvis are pleased to be able to offer a series of specialist tours from their Worldwide brochure so that you the adventurous traveller can sample the other side of our wondrous planet.

Experience the wonders of the Amazon from a jungle lodge in the Ecuadorian Orienté.

Discover the diversity of natural selection in the Galapagos Islands, or walk the savannahs of the African bush. Raise your awareness of the flora and fauna of the Costa Rican rain forests or watch the whales as they thunder from the seas off Patagonia.

Through different eyes appreciate the environmental beauty of the planet from rain forest to frozen seas in all of its natural majesty.

HAYES and JARVIS

A World of Experience

To request a brochure or receive further information
call: 0181 748 5050

Hayes & Jarvis (Travel) Ltd, 152 King Street, London W6 0QU

V1464

ACKNOWLEDGEMENTS

Thanks are due first to Trish Nicholson for her work in editing the Points on the Green Compass section of this book, amalgamating a thumbnail description of most of the world with some of the award-winning environmental tourism projects of recent years. She also contributed the section on Internet sites and drew on her own researches as an anthropologist for essays on tourism in Vietnam and the Philippines, and on wider cultural concerns.

My thanks also go to the very many people who offered advice or observations on particular aspects of travel and tourism. In particular, Tricia Barnett of Tourism Concern and Geoffrey Lipman, president of the World Travel and Tourism Council, were among those who gave generously of their time and opinions or took care to provide information on their own organisations and activities. Deborah Lurman of the World Tourism Organisation, Roger Higman at Friends of the Earth, Lynn Sloman of Transport 2000 were also helpful with suggestions and assistance for several sections, as were Hugh Somerville and his colleagues at the British Airways Environment Branch.

Frances MacDermott and her colleagues at Earthscan devoted their editorial production skills to the task of meeting late deadlines; Joanna Fraser headed the advertising team with customary energy and diplomacy. *The Sunday Telegraph* granted me unpaid leave for the final blitz on the manuscript, while Julia Braybrook, Sue Cheetham and Joyce Vetterlein provided invaluable assistance in their own fields. Finally, Sue Steward helped me through the domestic traumas of producing *The Green Travel Guide* for a second time, even while labouring on her own manuscript. To allow another author anywhere near your own word processor under such circumstances surpasseth understanding.

LIST OF BOXES

Irish hospitality begins in the air.

With more flights in and out of Ireland
than any of our competitors, and
the type of in-flight service you'd expect,
your visit really starts with us.

Aer Lingus 🍀

Ireland's National Airline.

Aer Lingus. Tel: 0845 3000 747.

ACRONYMS AND ABBREVIATIONS

ABTA   Association of British Travel Agents
AITO   Association of Independent Tour Operators
BAA   British Airports Authority
BCU   British Canoe Union
BHS   British Horse Society
BTA   British Tourist Authority
BTO   British Trust for Ornithology
CAFOD   Catholic Fund for Overseas Development
CALM   Conservation and Land Management Department (Western Australia)
CAMPFIRE   Communal Areas Management Programme for Indigenous Resources (Zimbabwe)
CART   Centre for the Advancement of Responsive Travel
CERT   Centre for Environmentally Responsible Tourism
CFC   chlorofluorocarbon
CITES   Convention on International Trade in Endangered Species (of Wild Fauna and Flora)
CNG   compressed natural gas
CO_2 carbon dioxide
CPRE   Campaign for the Protection of Rural England
CTC   Cyclists Touring Club
DETR   Department of the Environment, Transport and the Regions
ECoNETT   European Community Network for Environmental Travel and Tourism
EGA   European Golf Association
ETB   English Tourist Board
EU   European Union
FSC   Field Studies Centre
FTO   Federation of Tour Operators
IFTO   International Federation of Tour Operators
ILO   International Labour Organization
IPCC   Intergovernmental Panel on Climate Change
IUCN   The World Conservation Union
IWA   Inland Waterways Association
LPG   liquid petroleum gas
MCS   Marine Conservation Society
MoT   Ministry of Transport
NGO   non-governmental organisation

Dragon Bay

PORT ANTONIO

THE BEST KEPT SECERET IN JAMAICA...

There are many ways to reach Port Antonio, the true unspoilt Jamaica.

The closest international airport is Kingston - Norman Manley. A private transfer from Kingston to Dragon Bay takes approximately two hours. From Montego Bay the drive is approximately four hours, a great way to see Jamaica. Alternatively, from Montego Bay's Donald Sangster International you can take a twenty-five minute flight with Jamaica Express to Portland, then a twenty minute ground transfer by courtesy bus to Dragon Bay.

Once you arrive at Dragon Bay you will be welcomed by one of the friendly receptionists. Prior to showing you to your accommodation you are required to complete a registration form and leave an imprint of your credit card which enables you to make telephone calls and sign for incidentals during your stay.

For those who know Dragon Bay

well, there have been many improvements over the last two years. A total refurbishment of the property has been completed. All 30 villas have been fully upgraded with telephone and air-conditioned bedrooms, the thatched roofs have been replaced with terracotta tiles complementing the Mediterranean style setting. The honeymoon suite with four-poster bed was originally the private residence of Prince Alfonso Hohenlohe and the panoramic views of the turquoise sea are the ideal setting for a memorable Caribbean Wedding or Honeymoon experience to be cherished for ever!

Now located in the central building is a new 'British Bar', TV Room, Beauty Therapy Centre and Gym; and of course on the beach is the 'Cruise Bar' where the bar scenes in 'Cocktail' were filmed with Tom Cruise. In addition there are plans, in the not too distant future, to rebuild the 'disco' on the hill.

Dragon Bay goes green - in February

1997 the hotel was awarded a Certificate of Excellence for Progress in Environmental Management for significant improvement of the marine eco system of the Port Antonio Marine Park. The water quality in the area off Dragon Bay has improved to such an extent that the reef is steadily regenerating. To date this is the only known case of reef recovery in Jamaica, therefore snorkelling and scuba diving are excellent.

Dragon Bay
PORT ANTONIO

FOR INFORMATION OR RESERVATIONS CONTACT:
Dragon Bay, P.O. Box 176, Port Antonio, Parish of Portland, Jamaica, West Indies. Tel: +1 (809) 993 8514 or 8516/7 Fax: +1 (809) 993 3284
UK - The Caribbean Centre Fax: +44 (181) 940 7424
Email: jan@caribean.its.net
USA Reservations 1 800 6333284

NO$_x$	nitrogen oxide
PATA	Pacific-Asia Travel Association
RGS	Royal Geographical Society
RSPB	Royal Society for the Protection of Birds
RSPCA	Royal Society for the Prevention of Cruelty to Animals
RYA	Royal Yachting Association
SSSI	Site of Special Scientific Interest
TRAFFIC	Trade Records Analysis of Fauna and Flora in Commerce
TT	Tourist Trophy
UNEP	United Nations Environment Programme
UNEPIE	UNEP Industry and Environment Programme
UNESCO	United Nations Educational, Scientific and Cultural Organisation
VSO	Voluntary Service Overseas
WTO	World Tourism Organization
WTTC	World Travel and Tourism Council
WWF	World Wide Fund For Nature
YHA	Youth Hostels Association

INTRODUCTION

What's in a name? When the first edition of *The Green Travel Guide* was published in spring 1998, it stirred considerable debate – not least, over the title and its implications. Can you have 'green' – ie, environmentally sustainable – travel, tourism and holidays? Surely we know the damage that modern-day mass-transport and tourism does: polluted beachlines, once-undisturbed hillsides now scarred by the paths of numberless walkers, package-holiday jet planes churning out more pollution into the atmosphere, formerly tranquil fishing villages now concrete canyons that reverberate every summer's evening to the beery brayings of tee-shirted tourists? How can anyone taking a holiday think they can be environmentally responsible? The arguments long preceded the book, of course, and will continue to be debated: is it better, environmentally, for tourism to be confined into traditional holiday areas, leaving the rest of the planet relatively untouched by people travelling for their own enjoyment? Can any form of transport be described as green? Just how eco-friendly is so-called ecotourism? Are our holidays doomed to turn today's heaven into tomorrow's hell?

It is impossible – and certainly outside the scope of this book – to offer definitive answers to these questions. What this book tries to offer, however, are suggestions on how we can enjoy our travel and holidays while trying to ensure that we are as aware as we can be of the impact we are making – to become, in other words, 'green travellers', whether we are taking a traditional fortnight by the sea in Britain or ranging off the beaten track in the wilds of South America.

The book proposes two definitions of green travel. The first, as already suggested, is that we look at our normal holiday and travel habits from an environmental point of view, to see whether they can be improved. So in Chapter 1, we look at ways of becoming greener travellers, even when taking conventional holidays – looking more closely at how we can save time, energy and money, and at the same time enjoy our holidays more. Chapter 1 examines subjects such as the different ways we can travel when we go on holiday, the energy and resources we use, from the moment we decide where we want to go, to the day we return home. It also looks at some other issues that modern travel and holidaymaking raise, from human rights to sex tourism; from nature conservation to the clash of cultures.

The second type of green travel is the subject of Chapter 2 – the increasing range of holidays and breaks that are available for people who are interested in the environment in a broad sense. Here you will find details of holidays far from the stereotype of 'sand, sun and sex' (though these ingredients are not necessarily excluded): holidays spent working as a conservation volunteer amid the coral reefs of the Caribbean or on the canals of the English Midlands; wildlife watching in West Africa, or repairing dry-stone walling in the Yorkshire Dales. There are suggestions for spiritual breaks, healing and holistic holidays, as well as sections on such sports as sailing, surfing and cycling – all forms of activity where people enjoy being in a clean, healthy environment and are prepared to do their bit to keep it that way.

This edition of *The Green Travel Guide* is not intended as a conventional guide book, to take with you on your holiday. But in addition to offering information on how to be a greener traveller, and suggesting different types of green holidays, it has also been designed to help focus on and encourage some of the better examples of good environmental practice in holidaymaking around the world. To try to do this more effectively, this edition includes a round-the-world section, Section two: Points on the Green Compass, which looks briefly at the various environmental attractions for holidaymakers in Britain, continental Europe and further afield, and includes a selection of award-winning tourism schemes. We also include new information about groups and organisations that are campaigning to raise environmental standards – whether as pressure groups, trade organisations, governments or companies, updating some material from the first edition. And there is also a selection of Internet sites and suggestions for further reading.

Amid the reviews that greeted the first edition, one writer – surprisingly, in the members' magazine of a well-known environmental campaigning group – sounded surprised to find that there is a large body of academic writing on tourism. This book is not intended as an academic work, though it is, we hope, a serious contribution to an important debate. Nor is it intended to be excessively 'preachy'. You don't have to wear a hair-shirt to enjoy the environment – a mistake some green groups can sometimes be accused of making. Instead, we hope that *The Green Travel Guide* can help to suggest ways in which we can enjoy our holidays and our travel even more: by becoming green travellers. It is not a guide book to any country or region, nor the last word on any sport or pastime, but it does suggest sources of information for those.

Again, while *The Green Travel Guide* carries examples of holiday schemes and other projects that have won awards, as well as advertisements for holiday companies and other organisations, this does not imply any editorial endorsement. It goes without saying that no undertakings of favourable comment have been given, and no endorsement of any company, holiday, service or organisation advertising in this book is implied.

We hope that *The Green Travel Guide* will become a regular publication, helping to improve environmental standards in one of the world's biggest industries, while helping readers better enjoy their holidays and travel. We welcome comments from readers – whether on particular holiday experiences, or suggestions for other areas of coverage. Please write to *The Green Travel Guide*, c/o Earthscan Publications, 120 Pentonville Road, London, N1 9JN.

Note: In keeping with Earthscan style, while most addresses and telephone numbers given in *The Green Travel Guide* are for the United Kingdom, telephone numbers are given with the international direct dial prefix ie, '+44', and the local code in brackets, normally missing the initial '0' – eg, '(171)' for inner London, where callers within the UK will add the '0'. To avoid repetition, we omit the line 'UK' from addresses. Internet addresses omit the 'http://' prefix.

It's no use being the world's favourite airline if there's nowhere left worth visiting.

British Airways are holding the annual Tourism for Tomorrow Awards, which recognise environmentally responsible tourism around the world. Because we don't just look at things from 40,000 feet up. For further information contact: British Airways Plc, Environment Branch, Waterside (HBBG), PO Box 365, Harmondsworth, West Drayton, UB7 0GB.

BRITISH AIRWAYS
The world's favourite airline

THE BRITISH AIRWAYS 'TOURISM FOR TOMORROW' AWARD SCHEME

It is impossible to offer more than a subjective impression of praiseworthy attempts to combine environmental conservation around the world in the limited space of a book such as this. In this edition of *The Green Travel Guide*, therefore, we list at the end of each section in this part of the book, details of projects which have won awards in the Tourism for Tomorrow scheme, run by British Airways.

The lists of award winners at the end of each chapter are not intended to be read as league tables. The categories adopted here relate to the point of impact of award-winning projects, or to their strategic significance in the wider environment and development context. The listings offer benchmark examples of better or improved (as distinct from 'best') practice. Note that for every award winner there have been 15 to 20 projects nominated or shortlisted for awards, all worthy in their way of note and praise, to say nothing of ventures that have not so far put themselves forward for awards.

'The Tourism for Tomorrow scheme can't claim to have run a complete health check on award-winning schemes,' explains Dr Hugh Somerville, British Airways' Head of Environment. 'The judging panels, chosen from a broad cross-section of tourism and environment professionals, do examine winning entrants thoroughly and finalists for the Global Award are interviewed in depth by the Global Award judging panel. But there's no absolute endorsement implied by the awards. We simply recognise certain examples of better practice that look to the experienced eye of selectors as though they deserve to be applauded and emulated around the industry.'

The listings of award winners at the end of each chapter of Section Two of the Guide are grouped into countries, but in no specific order. Entries are based on citations supplied by British Airways, which has run the scheme since 1992, and by the Federation of Tour Operators, which mainly administered the scheme before then. For reasons of space, only those awards won since 1994 are included. Where available and appropriate, note is made of main tourism attractions or award-winning distinctions and latest contact details (where available) at the time of going to press. Enquiries should be made direct to listed companies and organisations, not to the publishers of this Guide. British Airways welcomes feedback from readers on any of projects listed here. Contact: British Airways 'Tourism for Tomorrow Awards', Waterside (HBBG), PO Box 365, Harmondsworth, West Drayton, UB7 0GB (Fax: +44 (181) 738 9850).

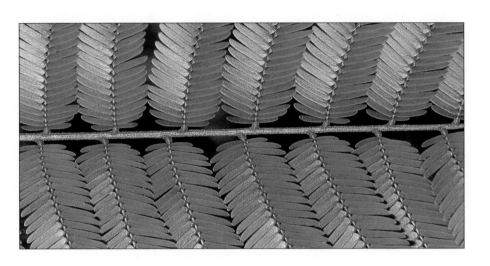

SECTION ONE
THE GREENER
HOLIDAY

CHAPTER 1

HOW CAN WE BECOME
GREENER TRAVELLERS?

Why do we take or keep holidays? It's not as simple a question as it sounds. Since the beginnings of ordered society, special times, dates and events in the calendar have become special, to be marked or celebrated, venerated or kept holy. It might be the time at which the seasons began to change – from dark winter to spring – or a date associated with a formal event in the religious calendar – a saint's day, perhaps. Most religions have a special day of the week, such as the Christian Sunday, which is traditionally kept special, as well as annual festivals, such as Easter, or the Muslim month of Ramadan. Today, in an increasingly secular world, we still cherish our holidays as times to enjoy ourselves, by ourselves or with friends, family and others.

Travel has also evolved as holiday activity. Just as medieval pilgrims journeyed to distant sacred sites – pilgrimages still followed today – so nowadays we try to take time each year to go away on holiday. And over the centuries, whether as a means of expressing wealth and classical education, for satisfying curiosity or indulging a sense of adventure, or simply taking a break from work in order to relax and revive ourselves, so holidays have become an important part of our leisure, even as they take different forms. In Classical times, wealthy Romans visited the temples of Greece, or marvelled at the buildings – already antiquities – of Egypt. In the 18th century, aristocratic young Englishmen took the Grand Tour of Europe, travelling through France and Switzerland, often with a tutor accompanying them, to complete their classical education amid the glories of Rome. It was a route to be increasingly followed by the middle classes in the 19th century, as Thomas Cook's tour company made use of the newly developed railways and steamships to take travellers further afield. In this century, amid the campaigns of trade unions and reforms of governments for working people to win the right to paid holidays, millions more have enjoyed holidays away from home – carried by train, by motor coach, by car or by passenger jet.

According to the World Tourism Organization (WTO), a United Nations body, the numbers of people travelling abroad rose from 25 million in 1950 to 563 million in 1995.[1]

1 WTO, *Tourism 2020 Vision*, 1998

In 1996, the figure rose to 595 million, and although the effects of the Asian economic crisis slowed down that growth, the WTO's most recent estimates are that in 1997 some 612 million people travelled abroad. When you consider that about 70 per cent of such journeys are made for pleasure rather than for business or other reasons, it becomes clear how important an industry travel and tourism has become. In 1997, the WTO estimates that tourism receipts represented almost one-third of the value of world trade in the service sector.[2]

2 WTO, *Tourism Highlights 1997*, 1998

This massive growth has economic implications. The World Travel and Tourism Council (WTTC) has estimated that by the year 2005, the travel industry will have created employment for 305 million people and be producing 11.4 per cent of world gross domestic product. Looking even further ahead, the WTO predicted in 1998 that annual international tourist arrivals will rise to 673 million by the year 2,000, top 1 billion by 2010 and reach 1.6 billion in the year 2020.[3]

3 WTO, *Tourism 2020 Vision*, 1998

At the same time, the tourism industry seeks to continue this pattern of growth. Advertising 'new' resorts and destinations as 'unspoiled paradises' all too often encourages customers by implication to go there before they are 'spoiled'. 'As the world becomes increasingly explored, and fewer "new" destinations are left for tourists to discover, there is a trend to travel to high places, under water, the ends of the earth or off the planet itself,' the WTO says.[4]

4 WTO, *Tourism 2020 Vision*, 1998

More tourists are taking guided mountain tours, more companies offering submarine excursions; more visitors travelling to the previously inaccessible polar regions. Some travel operators are even now talking of tourist trips in space – at first in ultra-high-altitude planes, experiencing zero-gravity, but within a decade by low-orbital rocket.

What does this increased travel and tourism mean for our environment? Of course, new developments in technology, resource management and regulating demand, such as more efficient jet engines, using solar power to generate electricity, installing toilets that use less water, or encouraging off-season tourism – all these can help reduce the impact on the environment of our fondness for travel. But even so, the toll of unregulated tourism and travel is a serious one:

■ An estimated 70 per cent of international travel trips are for pleasure. This can mean a vast expenditure of energy, and a colossal amount of transport-generated pollution. According to one estimate, air travel alone is responsible for at least 5–6 per cent of the global warming caused by the emission of 'greenhouse gas' pollution – and it could be as much as 10 per cent, more than half the global warming potential of the pollution caused by cars and other road transport. Together, aircraft and cars, two of our favourite means of travel when we go on holiday, are carrying a large part of the responsibility for the pollution that a majority of scientists now believe is causing change in the Earth's climate patterns, while car exhaust pollution is a major source of the smog-causing gases and chemical particulates doctors have linked with respiratory and other diseases.

■ Tourism – even the so-called eco-tourism of nature-watching – can put undue pressure on some of the world's most fragile natural environments. In Snowdonia, the Lake District and the Peak District, the tramping feet of tens of thousands of hillwalkers each year has caused serious erosion to some mountain paths. In the Galapagos Islands, off the Pacific coast of Ecuador, conservationists have been fighting a long drawn-out action to persuade the Ecuadorian authorities to limit the number of tourists admitted each year – currently around 60,000 – because of fears that the associated extra pollution, plus the sheer numbers of visitors tramping across the islands, could be a threat to the existence of rare species, such as the marine iguanas, giant tortoises and various bird species found there. Tourist litter, such as discarded plastic bags and bottles, kills unwary wildlife around the world. In Greece and some other Mediterranean countries, the building of tourist hotels and discos has disrupted turtles nesting on some nearby beaches.

■ The built environment of historic towns and cities can be degraded by unregulated, excess tourism. Some Italian cities are now taking measures to limit the numbers of tourist buses allowed into their centres, fearing that the noise, exhaust emissions and vibrations would damage ancient buildings.

■ Mass tourism can damage local cultures and economies. In East Africa, Maasai tribal people were moved from some of their traditional areas to make way for new national parks – a key attraction for tourists wanting to see the region's famous wildlife. In Kenya and in Goa, there have been cases of water sources traditionally used by local people being diverted to supply newly built tourist hotels and lodges. In Thailand and the Philippines, tens of thousands of young girls – and some young boys, too – have been caught up in the prostitution which initially sprang up to cater for American troops during the Vietnam War but which is now part of a 'sex tourism' industry, often controlled by criminal gangs. In more remote parts of the world, indigenous peoples fear that even the development of nature or 'eco-tourism' is part of a process that will threaten their lands and autonomy, leaving them as mere exotic sights for the tourists. Even in western Europe there have been protests that tourism, while benefiting local economies, can get out of hand. In November 1998, some islanders in Majorca planned demonstrations calling for a limit to further tourist developments, amid rows over new building, water shortages and the sale of large numbers of homes and farms on the island to foreign visitors.[5]

5 'Majorcans say no to any more tourism', *Independent on Sunday*, 8 November 1998

It can be a bleak picture. But just as there are positive signs – which we examine later in this Guide – that the travel and tourism industry, helped by green groups, conservation organisations and governments, is improving its performance, so the individual traveller or tourist can make a difference. A well-known environmental slogan for the green traveller is, 'Take only photographs, leave only footprints'. How can we achieve this (and even better, leave rather lighter footprints)?

Photo © VSO/Mark Hakonsson

Buying village crafts at a fair price supports the local economy

BOX 1.1

CULTURAL AWARENESS FOR TRAVELLERS

Mark Twain's assurance that 'Travel is fatal to prejudice' is valid only if we travel with an open mind and a willingness to accept and respect other people's ways of doing and thinking. The growing popularity of cultural and ethnic tourism, and the search for 'real' cultural experiences, leads the stranger into ever more intimate areas of people's lives. Watching a religious festival, witnessing a village wedding, or visiting a local home to see how people live, can be exciting experiences. But there can be a price to be paid by the host communities – loss of privacy; less time for food production, child care and other essential tasks, and the often unsettling comparison between the wealth and freedom of the tourist and their own quality of life.

Cultural responses to tourist exposure vary enormously and are greatly influenced by the scale and speed of tourism development, and the social and economic situation of the host community. For example, in some situations, traditions of hospitality and the need to preserve family honour may oblige local people to give more to strangers than they can afford. Rules of hospitality, based on mutual trust and reciprocity, are essential for the long term security and survival within and between many communities. But when hospitality, based on cultural values, is tapped by tourism based on commercial values, exploitation can easily result. The transience and observable wealth of tourists can also change local attitudes towards strangers. Locals may develop a 'tourist culture' and a 'catch while you can' approach to the tourist dollar which can result in aggressive selling and blatant over-charging.

When travel brochures highlight 'culture', they often make a special feature of local festivals and rituals. Indeed prices are usually higher for these dates. But such cultural events, often combining elements of burlesque with sacred rites, are usually more than just spectacles and colourful performances. They may act out important values and beliefs, and have deep spiritual significance for participants and the community as a whole. When such events become reoriented towards a tourist audience, market values can overwhelm cultural values which the rituals were intended to represent. In Marinduque Island in the Philippines for example, spectacular Easter rituals – Moryonan – which re-enact the Passion of Christ, were promoted by politicians as a tourist attraction. A new emphasis on quality of performance and presentation excluded many traditional participants, made significant changes in time and place of the rituals, and turned a street dramatisation into a formal staged performance. Only in the little town of Mogpog, where the local participants kept control of their rituals, is Moryonan enacted as it has been since the late 19th century. Although it is a natural process for all cultures to undergo change, where cultural representations are controlled by local communities themselves rather than by government or tourist agencies, change is more likely to retain values and meanings important to the community.

But culture is more than festivals and rituals, or even exotic foods and art forms. It is about how people perceive the meanings of their lives and how their lives are lived. These perceptions, beliefs and values are negotiated and acted out in every relationship and social encounter. So it is with tourists who are themselves representations of their own cultures. There is ample scope for misunderstanding, frustration and offence, though, thankfully, this can be reduced by the common sense and inherent courtesy of local hosts who make allowances for foreigners' lack of local knowledge. Maximising our own knowledge and courtesy will greatly enhance our understanding and enjoyment of other cultures.

Despite potential difficulties, close encounters of the cultural kind can be enriching on both sides if we take special care to make sure it is, and to avoid the 'human zoo' approach and the exploitation that goes along with it. The following suggestions are intended to help the discerning traveller achieve this balance:

Visiting Villages and Special Events

- Examine your motives for visiting villages, homes and rituals; idle curiosity or the fact that they are advertised may not justify disturbing people's work and privacy.
- Avoid wandering into fields, villages, or ritual places on your own. If you really need to get this close, find a guide who speaks the language and can negotiate permission, take his/her advice about how to behave and appropriate ways to show appreciation to your hosts.
- On set tours, check with the organisers that communities have agreed to the visit and are expecting your group; also check that they are being fairly compensated for their time and disturbance.
- Choose a tour company which employs and trains people from the villages as guides and interpreters.
- Buying village products can boost local income, but check first that items are produced for sale; poor people may feel pressed to sell household necessities or ritual objects because of their need for cash or to oblige visitors out of traditional hospitality.
- Ask your guide's advice about gifts to take on a village or home visit. It is usually better to give, for example, school materials or local food treats, as a group through a village leader or household head, than to encourage children to beg, or distribute sweets where there may be no dental service.
- Prepare yourself beforehand with background information and enough local phrases to at least respond to greetings and farewells with courtesy and respect.

Taking Photographs

- Always ask permission before taking close shots of people, ritual events, or special places like shrines. You don't have to speak the dialect, just pointing to your camera with a questioning glance is enough. If people seem at all reluctant, or look away, don't. In some cultures, for example among some hill tribes in South East Asia, babies and small children are believed to be at special risk if exposed to photography, so be careful not to cause unnecessary heartache through thoughtlessness.

■ People often appreciate being sent a copy of a photograph you have taken of them. They may ask, but it is nice to offer. But if you say you will do so, be sure to keep your promise.

■ Avoid using flash or spot lamps to photograph textiles, murals, temple interiors and so on, even if there is no official notice to say so, because it accumulates damage to pigments and surface finish. Instead, use a light, collapsible tripod and take a long exposure - you'll get much better results anyway. And don't use a flash in people's faces!

■ Ask before taking photographs from unusual angles; for some people, for example, ethnic minorities in Vietnam, a camera placed on the floor (to take a ceiling shot for example) is extremely offensive. This may apply to others too, so check before you click.

Shopping for Bargains

■ Shop till you drop if you must, but try to buy locally made products, and shop in locally owned outlets. That way, more of the economic benefits are retained by the community.

■ Where haggling over price is customary, this can be an enjoyable encounter for vendor and shopper alike, but don't beat people down too hard. It is not true that no trader will sell at a loss; both retention of personal dignity, and immediate needs for cash, can force vendors to sell goods at less than cost.

■ Ask your guide or other local people for guidance on prices, to avoid either being over-charged, or inadvertently exploiting others because your gender or status as a foreigner gives you greater bargaining power.

■ Travelling vendors, often women and children, can be among the poorest people and their need makes them particularly vulnerable. If you do not wish to buy, don't play around; be polite but firm in declining, so they can use their time more profitably on more enthusiastic shoppers.

■ Where there are many vendors, market stalls and local shops, don't give all your custom to only one, spread your purchases around to benefit others also.

Sight-seeing and Getting Around

■ Public transport is often crowded and in short supply. Drivers may try to give preference to foreigners, but be considerate of local passengers struggling to get to work or market.

- Some countries have a two-tier fare structure so that local people pay less than tourists for public transport. Pay up graciously, and don't assume this gives you special privileges.
- Dress respectfully at sacred places, and inside buildings or crowded spaces. For example, you may have to remove your shoes or cover your head, and women may need to cover their arms and shoulders. Carry a scarf and long-sleeved top to be prepared. As a general guide, shorts, sun-tops and skimpy summer wear are rarely suitable away from the beach. But ask and follow local advice.
- Avoid displays of conspicuous consumption – expensive jewellery and watches, state-of-the-art personal stereos. Apart from the possible incitement to robbery, it accentuates the gap between rich and poor and distances you from the cultures you came to experience.
- Keep handy a few photographs of family and friends back home; local people you meet and talk with will appreciate you sharing with them some aspect of your own culture.
- Take with you some postcards of your home area; these make ideal small gifts to show appreciation or to mark a friendly encounter.
- However friendly people are, to avoid causing offence or worse, don't hug and kiss everyone until you have checked out local customs on touching. Also non-verbal expressions often have different, even opposite, meanings in another culture. For example, don't use the thumbs-up sign in Greece (there, it is equivalent to the 'two-fingers' sign in Britain); or pat children on the head in Thailand (the head is a very special and spiritual part of the body); or point with your finger in Malaysia (it is considered very bad manners), but you can stick your tongue out in Tibet – it is the traditional form of greeting, especially in the remoter areas.
- Learn a few phrases of the local language. At the very least your stumbling efforts to show willing will raise a smile and break the ice.
- When things go wrong, being assertive and raising your voice is guaranteed to make them worse. Other cultures have different concepts of time and the situation may not be as straightforward as you think. In all of Asia and most of the developing world, a smile and a little humility go a long way.
- In many countries public places also have zones of privacy which should be respected. This is particularly so around public water pumps, and along river banks and canals where people may wash themselves and their clothes. Also, small shrines and other sacred sites may be in places you don't expect. Read about the culture, ask the locals, and be sensitive to what is going on around you.

Enjoy 'being there', and ensure that those you meet on the way have enjoyed your being there too.

Trish Nicholson

BOX 1.2

THE BAD AND THE UGLY

A sobering overview of the damage tourism can do is contained in *Beyond the Green Horizon*, a discussion paper on principles for sustainable tourism commissioned by the World Wide Fund for Nature in Britain from the organisation Tourism Concern. Among its points are:

■ Although there is increasing awareness of tourism's adverse impacts, its growth continues. Often the tourism industry is marked by short-term considerations. 'Tourism, perhaps more than any other activity, depends on quality human and natural environments and resources. Yet in general it is characterised by rapid, short-term development – the "boom-and-bust" syndrome – which more often than not damages those very assets it seeks to exploit and, having wreaked havoc, simply moves off elsewhere,' the paper says.

■ Tourism can be a powerful force for conservation – there are more than 5,000 national parks, wildlife sanctuaries and reserves around the world today, many depending on tourism for their financial support – but it can equally damage species and their habitats. In parts of the Mediterranean, for example, turtle nesting sites have been destroyed to make way for hotels.

■ Tourism development can destroy the natural resources that a local community depends upon. For example, in Indonesia, sewage pollution has damaged coral reefs in Bali, leaving beaches vulnerable to erosion. Transport pollution is blamed for damage to Alpine forests, leading to soil erosion, while tourist litter and human waste have contaminated the mountain streams in Nepal that locals depend upon for fresh water.

■ Local people are often the direct victims of tourism development. In Malaysia, for example, fishing families on the island of Langkawi were evicted to make way for new hotels. 'Powerful tourism interests have from time to time managed to persuade, buy or bribe governments and ministers and force people off their land,' says *Beyond the Green Horizon*. 'The story is repeated from Colombo (Sri Lanka) to Baguio (Philippines), from Bali (Indonesia) to Langkawi (Malaysia), from Honolulu to Hongkong.'

■ Local cultures can also suffer. Sacred sites make way for hotels or golf courses, traditional values are commercialised for the benefit of the visitor. 'Visitors to the Philippines may enjoy being treated to a "typical Filipino dance" with Filipino dancers wearing mock Hawaiiian grass skirts, clicking Spanish castanets and dancing who knows what … what this does to native culture is another matter.'

Of course, in the end, tourists and travellers also suffer from this process.

Source: Eber, S (ed) (1992) *Beyond the Green Horizon: Principles for Sustainable Tourism*, WWF

HINTS FOR GREEN TRAVELLERS

Before You Go

Do You Really Need That Holiday?

It might sound daft, but some of the reasons we give for taking a holiday suggest that there are better alternatives. Many of us can't wait to get away from work for our summer or winter breaks – but in some cases, if it is only the prospect of an annual holiday that makes a job tolerable, it might seriously be worth examining your job, and what it is doing to your physical or psychological health. Although much current employment is insecure, marked by short-term contracts, increased pressure and more work for smaller workforces, some people are finding an alternative in 'downshifting', or changing the way they work. Some are beginning to work part-time from choice, not necessity, possibly working from home, using computers to link them to their former office; as home-based freelances, consultants or self-employed workers rather than employees. While this trend is still that of a relative minority – and should be distinguished from those people who want traditional full-time employ-ment but are being made redundant as their bosses 'down-size' – the indications are that it is a growing one. In a recent book, *Getting a Life: A Downshifter's Guide to Happier, Simpler Living*, authors Polly Ghazi and Judy Jones point out that this new lifestyle has its own advantages and attractions. One advantage of such a way of living is that it releases you from the conventional constraints of employed work patterns. You may simply not feel the need for conventional holidays; or if you want to travel, you can do so at times of the year more convenient to you; away from the crowds.

A Question of Timing

It may not always be open to you, particularly if you have children, or are tied to taking your holidays at the same time of year, each year, but consider the advantages of holidays taken off-season. Economically, you can usually save money; and you will find you are not simply one of the crowd. That in turn means you are likely to be placing less pressure on the environment – leaving a lighter footprint – particularly if you opt for a holiday that is not so dependent on seasonal weather. You don't have to be a sun-seeker.

Short Breaks or Long?

If you can, consider the advantages of taking shorter breaks, possibly closer to home. Not using up your annual allowance in two or three blocks means less time until the next break, while shorter journeys are less energy consuming, and can often be made by public transport. Conversely, if you are planning a long-haul trip, see whether it is possible to take a longer holiday, possibly travelling off-peak: this has the advantage of giving you the chance to holiday at a more civilised pace, and in the long run can also cut down on the number of costly trips you may have to make. Rather than several intercontinental holidays to the same part of the world over two or three years, see whether it might be possible to arrange one longer excursion, with some of your travelling being done by rail, bus, boat, bike or even on foot.

Take a Different Type of Holiday

This is probably the option for people who are aware of the limitations of conventional holidays – the crowds, the pressure, the wearing damage to the environment – but are not taking the 'downshifting' route. Change your attitudes to holidays and you can not only benefit the environment, but as a Green Traveller enjoy yourself in ways you may not have thought possible.

Stay at Home

From time to time, particularly if you can take some short breaks or holidays, stay at home rather than travel simply because 'a holiday means going abroad'. You could be pleasantly surprised to find out a little more about the area where you live, or use local transport systems to make short journeys that reveal new attractions on your doorstep.

Take a Greener Holiday

There are alternatives to the conventional 'two weeks abroad, on the beach by day and in the bar by night' holiday – popular though that can be. Take your environmental interests further by exploring some of the many different types of break we discuss in Chapter 2 of this book. Go diving in the Caribbean – but as a volunteer working on a conservation project, helping scientists and local governments devise ways to preserve the coral reefs. Take a short break to learn a new skill, such as dry-stone walling with one of the conservation organisations that help preserve our historic buildings and landscapes. Work with other volunteers restoring a canal (they lack beaches, but not canal-side pubs). Support wildlife conservation through trips with some of the more responsible safari or wildlife-watching companies. Take a course with groups such as the Field Studies Council, learning new environmental, craft or arts skills. If you want to travel further afield, join one of the expedition organisations – in a remote wilderness, you may be able to help a scientific research project, at the same time developing your own self-knowledge. If you want a longer journey, consider taking a year or two off work – many employers support such schemes – on a volunteer or exchange scheme abroad. And if you fancy a more active holiday, give the beach a miss and take a holiday that puts you in touch with the countryside – hill trekking or hostelling, cycling or horse riding off the beaten track. For more information on these options, see Chapter 2, Greener Holidays.

Green Your Travelling

Whatever holiday you finally decide on, try following some of the suggestions in this chapter: they can help make a difference.

Package Holiday or Independent Traveller?

Another choice you may have before booking your holiday is whether to take an 'all-in' package, which will include your transport to your destination (usually the flight, together with any connecting bus or other service), accommodation and breakfast or other meal. Increasingly, however, the travel industry is seeing many tour operators seek to offer all-inclusive packages which give you more – three meals a day rather than just a pre-paid breakfast, together with such 'extras' as trips, outings to nearby attractions, and perhaps even something towards a bar bill. This form of one-stop shopping may have the attraction of giving you a full package for an apparently competitive price, but it is worth remembering that a disadvantage of many inclusive packages is that much of the profit is repatriated back to the company with whom you make the booking. It concentrates economic buying power in the hands of the tour operators, to the exclusion of many local people in the holiday destination, and it favours the bigger hotel chains, restaurants and local businesses which can become the tour company's favoured supplier. While this certainly can make for savings for the tourist, it can help distort local economies. The government in the West African state of The Gambia, for example, has expressed its concern at moves by European tour companies to move towards all-inclusive holiday packages.

Another reason for taking a more independent course in your holiday planning is that it may allow you to take a different means of transport, take more local decisions when you are actually on holiday, and also travel off the beaten track. Often a smaller, more specialist holiday company may be able to offer you something that may not be as cheap, but is more in tune with what you really want to do. And one advantage that smaller holiday or tour operators have is that they can cater for travellers with specialist interests. Travelling independently also means you generally have a chance to see more, and meet more people locally, while the environmental standards of your journey may also be higher. Many students, young people and others, for example, who take advantage of concessionary fares to travel around Europe by train, staying in hostels, camp sites or cheap hotels and eating in local cafes, are more likely to experience life away from the regular tourist tracks than holidaymakers who book a package, fly to their resort and seldom venture beyond it. And again, if you take a journey in your own time, at your own pace, it becomes less of a commodity, more of an experience to be savoured.

Booking your Holiday

You have an idea about the type of holiday you'd like, or maybe just where you think you'd like to go. But before you make the booking, there are other sources of information, to help you make up your mind.

Advertising

How truthful are the holiday company adverts? Some still employ the old images of 'undiscovered paradise', with pictures of glistening white beaches and sunny, clear blue skies. Obviously, commercial companies are not going to undersell their services, but you deserve to know more, particularly about a wider range of environmental issues that could affect your holiday. Some companies are better than others in this respect. In 1997, for example, the travel company Thomson began a marketing campaign that included more balanced customer comments, rather than the traditional over-the-top testimonials. A willingness by a travel or holiday company to include material about environmental issues is a sign that it takes them to be important. Abercrombie & Kent, a leading wildlife safari company, now includes guidelines issued by the Friends of Conservation group together with some of its advertising brochures. And in one example of no-nonsense prose, the Emerald Forest Expeditions company described how some of its trips into the rainforest of eastern Ecuador were not only chances for visitors to see the beauty and diversity of the region, but also 'to experience the deforested areas caused by the pursuit of petroleum in this fragile ecosystem, and the consequences of slash-and-burn agriculture. See first hand what is being done by the oil industry and how this experience can be used to educate others about the importance of conservation and preservation.' A similar refusal to avoid issues tourist brochures normally neglect comes in the 1998/9 brochure of Fundani Township Tours, a South African company. While its tours include the conventional trips to wildlife reserves, it doesn't omit to point out the sites where black South Africans were forcibly removed from their homes during the apartheid era. They describe one tour, of Port Elizabeth, as 'the tour of two contrasting worlds in one country – visit the bold, the beautiful and the ugly.' Some organisations now specialise in 'alternative' tourism, as a deliberate contrast to conventional holiday-making.

Green Schemes and Certification

In recent years, some tourism organisations and non-governmental organisations (NGOs) have begun to develop various training programmes and award schemes designed to improve environmental standards. When you study the brochures, or visit a travel agency, look for evidence of this. For example, the World Travel and Tourism Council (WTTC), an industry body with its headquarters in London, has set up the Green Globe programme, which aims to help travel and tourism companies improve their environmental standards. The programme helps participating companies exchange information about new technologies and best practice. Linked to this is Green Flag International, which also helps run training programmes. Reference to some of these schemes in holiday brochures indicates that the companies are trying to improve their environmental performances.

Some non-commercial groups have also set up schemes to publicise travel companies which are trying to improve. The Centre for Environmentally Responsible Tourism (CERT), has an Environmental Kitemark scheme, under which travel companies can use the scheme's gold, silver or bronze stars in their publicity material, as evidence of their commitment to better standards. To win these awards, the companies must publish their own environmental policies, make sure their staff follow them, and distribute CERT questionnaires and literature. In addition, the companies include a £1 donation to conservation projects in their holiday prices, and undertake to match the donation themselves. Holidaymakers' responses to the questionnaires help determine whether the companies win their stars.

Environmental Awards

They might not appear in holiday company brochures – though it is a good thing if they do – but there are also other awards that can tell you more about the environment where you may be staying. In Britain, the annual survey of beach and bathing water quality by the Marine Conservation Society (up to 1998, sponsored and published as The Reader's Digest Good Beach Guide), is carried out to criteria higher even than the European Union's Blue Flag awards scheme, whereby bathing waters are tested for their environmental health and safety. In Britain, the Blue Flag campaign is run by the Tidy Britain Group (on behalf of the Foundation for Environmental Education in Europe). The Tidy Britain Group is also responsible for the annual Seaside Awards, whose yellow and blue flags are given to beaches that are clean and safe and of the mandatory standard for water quality (though not necessarily the higher, guideline standard), set down by the European Union (EU).

Finally, there are awards given to individual tourism projects that mark specific environmental initiatives. Among these are the Tourism for Tomorrow Awards, which were originally set up by the British Tourist Authority (BTA) and the UK-based Federation of Tour Operators (FTO) in 1990, and which since 1992 have been sponsored and administered by British Airways. Each year, awards are given to regional and international projects which the competition's judges (who include environmental experts) consider show merit in raising green standards. Previous winners have included the coast-to-coast cycle path set up in northern England by Sustrans, and a Hawaiian project that succeeded in reducing tourist numbers on some beaches by restricting vehicle access, thus reducing the pressure on local marine wildlife. By themselves, such awards cannot guarantee environmental excellence, but they help persuade the holiday industry of the competitive merits of improving its performance. Look for these in the holiday brochures and other literature before you book.

Specialist Media and Other Organisations

In addition to the sources previously mentioned, as well as the more intelligent travel journalism in some newspapers and magazines or on radio or television, you may be able to get more information from such magazines as Holiday Which, Ethical Consumer, and the literature produced by specialist organisations such as Tourism Concern, which regularly publishes material on the effects of new travel and holiday developments. Other environmental organisations, such as Friends of the Earth, Greenpeace, the World Wide Fund For Nature (WWF) and similar groups, also publish magazines and other material, sometimes on tourism-related topics, that can be helpful. Searching the Internet is another way of helping you get more information about holidays or travel options (see the selection of Internet sites in Section Three).

One Internet service that is specifically designed to help improve environmental standards in tourism and travel is the ECoNETT project, the European Community Network for Environmental Travel and Tourism, an EU-funded initiative based at the WTTC's London office. It is designed to provide information for the general public, as well as more specialist material for the travel industry, tourist resorts, governments, academics and media. Its Internet address is http://www.wttc.org.

Checklist

■ What is the holiday company's – or the resort's – environmental record? Has it won any formal merits, such as a Tourism for Tomorrow award, or a Campaign for Environmentally Responsible Tourism star? Does it belong to the Green Flag or Green Globe schemes?

■ Does the company's literature make reference to the environment or local communities?

■ Does it give or invest any of its profits to local companies, charities, community or green groups? What is its 'fair trade' policy of ensuring local workers enjoy reasonable wages and conditions, or that more of the money tourists pay for their holiday stays in the destination country?

■ What advice does it give on environmental or conservation issues to prospective customers?

Of course, you may not get all the information you want, whether from specific holiday companies, or from the travel agency. It may even seem trivial to ask such questions, but by doing so, you are helping to raise the profile of environmental issues. In the face of customer pressure, the successful holiday companies are those that respond.

Getting Ready

Having decided what you are going to do and where you are going to go on your holiday, there are several important things you can do to get ready, other than the usual preparations: checking your passport is up to date, that you have any visas or vaccinations required, a suitable insurance policy, and so on. These are some of the preparations you can make to ensure that you travel – as a green traveller – lightly and with less impact.

■ Read yourself in. Apart from the suggestions in this book, you can acquire more information about environmental and other issues from a wide range of organisations and sources. Some of them are listed in Section Three of this Guide.

■ For the most encyclopaedic volume that any serious traveller should consult, *The Traveller's Handbook*, published by Wexas, a travel club that has an extensive environmental pedigree, is in a class by itself. For individual guide books relating to the country or region you are visiting, or for your own personal interest, be it wildlife, history or whatever, these are often a matter for individual taste. Of the more generally available country guides, the *Lonely Planet* series usually offers sections on local environmental issues and attractions. *The Rough Guide* series tends to give more information on local cultural and political considerations.

■ Take time to learn something about where you are going – the history, local cultures and other aspects of your destination, including any customs and sensitivities that should be observed. Before you book a holiday, it might also be appropriate to learn a little about the human rights situation in your possible destination. Although there are good reasons to debate the rights and wrongs of

holidaying in countries where human rights abuses occur – one school of thought argues that the presence of foreign travellers and holidaymakers can exert a liberalising influence, the other that a tourist industry finances and legitimises a corrupt regime – sometimes tourism directly supports the worst type of dictatorships. In the South-East Asian state of Myanmar (formerly Burma), there have been reports of communities being displaced and forced labour being employed on new state-sponsored tourism schemes.

■ Learn a little of the language, if appropriate. Even a few weeks may be sufficient to learn enough to get by – and a handful of simple phrases, from 'Hello', to 'Please' and 'Thank you', can make a good impression. The idea that being British abroad simply means talking slowly and loudly is an outdated stereotype: the more you fit in, the less intrusive you are. And being able to understand more of what is being said around you, or reading street and shop signs, market banners and restaurant menus, not to mention local newspaper articles (even if only the headlines), will allow you to take a closer look at the communities you are to visit.

■ Pack carefully, and in good time. Apart from reducing the stress of a frantic, last-minute departure, packing carefully should save you from carrying unnecessary weight, while also ensuring you are properly equipped for your travels. Every ounce you carry has to be paid for in terms of the fuel burned by your aircraft, car or bus – or the energy your body uses, if you are walking or cycling. Don't pack more than you need – even shampoos can be decanted into smaller bottles. But do make sure that if you are going to need specialist equipment that will be difficult to hire or buy at your destination, that it is ready in good time – binoculars or

cameras if you are going wildlife-watching, for example. If you are taking a trekking holiday, make sure your boots are broken in before you set off – you will pay for it in blisters, otherwise. Remove any excess packaging from new film, clothes or other items you are packing – it also saves weight, space, and means you are not taking litter around the world for someone else to dispose of. There is another consideration here – even if you are backpacking in remote regions, you don't have to rely on freeloading off your hosts, or depending on their sense of hospitality. Of course, ensure that any specialist equipment can be carried safely on a plane or other form of public transport.

■ When packing, a good, hardwearing rucksack can be longer-lasting and more appropriate than a suitcase. A well-made travel bag, or pair of boots, for example, are more likely to last than last-minute, unsuitable purchases that will soon be thrown away.

■ Consider whether there are any items you can take to your destination to give away. In some regions, a gift of pens or pencils to local children is preferable to handing out sweets. And being able to show a photograph or postcard of your own town or family back home is a good way to break the ice.

■ If you are travelling independently in remote regions, it is worth telling someone of your planned itinerary, and arranging to check in at various points.

■ Consider buying travel insurance from companies with environmental aims. Often it can also be cheaper than that offered by package tour companies.

Get Your Home Ready

Your home can still use up resources even while you are away. Environmentally, it helps to keep this energy and resource use to a minimum. Make a checklist:

■ Cancel the deliveries you won't need – papers, milk and so on. It saves money, cuts waste, and doesn't leave tell-tale signs of your absence.

■ If you are going away in winter, and leaving your home empty, turn your central heating off or down to its minimum setting if it is absolutely necessary to have some heating.

■ If you want to leave a light burning for security reasons, fit a time switch and a long-life, low-energy bulb. These can cost as little as £5–6, and should easily pay for themselves as they last much longer than a conventional bulb.

■ Make sure any animals you leave behind – and, if appropriate, any plants – are properly cared for. Delayed-action watering devices can now keep plants healthy, indoors or in the garden, without wasting water. Animals are best cared for by people, not machines, so enlist the help of a reliable flatmate, friend or neighbour. Don't overfeed fish (or any animal, for that matter) before you go on holiday.

Transports – of Delight?

The various types of transport you will use on your journey or holiday all have associated environmental consequences, whether in terms of the energy they use, the noise and exhaust emissions they generate, or the infrastructure they require. Precise comparisons are often difficult, but as a general rule, the greenest forms of travel are those which are most effective over shorter distances, such as walking and cycling, which is why a locally-based holiday is worth considering. Taking public transport, such as a train or a local bus, is also a better bet, environmentally. If you do fly, or drive, there are many ways of lightening the environmental load, whether by supporting those airlines prepared to invest in more energy-efficient aircraft, sharing a car or minibus, or – most common – varying your means of transport. Let's briefly examine some of your options.

Flying

Just as the railway and the steamship opened the era of cheap mass travel – Thomas Cook organised his first excursion, a railway day trip for a local Temperance Society, from Leicester to Loughborough, in July 1841 – so since the 1950s, the passenger jet aircraft has been largely the vehicle for the expansion of foreign travel. The economics of cut-price, package tourism has meant new horizons for generations, but air travel does carry an environmental price. Airlines argue that modern, more efficient aircraft may be more energy efficient than, for example, older cars – especially if the latter just carry one person. But several studies have shown aircraft generating many more grams of the 'greenhouse gas' carbon dioxide (CO_2), per passenger kilometre, than cars, buses or trains.

Of course, such figures by themselves can mislead: air travel is still the preserve of the relatively wealthy, and is currently used by a fraction of the numbers of people who use a car each year. But air traffic is growing – latest figures suggest by between 5 and 6 per cent per year – and according to one report, calculations carried out by scientists for the Intergovernmental Panel on Climate Change (IPCC) estimated that aircraft emissions could be responsible for anything between 5 and 10 per cent of greenhouse gas emissions.[6] Again, these figures have been challenged: aviation industry experts believe aircraft are probably responsible for about 2.5 per cent of CO_2 emissions.

6 *New Scientist*, 11 April, 1998

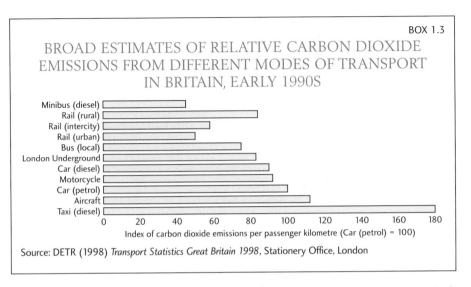

BOX 1.3

BROAD ESTIMATES OF RELATIVE CARBON DIOXIDE
EMISSIONS FROM DIFFERENT MODES OF TRANSPORT
IN BRITAIN, EARLY 1990S

Index of carbon dioxide emissions per passenger kilometre (Car (petrol) = 100)

Source: DETR (1998) *Transport Statistics Great Britain 1998*, Stationery Office, London

Equally a cause for concern, the nitrogen oxide (NO_x) emissions produced by aircraft cruising high in the troposphere are believed to contribute to global warming. There is still some scientific debate, however, about whether these emissions may also have a – probably lesser – cooling effect. Scientists are also trying to assess the effect of water vapour emissions from aircraft.

The growth in air travel has other implications than simply atmospheric pollution, important though that is. As the number of people travelling by air increases, so the number of aircraft and flights rise too. This in turn leads to greater ground traffic around airports, more land given over to airport building, and consequent concerns about the loss of green space, noise and increased pollution levels in the vicinity. Some environmental groups have predicted that protests over the growth and impact of air traffic could develop in the early years of the next century, rivalling the intensity of earlier campaigns against excessive road building in the 1990s. In November 1998, an international campaign was launched by some green groups calling for increased taxes on aviation fuel. 'We are in the position with aviation now that we were with cars in the 1970s,' Paul de Clerck of The Netherlands Friends of the Earth told *The Observer* newspaper. 'Twenty years ago it was almost impossible to interest the car driver in the pollution he created. Now every driver is aware. But while the car is slowing down for the red light, if you like, the plane is overtaking it on the outside.'[7]

7 'Pollution battle takes to the skies', *The Observer*, 8 November, 1998

BAA
130 Wilton Road
London SW1V 1LQ
T: +44 (171) 834 9449
F: +44 (171) 932 6699

British Airways
Environment Branch
Waterside (HBBG)
PO Box 365
Harmondsworth
UB7 0GB

Aviation Environment
Federation
Sir John Lyon House
5 High Timber Street
London EC4V 3NS
T: +44 (171) 329 8159
F: +44 (171) 329 8160
E: 101455.1475@
compuserve.com

One issue likely to become increasingly politically sensitive in the next few years, is how individual countries' airlines account for the greenhouse gases they emit. International conferences on how to tackle global warming – at Kyoto, Japan, in 1997 and Buenos Aires, Argentina, in November 1998 – did not resolve this issue, instead referring it to consideration by the International Civil Aviation Organisation, a decision criticised by green groups.

Meanwhile, the controversy over plans to build a fifth terminal at London's Heathrow Airport – the world's busiest – continues. A public inquiry on the issue became the longest in British legal history in 1998. BAA (formerly the British Airports Authority) say the development is essential to meet the increasing traffic pressure on the airport, avoid further delays to passengers over the next decade and to prevent the loss of valuable custom to airports on the European mainland. Opponents say it will cause further environmental damage and increase air traffic.

There are some positive developments in air travel, however. New engine technologies and aircraft design have doubled efficiency over the last decade, and the most modern jets now burn much less fuel per mile than they did ten years ago. Similarly, a combination of new technology and stricter legislation has also led to a new generation of quieter planes, conforming to new 'Chapter Three' noise standards. Airlines that believe they are leading the field in this area have begun to call for tougher action against their noisier rivals. British Airways, KLM, Scandinavian Airlines, Quantas and Air New Zealand are among the airlines to have invested in quieter, more energy-efficient planes in recent years. Some of the smaller charter lines and less affluent national carriers do not, however, despite the prospect of growing environmental costs and financial penalties – a number of airports (Sydney, Australia, is a prominent example) now impose stiff fines on planes exceeding set noise levels. A number of airlines have also sought to avoid the international agreement that would phase out noisier 'Chapter Two' planes by 2005, however, by fitting 'hush kits' which only marginally comply with the tougher 'Chapter Three' regulations.

In Britain, companies such as British Airways now publish annual environmental reports, listing their attempts to 'green' their performance: among them, attempts to increase fuel efficiency (more than 90 per cent of an airline's energy bill is

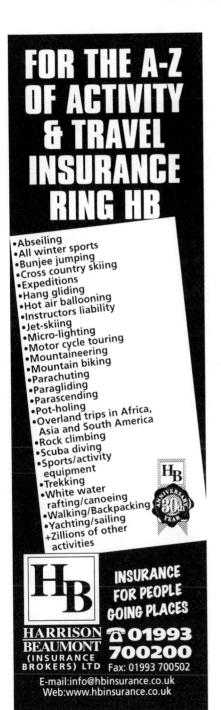
normally on kerosene for aircraft); reducing ground pollution; encouraging recycling or more efficient use of materials; cutting noise and ground traffic congestion. Other airlines publishing similar reports include Iberia, KLM, Air France, SAS and Lufthansa. Environment groups such as the Aviation Environment Federation, Transport 2000 and Friends of the Earth issue their own material as part of their various transport campaigns – needless to say, the two sides do not always agree (particularly over the planned Terminal 5 at Heathrow), but the ongoing debate is a sign of engagement.

Tim Johnson, director of the Aviation Environment Federation, believes that from a traveller's viewpoint, as well as being aware of aviation's environmental effects, key issues to consider include the following:

■ *There are alternatives to short-haul air travel. The advent of the Channel Tunnel has cut train times from Britain to western Europe; and trains take passengers closer to the main city centres than air travel.*

■ *If flying long-haul (or flying at all for that matter) it is worth finding out from airlines the type of aircraft being used: there are considerable differences between the noise and emissions performance of aircraft within each class – some airlines are better than others!*

■ *When travelling to an airport, use public transport whenever possible: the single largest source of emissions at an airport is still road traffic. In south-eastern England, a new development in 1998 was the*

opening of the Heathrow Express train service now linking Heathrow to London's Paddington Station. It is much faster, though more expensive, than taking a Tube train on the Underground – but both are environmentally preferable to driving.

The Car

An extension to popular democracy, a lifeline to people living in remote or rural areas – or the single biggest threat to our environment? The car has been called all these things. Certainly its impact on our lives has been extraordinary, however, shaping where and how we live, work, shop and take our entertainment. Arguably, the campaigns against a series of new road schemes in the late 1980s and 1990s – including the Newbury bypass, the M11 extension, the planned (and withdrawn) dual-carriageway road through Oxleas Wood, south-east London – did more to focus popular attention on environmental issues during the period than almost any other. While this Guide is focused largely on holiday travel, it is important to realise that driving by car has environmental consequences during the rest of the year, and the more we can reduce our reliance on it, the better. As car use has grown since the 1950s, so too have the numbers of traffic accidents; while planners have accentuated the trend: more out-of town shopping centres, in many cases sucking the economic life out of older town-centres; greater hazards and longer journeys for pedestrians; increasing concerns about traffic-related pollution and the personal consequences of a society increasingly travelling by car. We walk less, are less fit as a result, our streets and local communities are less social. Getting out of your car is therefore an environmental imperative, as the British government conceded in 1998, when it published a White Paper spelling out its desire for moves towards an integrated transport system.

If you travel by car on holiday, remember the following points:

- *Don't use the car when you needn't.* Walk to local shops or sites, or use local public transport.
- *Care for your car.* Regular maintenance and servicing can reduce your car's emission levels, and is in any case necessary to ensure that you meet MoT standards. In particular, make sure that the carburettor is properly adjusted for the most efficient fuel mixture, and that both spark plugs and filters are clean. In

the long-term, it is worth considering the possibilities of cars using cleaner fuels – low-particulate diesel, liquid petroleum gas (LPG), compressed natural gas (CNG), ethanol – and, as they become more widely used, electric vehicles. Check that tyre pressures are appropriate – this can save fuel by reducing tyre friction.

■ *Share the journey.* Just as car-sharing at home or at work is environmentally beneficial (as well as being more sociable), so sharing a car with fellow holidaymakers will reduce costs as well as congestion and pollution.

■ *Travel lightly.* The less weight you carry, the less fuel your car will burn. Carrying a roof rack – even an empty one – can reduce a car's aerodynamics, increasing fuel consumption by up to 30 per cent, depending on how well it is loaded. If you are carrying a roof rack, the AA recommends loading luggage as low as possible. 'Wrapping the luggage in plastic sheeting improves fuel economy by 2 per cent,' the AA said in advice to holidaymakers in 1998. 'If you are staying in the same place, it is worth removing the roof rack before driving to beaches and tourist attractions – but make sure you don't lose any of the bits.' In research for its 'Fuel for Thought' campaign, the AA found that by travelling with a window open, carrying roof luggage or using air-conditioning wastefully, drivers could increase their travel costs by more than 25 per cent. 'A small car travelling from London to Exeter and back can add at least £6 to its petrol bill if windows are left open or the air-conditioning is left on, it carries a loaded roof rack, and its tyres have not been pumped up to compensate for carrying passengers and extra load,' David Lang, the AA's chief engineer, said at the time. 'That rises to £7 for a medium car.'

- *If you hire a car,* bear the above points in mind – where possible, hire a car with a catalytic converter, capable of running on unleaded petrol, and ensure it is well-maintained.
- *Drive efficiently, as well as considerately* – remember, local conditions may be different from those you are used to, when you are on holiday. Both the AA and the Environmental Transport Association have issued advice for environmentally-conscious holiday motoring:; among the points they stress are keeping your speed down (keeping below 60mph reduces emissions and saves fuel); driving smoothly, anticipating other drivers' actions; taking an advanced driving course to improve your road-skills; switching the engine off in heavy traffic jams, or where you are stationary for more than a minute, particularly in towns; driving in as high a gear as possible (this also saves fuel).
- *Plan your route in advance.* Information from motoring organisations and local TV and radio can help you avoid traffic congestion, and hence reduce your time on the road, as well as the amount of fuel you burn.
- *If you park in the sun,* use a windscreen shade and open up the car's windows and doors for a few moments before driving off – this will bring down the interior temperature, and reduce the need for air-conditioning.
- *Join and support* organisations pressing for more environment-friendly transport options. This includes the Environmental Transport Association. Like the AA and RAC, it offers such services as breakdown assistance and various forms of insurance, but it also campaigns specifically for alternatives to car transport, as well as offering services to cyclists. It publishes a guide to the best (and worst) cars, from an environmental point of view), and also helps organise such events as Green Transport Week and the National Car-Free Day.

Environmental Transport
Association
10 Church Street
Weybridge KT13 8RS
T: +44 (1932) 828 882
F: +44 (1932) 829 015
URL: www.eta.co.uk

Rail – Letting the Train Take the Strain

The privatisation of Britain's railways in the last years of the Conservative government of John Major has helped increase the number of passenger journeys made by rail, but by late 1998 complaints about late or cancelled services, poor levels of information, service and comfort on board were running at all-time highs. A seemingly bewildering number of new train companies now compete for traffic on some routes, and while public subsidies are due to decline, fare increases have continued. All in all, not the most propitious of states for a transport network that should be one of the most environmentally beneficial. Meanwhile, while the Channel Tunnel and Eurostar train services have offered a real alternative for travellers, as well as further opening access to continental Europe's rail network, there is a mixed picture in many parts of the world for railway users. Faster services in parts of western Europe; cuts in services in some eastern regions. In the US, the shift to car or air journeys has left Amtrak services a shadow of one of the country's former glories.

But train journeys are still an excellent, environmentally-preferred option for middle-distance and longer journeys, and should be considered for your holiday plans. Though generating the electricity required to power a modern train engine may pose its own environmental issues – in France, much comes from nuclear energy, for example, while other countries' power stations burn fossil fuels – the train is generally estimated to be less polluting, in terms of passenger kilometres, than cars or aircraft, particularly at lower speeds. Cycling and walking organisations – such as the Cyclists' Touring Club, the London Cycling Campaign, the Ramblers' Association and the Youth Hostels Association – are among the many groups that offer information on holidays and journeys that can link with railway stations and train services (see Chapter 2, Greener Holidays, for details of some of these organisations). And for students and young people, the cheaper fares offered on Europe's railways offer some of the best opportunities for holiday travel. Rail passes are also available, offering cheaper travel across international borders, or other domestic reductions, in most parts of the world.

On the Right Tracks

- Support organisations such as Transport 2000, Save Our Railways and your regional Rail Users' Consultative Committees which campaign for improved rail services.
- If planning a holiday, think of taking a train rather than driving or flying, particularly for short or middle-distance journeys.
- Take advantage of cheaper tickets by using various student rail or pre-booking schemes. Shop around; since rail privatisation in Britain you need to be persistent to get full information from the national rail inquiries service of different train services and ticket prices that may be available.
- Consider using the train as part of a walking or cycling holiday. Consult the various cycling and walking organisations (as well as the rail companies) for details.
- Whether travelling by train, bus or other forms of public transport, keep personal stereos personal. They may keep you entertained, but if the stereo's earpieces are not particularly well-fitting, or you're simply playing it too loud, then other passengers within earshot have every right to be annoyed. Noise pollution is still pollution even if you are producing it.

Ship

Other than taking a cruise, or sailing recreationally, it is still possible to use marine transport as part of your holiday. Ferry services remain important in Britain, despite competition from air and (since the Channel Tunnel's completion) rail. It is also still possible to sail as a passenger on some

Strand Travel and
Voyages
Charing Cross Shopping
Concourse
The Strand
London WC2N 4HZ
T: +44 (171) 836 6363
*Offers information on
passenger-carrying cargo
ships*

commercial cargo vessels, which offer a different perspective on travel. (For environmental aspects of sea travel and marine holidays, see Chapter 2).

Bus and Coach

One of the most familiar forms of public transport can also be one of the best ways of getting around. In terms of fuel efficiency per passenger mile, the bus beats a private car. And in terms of congestion, a bus is a much more practical way of taking large numbers of people into or out of town. Travelling by bus or coach can also be a much better way of seeing the countryside at a slower pace than by train, and for meeting local people. But there are points worth remembering:

■   Travel light. Every ounce you carry will add to the fuel load – and usually coaches and buses have limited storage space. Don't let your back-pack or case get in the way of other passengers.
■   Coach parties should take care not to disrupt local life. Park away from popular sites and walk, rather than add to local traffic congestion. Try not to swamp local cafes or bars – split up, and divide your trade between local shops.
■   If you are travelling abroad by bus, try to avoid travelling in groups so large that you force local travellers off.

Cycling

One of the most environmentally benign forms of travel – and for journeys of a few miles or less, particularly in towns, one of the more efficient – cycling is also an excellent way of going on holiday, by itself or with another transport mode. It has the advantage of being a form of recreation as well as a means of transport – particularly if the weather and road conditions are clement. Although cycling holidays are discussed in Chapter Two, Greener Holidays, there are more general points as well:

Pedal Power

■   Keep your bike well maintained. Brakes, tyres, chain, gears, handlebars and seat – whether you cycle year-round or on holiday, it is worth knowing how to look after your bicycle, to give you extra independence, and to stay safe. Wear a safety helmet wherever appropriate (sadly, that seems almost everywhere today).
■   If you hire a bike on holiday – and it is often the best form of transport on holiday – make sure it is the right size for you, and that it is in good working order.
■   At night, be seen and be safe. Use lights front and rear, and wear reflective gear.
■   If you ride off-road, don't contribute to eroding paths or tracks; respect wildlife sites – don't disturb nesting birds, or ride through undergrowth.
■   Join and support some of the cycling organisations campaigning for better conditions for cyclists (and which offer widespread advice on cycling holidays and touring – see Chapter 2 for details).

Walking

Most forms of walking holiday – rambling, trekking, hiking and so on – are discussed in Chapter 2. But walking can be the best way of getting around during any holiday, even though town planners are making urban pedestrians an endangered species in some cities. Walking is the best way to see most cities or parts of the countryside, but whether in town or country, there are some points to remember:

The Pedestrians
Association
126 Aldersgate Street
London EC1A 4JQ
T: +44 (171) 490 0750
F: +44 (171) 608 0353

- ■ Whether at home or abroad, observe local traffic regulations. Many countries have stricter laws on jay-walking than the UK.
- ■ Crowds of tourists walking in cities can be a bugbear to local people if they block the pavements. Be considerate, particularly if you are carrying a back-pack.
- ■ Help organisations such as the Pedestrians Association campaign for better conditions for walkers in your town or city – it will be encouraging greener travel for visitors, too.

While You Are Away

Save Energy

Whether you are staying overnight in a hotel or renting a holiday cottage for a fortnight, you can almost certainly help reduce the environmental footprint of your travel by saving energy. This may also save you money, but even if your hotel bill does not include any element for the power you use, the hidden costs of wasting energy can be high, particularly if you are travelling in a country where power supplies are limited. Here are some suggestions:

- ■ If you are staying in a hotel, ask for a room where you can control your heating or air-conditioning – or find out where the controls are. You can usually regulate the temperature to ensure that you stay comfortable, but without using so much power. For example, in warm climates, you should always turn the air-conditioning off when you go out, and only run it at a low level when you are in your room – indeed, most people can survive surprisingly well without it.
- ■ Central heating is often another way of wasting energy. If your room is too hot, don't just open a window to cool down – turn the heating down or off – and always turn it off when you go out. The simplest way to keep warm in a cool climate without turning up the heat is simply to put on a sweater or, at night, ask for an extra blanket for your bed.
- ■ Don't leave a television on standby overnight, or when you leave your room.
- ■ If you are making yourself a cup of tea or coffee, don't overfill the kettle. Heat only the amount of water you need.

- Turn unnecessary lights out at night. Apart from saving energy, you are also cutting the amount of light pollution which helps obscure the night sky.
- Ask about the hotel's energy policy before you book – or look to see if it is mentioned in any brochure. Many hotels are increasingly aware of the need to cut their fuel bills and operate energy saving schemes. In some parts of the world, hotels are beginning to use clean or renewable energy – such as solar-power from roof-mounted panels. The Inter-Continental Hotels and Resorts Group is an example of one company which has improved its business efficiency at the same time as its environmental policy. Between 1988 and 1995, it cut energy costs in its hotels by 27 per cent. It also adopted a policy of replacing CFC refrigerants – gases that can damage the Earth's protective ozone layer. The company encourages its managers and staff to come up with new environmental initiatives, with an annual award scheme, inaugurated in 1996 when the Hotel Inter-Continental Zagreb was honoured for its success in moving away from a coal-burning power policy. At the same time, Varuna Fernando, a regional chief engineer based at the Hotel Inter-Continental Nairobi, was commended for his work in producing a booklet on energy conservation in hotels as well as a guide to environmental auditing. Where hotels mention their environmental policies, it is worth encouraging them, just as it worth supporting locally owned and managed hotels, restaurants and cafes, to ensure more of your tourist expenditure stays within a local community.

Water

Recent drought years in Britain have brought home the message that water supplies are not limitless, even in a country known proverbially for its rain. The need to conserve water supplies is even more pressing in warmer, drier climates – particularly if water is being diverted for tourists. According to the United Nations, the amount of water needed to satisfy the average demands of 100 tourists in a typical hotel for 55 days can maintain 100 rural families for three years. Access to water has always been critical for societies: some environmentalists and UN leaders have warned that it could become a flashpoint for future 'water wars'. In East and southern Africa, southern India and in South-East Asia, there have been examples of local people losing their water to new hotels or tourist resorts. Such organisations as Tourism Concern, or human rights groups, can provide more information of such cases. Apart from shunning the more blatant developments, the individual traveller can help save water by simple methods:

- A shower normally uses a third of the water that filling a bath requires (though power showers can use almost the same amount as a bath).
- Don't allow a tap to run freely with the sink unplugged while you are washing clothes, shaving or cleaning your teeth.
- Many hotels now operate schemes whereby guests are asked whether or not they want towels (and in some cases, bed linen) changed daily. Support such schemes. Laundering towels and linen each day uses large amounts of water and detergents, some of which may pollute water courses.

- If you have taken your car on holiday (not always the best choice, as we have seen), use a bucket of water to clean it rather than an automatic car wash.
- If you are taking a golfing holiday (see Chapter 2), choose resorts where the courses have policies designed to conserve water.

Noise

Most people like to relax and enjoy themselves, especially on holiday. But, just as at home, it is worth checking your noise, to ensure you're neither spoiling someone else's holiday, or disturbing local people. Excess noise, particularly in remote areas, or at night, may also disturb wildlife. The noise and light of tourist discos in some Greek resorts has been shown to disrupt nesting and hatching behaviour of some turtle species, for example.

Waste and recycling

Cutting back on waste packaging, together with the amount of waste you throw away, can help reduce your environmental impact. This is particularly important in resorts where waste recycling or disposal is difficult or environmentally damaging. Small island holiday resorts, for example, may have limited resources to dispose of waste, and elsewhere garbage dumps threaten to pollute water supplies or damage local wildlife.

- Keep your packing to a minimum before setting out on your travels. Discard waste packaging – preferably for recycling – before you set off.
- If your hotel or holiday accommodation has a recycling scheme, use it.
- Many hotels – and airlines, for that matter – offer individual bottles or jars of shampoo, soaps and other toiletries. It can be useful to cut down on the weight of your luggage by using a refillable container for such products, but otherwise don't use them – they create excess packaging which ultimately means waste.
- Dispose of any waste carefully – especially such items as discarded razor blades, used sanitary towels or condoms.
- If you are going to be out in the sun, choose a sun block that is preferably made from organic ingredients. Excessive use of sun oils and creams has caused water pollution in some holiday resorts. A hat, t-shirt or long-sleeved shirt can often be as useful in protecting you from harmful exposure to the sun – remember, skin cancer rates are rising in the wake of changing holiday habits and the damage to the Earth's ozone layer in recent decades.

Eating and Drinking

Wherever you are staying on your travels, try to eat and drink local produce. Apart from extending your experience, you are also contributing to the local economy, and reducing your dependency on expensively imported western foods. Flying western convenience meals into Africa, Latin America or Asia contributes to the mounting cost of what environmentalists call 'food miles', and takes money out of local economies. Try to observe local cultural customs as far as food is concerned – some cultures look askance at eating pork, or drinking alcohol, for example – and public drunkenness is usually simply bad behaviour, wherever you are.

Sex. And Drugs...

Sex and travel have a long-standing connection: released from local conventions or restraints, social behaviour can change. As Byron wrote in his poem 'Don Juan' (Canto LXIII), not without a certain northern prejudice:

> *What men call gallantry, and the gods adultery,*
> *Is much more common where the climate's sultry.*

Even so, while the relative freedom of a holiday can have its pleasures, it is worth remembering:

- Respect local cultures and traditions and behave appropriately in public if you are with your partner.
- Aids and other sexually-transmitted diseases are widespread, and potentially ruinous. In many parts of Africa and in other developing regions, Aids is still destroying lives, communities and economies. Take precautions against sexually-transmitted disease, as well as unwanted pregnancies on holiday. If you have casual, adult sex abroad (or at home, for that matter), make it safe sex: use a condom.
- 'Sex tourism' has become a major, disfiguring phenomenon in some tourism destinations. It is estimated that with the increase in global travel, millions of young women, and many young men and children, are now working in various aspects of the sex trade, often under the control of criminal gangs. Around the world, various charities and pressure groups are campaigning for curbs on the abuse of children in sex tourism: in Britain, ECPAT UK is a leading organisation in this campaign (see the section on sex tourism in Chapter 16). On holiday, find out local laws on prostitution and respect them. If you see evidence of child sex tourism, contact local health or police authorities (in Britain, you can report your suspicions, in confidence, to the National Criminal Intelligence Service on a hotline: 0800 555 111).

Protecting wildlife

We have already seen how tourism development has sometimes been at the expense of environments and wildlife around the world. You can help protect the local environment wherever you are in many ways, as we have already seen. But in addition to choosing the best options in terms of transport, saving energy and resources, there are specific ways in which we can help preserve wildlife while we are on holiday:

- Watch out for wildlife while you are travelling – especially driving. In remoter areas, wildlife can be found on or by the road. Take care, especially at night, or if you are driving off-road.

■ Find out about local wildlife, so that you can avoid disturbing nesting or feeding sites.

■ Don't feed wildlife, unless it is obviously either necessary (in extreme weather conditions, for example) or permitted locally. Otherwise, you may risk poisoning some animals with inappropriate food; habituate them to rely on feeding; or encourage potentially dangerous encounters with animals foraging for food. If you are camping, for example, keep food wrapped up and away from animals that might otherwise be attracted to your camp. And dispose of waste food where it will not attract or endanger wildlife.

■ Don't encourage local customs that lead to the mistreatment of wildlife – beach photographs with captive chimpanzees, for example, or the keeping of dancing bears in parts of Asia. Report any examples of animal cruelty to your tour guide, local police or animal welfare organisations, and if the matter is serious, or your complaints are not acted on, pass on your concerns to animal welfare organisations and your holiday company on your return home.

■ Be wary of buying animal products or souvenirs. Many wildlife products cannot be brought home, under the terms of the CITES treaty which is designed to protect endangered species. International trade – even domestic trade, in some cases – in such products as elephant ivory, turtle shell, reptile skins and many live animals, can be illegal. By buying such souvenirs you could be encouraging the poaching of such animals, and your souvenir could be confiscated by Customs – you might even face prosecution. Always ask a responsible person – your guide, the local authorities – before making any such purchase. Better still, if you have any doubt, don't buy. In Britain, organisations such as the World Wide Fund For Nature (WWF-UK), the wildlife trade monitoring organisation TRAFFIC, the local Customs and Excise office, or the Department of the Environment, Transport and the Regions can all give advice.

Coming Home

The end of your holiday should not just be about spending the last bit of foreign currency and flying home, overladen with duty-free booze, grumbling about the service and delays at the airport. Make a point of formally thanking and taking leave of the people you've met, and, equally, reflect on your holiday. Be prepared to pass on information about what you have learned on holiday – whether it is something you can act on next time, or take up with an environment or development group:

■ Before you leave, dispose of any waste or litter thoughtfully. The idea is always to travel lightly, but not leave a mess for someone else to clear up.

■ Leave a tip or gift to people who have helped you, wherever this is appropriate or in keeping with local culture or tradition. Sometimes this is best done by making a donation or contribution to local charities, schools, environment or development organisations.

- Take the addresses of people you have met, and keep in touch if you can. If travel is about making social and cultural connections, this is a way of broadening friendships.
- Some airports and airlines operate charity schemes, collecting unwanted foreign currency. Support them.
- On your return home, pass on any concerns you may have had about environmental or social issues, to your tour operator, local environment group or other organisation, as appropriate.
- Think about your holiday or your travel, and incorporate any new understanding into your daily life. Your travelling does not end simply when you close your front door behind you.

CHAPTER 2
GREENER HOLIDAYS

This chapter looks at different types of holiday or breaks from everyday work that appeal to green travellers – all those with an interest in the environment in its broadest sense. Whether you want a sporting holiday enjoying the waterways, want to explore the natural or built heritage of the countryside, or whether your aim is a quieter vacation, spent in spiritual recreation, or a period of volunteer work or education, the following pages should give you new ideas, as well as environmental guidelines for enjoying your holiday to the full.

WILDLIFE WATCHING

Watching wildlife is a pleasure, pastime and sometimes a near obsession with many people. The success of several generations of television natural history programmes is mirrored by the hundreds of thousands who join or support organisations that range from the Royal Society for the Prevention of Cruelty to Animals (RSPCA) and the Royal Society for the Protection of Birds (RSPB), through to internationally-focused groups such as the World Wide Fund For Nature (WWF) or more species-specific organisations such as the Whale and Dolphin Conservation Society. Watching wildlife can also stimulate interest in, and support for, wider environmental and conservation interests. But an increasing number of people are now combining their interest in wildlife watching with holidays specifically designed to cater for them. Of course, the fact that you are going to watch wildlife doesn't mean that you forget about the other green guidelines for travellers – in fact it means you take on other responsibilities, too. But such holidays can equally produce hours of absorption, new knowledge and moments of sheer joy in the diversity of the natural world.

Bird Watching

Royal Society for the
Protection of Birds
(RSPB)
The Lodge
Sandy
Bedfordshire SG19 2DL
T: +44 (1767) 680 551
F: +44 (1767) 692 365
URL: www.rspb.org.uk

British Trust for
Ornithology (BTO)
The Nunnery
Thetford
Norfolk IP24 2PU
T: +44 (1842) 750 050
F: +44 (1842) 750 030

Ornithology is one of the most popular passions in Britain, and the interest is shared around the world. The RSPB is one of the largest conservation NGOs in the UK, and uses the income from its membership as well as charitable donations and the fees from visitors to its bird reserves to maintain a network of reserves around the country. Volunteer assistants are always required. The RSPB produces voluminous literature on bird watching, including advertising for bird-watching holidays in the UK and abroad in its members' magazine. Other publications, such as BBC Wildlife, also carry such features. Because of their concentrations of more exotic species, especially of migratory birds, the wilder regions of northern and southern Spain, or the West African coastal state of The Gambia, are becoming particularly favourite destinations for ornithological tours, especially for those who want also to enjoy the countryside or the beach, but bird watching for a wide range of species is possible in most countries. The British Trust for Ornithology (BTO), together with the various county Wildlife Trusts, are further good sources for information on where to watch birds – they also welcome volunteer help on reserves and conservation and research work.

- When you go bird watching, be sure you are dressed suitably for the conditions – that may mean waterproof clothing and strong, possibly waterproof, boots or shoes. This particularly applies in remote regions, including marsh and estuary sites, where weather conditions can change rapidly.
- Learn how to identify birds from the material published by the RSPB, BTO and other organisations. Many bird reserves have illustrated posters or signs to help you. There are also holiday and weekend courses on bird identification (see section on environmental education later in this chapter).
- Carry a good, pocket-sized guidebook to help you identify the birds you see.
- Choose an appropriate pair of binoculars or a telescope, so you can watch birds at a distance without disturbing them (in many cases, it is the closest you are

likely to get to some species). The RSPB publishes a series of leaflets – *Selecting Your Binocular, Selecting Your Telescope,* and *Care and Use of Binoculars and Telescopes* – and there are usually regular reports and testings of new makes in the pages of the various ornithological magazines. Take care before you buy a pair of binoculars – a good shop will let you take your time and try out a number of pairs – particularly if you are buying second hand, when you should look closely for any sign of scratched lenses, wear to moving parts and the ease of focusing. All binoculars will carry a set of two figures, indicating their specification. The first refers to the magnification – usually it is between seven and ten, with the second figure referring to the diameter (in millimetres) of the objective lens. Generally, the larger the lens, the more light it lets in – in other words, the image will be brighter and easier to see. Even so, these figures are only guides to how good the binoculars are – a well made pair of 10 x 40 binoculars might give a better image than a pair of 10 x 50 made with inferior materials, for example. Sometimes there are letters after the two sets of numbers: a 'B' means that even if you wear spectacles, you should be able to use the binoculars without a significant loss in the field of view. Broadly speaking, the lower the magnification (eg 7x), the brighter will be the image, the lenses focus closer, the depth of field will be greater, and the easier the binoculars will be to hold. By contrast, the higher the magnification (eg 9x or 10x), the more suitable the binoculars will be for long-range work, usually using a tripod or other form of rest. More recent models have a zoom facility, allowing you to 'home in' on an object. A drawback to some of these makes is that they need to be held very still, and have a reduced depth of field. Take advice on what sort of bird watching you will be doing before buying a pair of binoculars, as they can be expensive.

■   Don't let your enthusiasm to see a rare species – a visiting migrant bird, perhaps – lead you to getting too close: birds can be startled or stressed, and may be particularly vulnerable after a long flight, when nesting or rearing chicks, or after particularly bad weather.

■   Do not disturb nests. Apart from the effect on the birds, you could be liable to prosecution in those countries where egg collecting is against the law.

■   Report any injured birds to the appropriate local organisations – RSPCA, RSPB – as well as any threat to the environment, such as fire or pollution (see entry on British Waterways and the Environment Agency hotline).

■   Join and support some of the ornithological organisations. It can be advantageous to you – RSPB members get free admittance to the society's reserves, for example – and it helps the conservation groups in their work.

Safaris and Wildlife Photography

These days, most holidaymakers joining a safari will be 'shooting' wild animals with nothing more harmful than a camera. A diet of wildlife films has given a new generation the enthusiasm for wildlife that makes them want to watch and enjoy seeing animals in their natural habitat. The travel industry believes that such niche-market tourism is going to become more important, economically, in the next century, as people place greater emphasis on the importance of 'experience' in their holiday expectations. Equally, those countries with important biodiversity reserves – wildlife and wildlife habitats – are increasingly seeing them as resources which must be exploited economically. What this means is that, while the 'Great White Hunter' safaris of the past – where hunters sought to amass trophies of the animals they had killed – are replaced by wildlife watching holidays, there will be new forms of pressure on the environment in those areas of the world.

There have already been sufficient examples of the problems of this kind of 'eco-tourism'. In East and Southern Africa, for example, tourists keen for excitement have been known to urge their tour-bus drivers to chase cheetahs, 'to see how fast they really run'. Some of the national parks in Kenya have suffered damage from too many buses concentrating in the same area – half a dozen or more such vehicles circling a bemused lion – with the danger of disturbance to wildlife as much as the erosion of trails and tracks.

Nor is it just the wildlife that can suffer from unplanned, unsustainable tourism development. In many parts of the world, from East Africa to Nepal, there have been conflicts where national parks or nature reserves have been created, if this means people losing their access to traditional hunting grounds. And the creation of tourist lodges in remote areas can lead to new pressure on water and power supplies. Lastly there is the danger that tourists see local tribal peoples as a different form of wildlife, treating them as simply another photo-opportunity.

Friends of Conservation
Sloane Square House
Holbein Place
London SW1W 8NS
T: +44 (171) 559 8790
F: +44 (171) 559 8792

The more responsible safari and wildlife watching companies now see it as important to remind their customers of the importance of good environmental behaviour. Abercrombie & Kent, for example, a travel company that arranges trips to Africa, Latin America and other parts of the world, includes guidance notes to travellers within its travel brochures and literature. The Friends of Conservation organisation, which brings together various travel companies and organisations, has organised training and publicity material for tour guides as well as tourists, and uses the revenue it gathers from various tourism sources to help conservation programmes such as anti-poaching drives in Kenya's Maasai Mara region. Other companies too have begun to insist that a proportion of tourist revenue goes to local communities. These are initiatives to be encouraged.

■ If you are thinking of taking a safari holiday (either by itself, or as an excursion during a trip abroad), choose organisations which put a premium on good conservation practice, and which put some of their income back into local communities. Ask for this information before you book.

- On a safari holiday, remember not to waste local resources that may be in short supply.
- Ask for local food rather than expensively imported western meals.
- Make sure you have the appropriate equipment for your safari before you set out – clothing (including boots or hats), as well as cameras, binoculars or other gear. Check, too, on any medical requirements before you set out, rather than making demands on local medical facilities.
- On safari, don't encourage your drivers or guides to get too close to wildlife to the point where you are endangering or stressing the animals (don't chase cheetahs, for example, or knowingly get between an animal and its young). Avoid 'convoys' of tour vehicles.
- On safari, always follow the advice of your guide or expedition leader. This is usually for your safety as well as that of the other safari members – and occasionally of the wildlife you are watching. This is particularly important in specialised safaris such as gorilla watching, for example, where there are restrictions on the numbers of people that can visit the gorillas at any one time and limits to the amount of time they can spend near the animals. Do not ignore your guide's advice, or seek to bribe guides for greater access to wildlife.
- In national parks and other areas, stay on the designated paths and, unless specifically permitted by your guide, stay in your vehicle – this is partly for your own safety, but also to prevent too much pressure and stress on wildlife.
- Don't feed wild animals while on safari; it could be bad for the wildlife, or – should the animals become habituated to such feeding – it could put them, as well as other people, at risk.
- Don't discard any litter on safari; don't risk starting a fire by discarding cigarette butts, or broken glass. Keep water courses unpolluted.
- If you are taking photographs of the wildlife you see on holiday, put a little work in beforehand, to ensure you don't waste large amounts of film. Discuss with your safari guides what type of pictures are possible, and study the work of other photographers beforehand. This will help avoid disturbing wildlife if you have to change position.

■ Take your time on safari. Watching wildlife is not something that can be squeezed into a pre-set timetable. The joy of being in any countryside, especially if you are watching birds, mammals or whatever, is nature's unpredictability. Studying the behaviour of a smaller, less celebrated animal can be just as rewarding – if not more – than chasing through the bush trying to tick off the more exotic 'Big Five' species (lion, elephant, rhino, buffalo, leopard), just so you can say you've seen them.

TRAFFIC International
219c Huntingdon Road
Cambridge
Cambridgeshire CB3 0DL
T: +44 (1223) 277 427
F: +44 (1223) 277 237

■ Don't buy souvenirs made from endangered species – ivory, turtle-shell or parrot feathers, for example, or live animals. Remember, international trade in many endangered species is illegal, under the CITES convention. You could be encouraging poaching, and your souvenir could be confiscated on your return home. If in any doubt, ask your tour guide, operator or local authorities for more information. In Britain, up to date information on what wildlife products can be brought home as souvenirs is available from the local offices of the Department of the Environment, Transport and the Regions (DETR), Customs and Excise, or from TRAFFIC International, the organisation set up to monitor the wildlife trade.

■ Deal fairly with local people: they are not an exotic wildlife attraction. Ask permission before taking their photograph, follow local conventions on tipping or bartering in markets, and respect their homes and culture, including religious or sacred sites, as well as the symbols of nationhood or sovereignty, including flags or currency. Learn at least a little of the local language, and try to use it.

Whale and Dolphin Watching

Whaling was once an enormously profitable economic activity – Heathcote Williams's epic poem *Whale Nation* records its extent, from providing fuel to food to corsetry in early 19th century communities. Now, while whaling is effectively confined to Japan and Norway (as well as the annual killing of whales in the Faroe Islands), whale and dolphin watching is an increasingly important tourist activity, generating income for many coastal communities around the world. Whales and dolphins have become important symbols of the environmental movement – sometimes romantically so – and interest in watching them at close quarters is growing. Between 1992 and 1997, the number of countries where whale watching is a significant tourist activity more than doubled, to 65, with the numbers of watchers increasing by an average of 10 per cent per year. In 1994, 5.4 million people went whale watching, generating an estimated revenue of $311 million. By 1998, those figures had grown – an estimated six million whale watchers were supporting an industry worth about £310 million a year. According to research carried out for the UK-based Whale and Dolphin Conservation Society, whale watching is now carried out in about 300 communities around the world, in many cases providing valuable tourist income to otherwise depressed areas. But equally importantly, the study found that in many instances, 'whale watching helps to foster an appreciation of the importance of marine conservation, as well as providing a ready platform for researchers wanting to study cetaceans or the marine environment.'

Wherever whales and dolphins can be found it is possible to watch them, though for practical purposes this is best done close to shore. In Britain, it is possible to see dolphins off the coast of Cornwall and along the west coast of Wales, as well as in the Hebrides. Whale watching off northern Scotland, it is possible to see minke whales, orcas, and even some rarer species. In the US, the New England whaling towns described in Melville's epic, *Moby Dick* now support thriving whale watching tours, while on the west coast, thousands of people go each year to watch the annual migration of gray whales from the feeding grounds of Alaska, along the coast of British Columbia, Canada, and south to the breeding lagoons of Baja California, in Mexico. Maori communities in New Zealand now run whale watching tours, and the sight of hump-back whales breaching the surface, hurling themselves into the air and then crashing back to the sea is one of the more extraordinary moments of whale-watching off Hawaii.

While in the last decade the hardy have braved the cold waters of Ireland's Dingle Bay, or the North Sea near Amble, on the Northumbrian coast, to swim near dolphins that have taken up temporary residence, swimming with dolphins is a regular occurrence in some warmer climes. In several parts of Florida or the Caribbean, such

The Whale and Dolphin Conservation Society can offer information on whale watching holidays, as can such companies as the Bristol-based Wild Oceans, which specialises in environmental expeditions, sometimes assisting groups such as the Oceanic Society in collecting and recording data on the animals you see.

Whale and Dolphin
Conservation Society
Alexander House
James Street West
Bath BA1 2BT
T: +44 (1225) 334 511
F: +44 (1225) 480 097
URL: www.wdcs.org

encounters are now marketed as attractions for visitors, while at Monkey Mia, Shark Bay in Western Australia, dolphins regularly swim so close to shore that visitors can wade out among them. For some people, swimming with dolphins can be a psychologically therapeutic experience – lifting depression and being of profound benefit for some, while for even the sceptic it is an extraordinary experience, coming close to an animal in its own environment.

However, there are an increasing number of governments and conservation groups who have begun to counsel caution. It is possible to put marine mammals under stress from such encounters, they argue. In October 1998, a conference was held in the Azores to debate draft proposals for new laws from the Portuguese islands' authorities to tighten controls on whale watching, limiting the numbers of boats involved and the distance they must keep from the whales, and also proposing a ban on tourists swimming with whales. Elsewhere, governments of countries such as the US, New Zealand, Canada and South Africa have tough restrictions designed to avoid harassment of cetaceans.

- Choose an experienced, responsible operator. If you are taking a short whale or dolphin watching trip as part of your holiday, make sure the boat operator does not cause any distress or danger to the animals you are watching.
- Before you set off, a good operator should explain safety procedures and rules of behaviour. At sea, they should give an informed commentary on the wildlife you are watching.
- Don't feed whales or dolphins, or allow litter to be thrown overboard in their waters. Avoid making noise – these animals are known to be acutely sensitive to disturbance.
- If you are swimming in the vicinity of dolphins or porpoises, do not try to touch them (it is unlikely they would allow you to anyway), or pursue them. If they want to approach you, they will. Boycott any enterprise where dolphins are confined in swimming or petting pools, or netted-off lagoons.
- Don't forget: binoculars, camera and film (a waterproof bag is helpful on board and you will need a special underwater camera for shots in the sea), adequate weatherproof clothing, sea-sickness tablets, sunblock (preferably made from natural, non-polluting ingredients) and a hat (both for cold as well as sunny climates).

The Whale and Dolphin Conservation Society also recommends the following:

- Always let the dolphins decide what happens. Keep your distance in a boat – no closer than 100 metres. If the dolphins want to come closer it is up to them.
- Keep the boat engine in neutral if dolphins are close to the boat, or you are uncertain as to where they are – a running propeller can cause serious injuries. Never run head-on towards dolphins, and avoid repeatedly changing direction and speed, or revving the engine. If dolphins keep heading away, they almost certainly want to keep their distance, or to lose you.
- Never move between dolphins and their young.

CONSERVATION HOLIDAYS

Conservation holidays and short breaks are becoming increasingly popular. In essence, they are an opportunity to enjoy yourself while working on projects at home or abroad, with a conservation or environmental purpose. As a result, you can not only have time in an environment that can be anything from a Central American coral reef to a Midlands canal, either helping with practical conservation or restoration work, or assisting academic research. You will usually learn new skills, make new friends and return from a holiday feeling the time has been spent with a real purpose – the opposite to many 'beach and bars' holidays. Even so, many conservation holidays do set aside time for you to relax as well as work, which is possibly another reason for their appeal.

Volunteer conservation work is not just for, or in, the countryside. BTCV has recently published The Urban Handbook (£14.95), a practical guide for community conservation work, ranging from planting wildflower meadows in city sites to safely disposing of burnt-out cars.

British Trust for Conservation Volunteers (BTCV)

The British Trust for Conservation Volunteers (BTCV) brings together more than 95,000 volunteers from all sections of the community to protect and improve their local environment. It has more than 100 offices across the country and a membership of over 1,958 local, school and community groups – figures swollen in 1998 when BTCV amalgamated with the Scottish Conservation Projects Trust. BTCV publishes regular Natural Break brochures, listing short holidays that include repairing and building dry stone walls; coppicing woodland; conserving coastal sand dunes and their sensitive nature sites by building boardwalks, planting grasses and erecting sand trap fencing; conserving ancient hay meadows; restoring ponds and helping to safeguard important archaeological sites. Short holidays usually last a week; short breaks are most often over a weekend. Apart from a sense of achievement, and the enjoyment of working in the countryside, such

Photo © Jane Alexander/BTCV

Stepping up. A group of BTCV volunteers help prevent path erosion in Durdle Door, Dorset

43

BTCV (British Trust for
Conservation Volunteers)
36 St Mary's Street
Wallingford
Oxon OX10 0EU
T: +44 (1491) 839 766
F: +44 (1491) 839 646
URL: www.btcv.org.uk

Scottish Conservation
Projects (SCP)
Balallan House
24 Allan Park
Stirling FK8 2QG
T: +44 (1786) 479 697
F: +44 (1786) 465 359

BTCV/Gwarchodwyr
Cefn Gwlad
Wales Conservation
Centre
Forest Farm Road
Whitchurch
Cardiff CF4 7HJ
T: +44 (1222) 520 990
F: +44 (1222) 522 181

Conservation Volunteers
Northern Ireland (CVNI)
159 Ravenhill Road
Belfast BT6 0BP
T: +44 (1232) 645 169
F: +44 (1232) 644 409

Conservation Volunteers
Ireland
PO Box 3836
Ballsbridge
Dublin 4
Eire
T/F: +353 (1) 668 1844

holidays and short breaks can be a means of learning a new skill. Accommodation ranges from local farms to historic houses, meals are usually prepared and taken communally, there is time off to enjoy the area in the evenings, and volunteers are encouraged to work at their own pace! Lower prices are usually charged to students, retired people and the unwaged.

BTCV also organises international conservation working holidays: the 1998/99 brochure lists projects including restoring traditional fishing huts in Iceland; helping naturalists radio-tracking wolves in Poland; building a tortoise breeding centre in Senegal; constructing solar-powered cookers in Spain; repairing mountain trails in the US and building nature trail boardwalks by the shore of Lake Erie in Canada. Some volunteers camp in their own tents, others stay in bunkhouses, farms or self-catering holiday homes. Free time is for exploring the local countryside, meeting local people and enjoying local food and drink. One project – working in a 'sustainable village' project at Gomorszolos, in north-eastern Hungary – is designed to help build sustainable rural economies – volunteers spend time helping with organic farming, house and fence building as well as other projects. In the Irish Republic, the organisation Conservation Volunteers Ireland also runs one-day, weekend and week-long projects. At present, this also includes a Millennium Urban Forest campaign, aimed at planting 50,000 new trees.

The National Trust

The National Trust is another organisation which offers conservation holidays. As befits the Trust, which now owns or manages historic properties across Britain, its Working Holidays are located in some of the more magnificent country properties. These range from country houses to Hadrian's Wall. The holidays are designed to offer a broad sweep of activities, ranging from moderate to strenuous, for people aged from 17 to 70. In addition to those which might be expected to be offered by an organisation which manages so many historic properties – cobble-laying, dry-stone walling, charcoal-making, gardening and woodland management – there are often one-off events which may attract those with an interest in heritage or the arts. In 1998, for

Photo © National Trust Photographic Library/Chris King

A National Trust Working Holiday team enjoy the collaborative effort of building a fence at Scotney Castle, Kent

example, the Trust sought volunteers to help set up the world's largest temporary sculpture trail, in West Yorkshire, and wanted assistants to help organise a week of concerts at Powis Castle, Wales, and open-air concerts at Petworth Park in West Sussex. It also advertised for helpers to clear the store rooms at Saltram Park, Plymouth – an 'Aladdin's Cave' of war-time treasures.

'Working Holidays play a vital part in the National Trust's countryside conservation programme,' the Trust says. The programme, now in its 32nd year, is arranged so that each project is supervised by trained volunteer leaders. Since their inception, more than 65,000 people have taken part in Working Holidays. The first project was at Lapworth on the Stratford-upon-Avon Canal. 'The accommodation consisted of a barn with a single cold tap. Nowadays, accommodation is much more comfortable, and most base camps offer hot showers, bunk beds, central heating, and fully

National Trust Working Holidays
PO Box 84
Cirencester
Glos GL7 1ZP
T: 0891 517 751
(Calls charged at 50p per minute within the UK)
(For a brochure, enclose two first-class stamps)

equipped kitchens within renovated buildings, set in attractive locations,' the Trust says. Working Holidays last from two to ten days and cost from around £45 per person per week. Those who take part in week-long holidays are given a National Trust admission card, giving free admission to Trust properties for a year.

Earthwatch Institute

'Earthwatch is an innovative way of matching the needs of scientists with the interest of the public,' says the organisation's British head, Andrew Mitchell. 'Many people long to use their holiday time in a more useful way, and scientists involved in crucial field research need committed, interested assistants.'

Earthwatch Institute
57 Woodstock Road
Oxford OX2 6HJ
T: +44 (1865) 311 600
F: +44 (1865) 311 383
URL:
www.uk.earthwatch.org

Earthwatch International
680 Mount Auburn
Street
PO Box 403
Watertown
Massachusetts
MA 92272–9924
USA
T: +1 (617) 926 8200
F: +1 (617) 926 8532
URL: www.earthwatch.org

More expensive, but more far-flung in their location, the holidays offered by the Earthwatch Institute combine many of the traditional elements of the foreign holiday – time off for the beach, visiting local sites of interest – with the volunteer element. Earthwatch was founded to help fund science-based conservation research. It has now expanded to the point where it sends travellers around the world each year to assist scientific researchers. Since 1972 it has

Photo © Earthwatch

An Earthwatch volunteer counts eggs laid by a leatherback turtle

Photo © Earthwatch

Earthwatch volunteers assist scientific researchers monitoring wild dolphin societies

supported more than 1,920 projects in 118 countries, and estimates it has thereby contributed some 5.8 million work-hours to field research.

Past projects have included assisting researchers assessing the effects of tourists swimming with dolphins in New Zealand; investigating the impacts of acid rain on the forests of Bohemia; gathering census data on proboscis monkeys in Borneo; studying traditional herbal medicine in Argentina; and measuring pollution off the Russian coast in the Sea of Japan. Accommodation on such holidays has ranged from bed and breakfast hotels for those assisting archaeologists excavating Irish villages abandoned during the 1840s potato famine to bunk beds in cabins aboard a ship surveying underwater volcanic vents in the Antarctic.

Some Earthwatch-aided expeditions are closer to home: recent projects have included helping palaeontologists surveying dinosaur tracks in Yorkshire. Earthwatch also organises shorter one-week programmes and Discovery Weekends, including helping excavate mammoth remains in Oxfordshire. Some language or other specialist skills are required for some Earthwatch volunteers, who pay an annual membership fee of £25 (£15 for students; £45 for non-EU members), as well as the cost of their particular trip, which can be over £1,000 for more remote locations.

Sea Life Surveys

Sea Life Surveys
Dervaig
Isle of Mull
Argyll PA75 6QL
T: +44 (1688) 400 223
F: +44 (1688) 400 383

Specifically for those interested in learning more about the UK's marine wildlife, Sea Life Surveys run survey tours of the waters of the Inner Hebrides. While helping with observations and record-keeping for the Hebridean Whale and Dolphin Trust, the volunteers watch animals including minke whales, dolphins, porpoises, seals and other species. The short trips – ranging from a weekend to one week – also include lectures and land-based nature trails.

Coral Cay Conservation

Coral Cay Conservation
154 Clapham Park Road
London SW4 7DE
T: +44 (171) 498 6248
F: +44 (171) 498 8447
URL: www.coralcay.org

As the name suggests, Coral Cay Conservation helps preserve marine ecosystems, by bringing together local scientists with volunteers who help monitor and record conditions around coastal habitats. The organisation has worked extensively in Belize, Central America, and also operates in the Philippines, but other projects have either included, or are planned, in Borneo, the Seychelles and the

Red Sea. Volunteers assist with reef surveys, collecting data on the health of various marine species, helping local authorities to draw up and maintain conservation programmes. In 1999, land-based projects are also planned for the Philippines – and possibly the Seychelles – helping conserve rainforest regions. The cost for trips lasting from two weeks to three months ranges from £650 to £2,550, depending on location, and excludes international air fares. Coral Cay Conservation also produces impressive reports on the marine environment, as well as organising regular meetings in Britain, and an annual two-week sub-aqua survey in the Scilly Islands.

Waterway Recovery Group

The admirably single-minded dedication of the Waterway Recovery Group each year mobilises volunteers who work for a weekend or a week helping to restore Britain's canals. The group's supporters share many enthusiasms – including a healthy appetite for beer and mud, if its newsletters are to be believed – and have helped restore many inland waterways abandoned this century. As well as being important links and habitats for wildlife, canals are valuable amenity resources, for quiet recreation in cities as well as the countryside. Their restoration is also a pointer to providing greener transport channels, though it is unlikely, given the narrowness of most canals in Britain, that domestic waterways will ever rival their continental equivalents for carrying freight. Even so, the Waterway Recovery Group's regular camps are enjoyable working breaks, helping to restore industrial history. Work – no previous experience is required – includes clearing canals and their banks, of silt, rubble and excess vegetation; restoring or rebuilding bridges, locks, brick and stonework. For people enrolled in the Duke of Edinburgh Award scheme, taking part in a Canal Camp can also help gain a qualification. Each year, various groups who have taken part in the camps organise reunions, testifying to their popularity. As one volunteer recorded of a group that included school and college students, a nurse, an engineer, a college lecturer, a computer consultant and a retired shipwright: 'Almost all of them snored all night long, and burnt the pans when it was my turn to wash up – but by the end of the week I felt I'd gained a whole load of new friends.' Canal camp volunteers must normally be aged between 17 and 70, and reasonably fit. Prices run from £35–45.

Waterway Recovery Group
c/o The Inland Waterways Association
PO Box 114
Rickmansworth
Herts WD3 1ZY
T: +44 (1923) 711 114
F: +44 (1923) 897 000
URL: www.waterways.demon.co.uk

A new publication, *Green Volunteers*, edited by Fabio Ausenda, gives a more comprehensive guide to voluntary work in nature conservation, including more long-term projects, especially those involving wildlife abroad. Published by Green Volunteers, Via Valenza, 5, 20144 Milan, Italy, it is distributed in the UK by Vacation Work Publications, 9 Park End Street, Oxford OX1 1HJ; price £9.99.

Environmental Management, Volunteering and Campaigning

Some groups use volunteers for short or long-term help with their environmental activities. The RSPB, for example, relies on the support of its members to help run some of its nature reserves and research programmes, as well as leading local community groups. The RSPCA and the People's Dispensary for Sick Animals (PDSA) also get sterling support from volunteer workers at their veterinary centres, shops and animal shelters. And green campaigning organisations, such as Friends of the Earth or Greenpeace, similarly rely on volunteer workers for some of their activities. These are not holidays, but are worthwhile ways of spending free time.

LONGER-TERM VOLUNTEERING

Voluntary Service
Overseas
317 Putney Bridge Road
London SW15 2PN
T: +44 (181) 720 7200
F: +44 (181) 780 7300
URL: www.oneworld.org/
vso/

British Executive Service
Overseas
164 Vauxhall Bridge Road
London SW1 2RB
T: +44 (171) 630 0644
F: +44 (171) 630 0624
E: team@beso.demon.co.uk

Community Service
Volunteers
237 Pentonville Road
London N1 9NJ
T: +44 (171) 278 6601

*The International Directory
of Voluntary Work,*
published by Vacation
Work Publications, is a
useful and regularly
updated source of
further contacts and
advice.

While the volunteer conservation or environment work considered in the previous section is usually short-term, not usually lasting more than a few weeks, and with a strong sense of holiday about it, longer-term voluntary work appeals to many people who want to travel. Several organisations exist specifically to harness volunteers' skills with opportunities abroad, or in serving a wider community at home. Many organisations, including churches, charities and other agencies, seek volunteers for work around the world, whether as teachers, engineers, medical workers or a whole host of roles. Most placements are for lengthy periods of a year or more. Remuneration varies; some organisations offer a salary as well as paying travel, board and lodging. Others require the volunteer to raise sponsorship funds. The most satisfying reward, however, is the work you do, and the benefit it brings to you and to others.

Perhaps the most well-known of the volunteer organisations is Voluntary Service Overseas (VSO), which sends skilled personnel abroad for periods of two years or more for development work that ranges from agriculture to teaching, to youth activity training. The work can be as exotic as camel herding in Tanzania (a British agricultural student was the successful volunteer), to teaching English (curiously, in recent years, a shortage of qualified British teachers of English has meant VSO has had to recruit English teachers from Holland and other countries). Community Service Volunteers seek mainly to place volunteers in community work in Britain; British Executive Service Overseas is a service that sends professional workers, usually recently retired, abroad on short-term placements, advising on projects that utilise their

Photo © VSO/Gavin Cawtha

A volunteer discusses local fisheries knowledge as part of a VSO project in Carigara, Leyte, The Philippines

professional, managerial or commercial skills (one recent volunteer found himself managing a factory in Central America; a British journalist spent a week helping a struggling Ukranian newspaper develop its business and marketing plan; another volunteer worked with a local NGO in Nepal gathering information on bonded labour).

The National Centre for Volunteering operates an inquiry service for potential volunteers, both for short-term or longer periods of work, as well as offering some skills training. Its extensive information reserves can give lots of ideas about volunteer work in urban as well as rural areas, in areas including working with young people, in sport, arts and heritage, the environment, health and social care.

National Centre for Volunteering
Regent's Wharf
8 All Saints Street
London N1 9RL
T: +44 (171) 520 8900
F: +44 (171) 520 8910
E: centrevol@aol.com
URL: www.volunteering.org.uk

Vacation Work Publications
9 Park End Street
Oxford OX1 1HJ
T: +44 (1865) 241 978
F: +44 (1865) 790 885
URL: www.vacationwork.co.uk

HERITAGE HOLIDAYS

Many people enjoy visiting historic cities, towns and houses; it may sometimes be a vicarious experience, but if your visit or holiday can at the same time help preserve part of the built environment it can also be a genuine contribution to

Photo © Julia Bayne/Sustrans

A cyclist stops outside The Pump Room to admire Bath Abbey – a masterpiece of Perpendicular Gothic style, begun in 1499 by Bishop Oliver King

conservation. Unfortunately, while mass tourism has brought many people to enjoy the sights of such historic cities as Venice, Rome, Bath or Bruges, it has also bought the potentially destructive pressures of tourism, as well. Many historic town centres now suffer from traffic congestion and air pollution exacerbated by tourist numbers. The rash of unattractive tourist shops; the sprawl of car parks; even the cumulative impact of thousands of feet or hands on historic pavements, staircases and balustradings – all this can degrade historic urban environments, or even more remote buildings.

Heritage Hints for Green Travellers

- *Join and support organisations* such as the National Trust, the Landmark Trust or Common Ground, which either manage or campaign for the conservation of historic buildings, landscapes or localities.
- *Time your visit to a heritage site carefully.* Take advantage of off-season entrance fees, or transport fares, where possible.
- *Take your time,* rather than rushing from place to place. This author, while waiting outside the British Museum, overheard a visiting American tourist tell a companion how he had 'managed to do the Louvre in an hour and 27 minutes...' Select an itinerary which will enable you to visit heritage sites slowly, giving you time to appreciate them.

■ *Use public transport wherever possible.* In Bath, the British city designated a World Heritage Site for its mixture of Roman remains and Georgian architecture, the National Trust has pioneered an experiment at Prior Park, a 250-year-old, 28-acre garden, given to it in 1993. Together with Bath City Council, the Trust has actively set out to discourage motorists from using their cars to visit the gardens. Save for a limited number of spaces for the disabled, there is no car park. Instead, visitors are encouraged to use a regular bus service, connecting with the city's railway station.

■ *Respect your surroundings.* Many historic buildings, landscapes and gardens attract hundreds of thousands of visitors, putting pressure on footpaths, lawns, grass verges and plants. Wear appropriate footwear for venerable floor coverings, or wet grass. Take photographs, but not plant-cuttings! Indoors, observe any restrictions on flash-photography – it can damage some paintings, textiles or other historic materials (as well as being a pain for other visitors). On some sites, including nature reserves or farmland, dogs may not be permitted.

In addition to the various guides and handbooks produced by such organisations as the National Trust, English Heritage and the Historic Houses Association, an excellent guide to heritage properties in Britain is *Hudson's Historic Houses and Gardens*, published annually by Norman Hudson & Company of Upper Wardington, Banbury, Oxon OX17 1SP, which helpfully includes details of houses and monuments open all year.

For those wanting to visit sites of historic interest abroad, the National Trust also produces a Travel Collection, available from Page & May, 136–140 London Road, Leicester LE2 1EN, T: +44 [116]250 7676. The Trust benefits from every holiday booked through the programme.

English Heritage

English Heritage, the official agency charged with preserving historic sites and buildings ranging from the ancient monument at Stonehenge to Civil War battlefields, produces a visitors' handbook (£4.95) to well over 400 properties across the country. English Heritage has been attempting for many years to improve conditions at Stonehenge, both for the monument as well as for visitors. In 1998, the government announced it was minded to support English Heritage proposals to move a nearby major road into a 'cut and cover' tunnel, to prevent constant heavy traffic from further destroying the peace of one of England's most historic sites.

English Heritage
23 Savile Row
London W1X 1AB
T: +44 (171) 973 3000
Enquiries: 973 3434
F: +44 (171) 973 3001

The National Trust

One of Britain's best-known conservation organisations, the National Trust was founded in 1895 to preserve places of historic interest or natural beauty. It now owns more than 603,000 acres (244,000 hectares) of countryside, with 565 miles of

Photo © National Trust Photographic Library/Ian Shaw

A National Trust volunteer learns the age-old skill of dry stone walling

National Trust holiday cottages:
Holiday Booking Office
PO Box 536
Melksham
Wilts SN12 8SX
T: +44 (1225) 791 199
(Include £2 contribution for brochure production, p&p)
National Trust for Scotland
5 Charlotte Square
Edinburgh EH2 4DU
T: +44 (131) 226 5922

coastline, and some 250 historic houses, gardens and industrial monuments or mills. A special, indeed unique, feature of the Trust is that it can declare its land inalienable, so that it cannot be sold, mortgaged, or compulsorily purchased without special permission from Parliament. The Trust has also introduced a range of conservation measures to protect its site: at Orford Ness, Suffolk, only 96 visitors a day are permitted to the remote shingle spit, which is home to rare breeding and migrant birds.

Other than visiting the Trust's historic properties, details of which are available in its annual handbook and other literature, you can take short breaks working as a volunteer (see above under Conservation Holidays). It is also possible to stay in more than 240 holiday cottages owned or managed by the Trust in England, Wales and Northern Ireland (the National Trust for Scotland also offers holiday cottages). These buildings range from a Cornish manor house to a converted 15th century Kent stable.

The Landmark Trust

The Landmark Trust, set up in 1965, is an independent charity which conserves smaller buildings of historic and architectural interest – often after rescuing and restoring them from conditions of neglect – and rents them to the short-term, self-catering visitor. Landmark Trust buildings, which are not normally open to the public on a regular basis, include an 18th century Scottish summer house built in the shape of a gigantic pineapple, estate gatehouses, follies, converted religious buildings, lighthouses and other edifices. Among the more extraordinary, Appleton water tower is a Victorian landmark near Sandringham, Norfolk; Beamsley Hospital is a circular almshouse, dating from Elizabethan times; and Kingswear Castle is an imposing building, completed in 1502, overlooking the mouth of the River Dart in Devon, with a Second World War blockhouse next door. The Landmark Trust does not produce a free brochure of its properties, but publishes a handbook, costing £9.50 in the UK, refundable against any booking (£12 elsewhere in Europe, £22 in the US – $21.50 from the Vermont address – the Middle East, Central Asia and Africa, £26 in Australasia and the Far East).

Historic Houses Association

Two-thirds of Britain's built heritage remains in private hands. The Historic Houses Association represents many of the owners of such houses and gardens, more than 300 of which are open to the public. The HHA membership department issues an information pack for members of the public.

Windmills and Watermills

A sometimes overlooked aspect of the built heritage is the many surviving windmills and watermills that dot parts of the British countryside. As interest in clean, renewable energy is increasing, it is perhaps appropriate to include them in this section. National Mills Day, usually held on a Sunday in May, is aimed to focus attention on the need to keep such buildings working. In 1998, 300 mills were opened to the public, encouraged by the Wind and Watermill Section of the Society for the Protection of Ancient Buildings.

The National Trust
36 Queen Anne's Gate
London SW1H 9AS
T: +44 (171) 222 9251;
Info: +44 (181) 315 1111
F: +44 (171) 222 5097
URL: www.nationaltrust.
org.uk

The Landmark Trust
Shottesbrooke
Maidenhead
Berkshire SL6 3SW
T: +44 (1628) 825 925
F: +44 (1628) 825 417

The Landmark Trust
RR1
Box 510, Kipling Road
Brattleboro
Vermont 05301
USA
T: +1 802 254 6868
F: +1 802 257 7783

Historic Houses
Association
Heritage House
PO Box 21
Baldock
Herts SSG7 5SH
T: +44 (1462) 896 688
F: +44 (1462) 896 677

Society for the
Protection of Ancient
Buildings
37 Spital Square
London E1 6DY
T: +44 (171) 377 1644
F: +44 (171) 247 5296

EXPEDITIONS

Brathay Exploration
Group
Brathay Hall
Ambleside
Cumbria LA22 0HP
T/F: +44 (15394)
33942
E: brathay.exploration@
virgin.net

In a world shrunk by discovery, jet transport and the television age, expeditions are still a way for the intrepid traveller to help advance scientific knowledge, as well as self-awareness. But these days, expeditions are organised with a professionalism that would surprise earlier generations. The need to raise or conserve funds means that a volunteer keen to help out (and often to raise their own finance), is often welcome. Contemporary expeditions have also evolved to a point where some commercial or charitable expedition organisers balance self-development for expedition members along with the scientific, conservation or development elements in the expedition itself.

Photo © Trish Nicholson

Shishipangma trek camp, Tibetan plateau

Raleigh International
Raleigh House
27 Parson's Green Lane
London SW6 4HZ
T: +44 (!71) 371 8585
F: +44 (171) 371 5116
E: info@raleigh.org.uk
URL: www.raleigh.org.uk

While for some people, therefore, expeditions are a form of adventure holiday, many organisations see them as a way of helping conservation or development projects in Britain or abroad, while at the same time training expedition members in skills and self-development. Raleigh International, for example (formerly Operation Raleigh), takes young people abroad on a variety of projects, most of which involve working with local people. The Brathay

Exploration Group mixes 'adventure and fieldwork', running expeditions each year to destinations that have included (or are planned to include) mountain bike touring and climbing in Ethiopia, trekking in the highlands of Yemen, and exploring the possibilities for developing walking tourism in the Karst hills of south-western China. Expedition members – who may have to raise £250–2,000 towards the cost of their trip, depending on its location – have the chance to undertake qualifying work for the Duke of Edinburgh Award Scheme. Trekforce Expeditions, a London-based branch of the International Scientific Support Trust, raises funds for various conservation projects (including, for example, establishing a health care centre in rural Kenya, or working to save orang utans in Indonesia), and organises volunteer trips in support of them. Costs may range from £2,350 for a six-week expedition, to £3,500 for a five-month placement. The Wilderness Trust, inspired by the work and teachings of Laurens van der Post, organises self-financed 'education journeys and camps', in the remoter regions of the world, including South Africa, Nepal, British Columbia, Italy and Lapland. According to Chris Blessington, the organisation's director:

Trekforce Expeditions
34 Buckingham Palace Road
London SW1W 0RE
T: +44 (171) 824 8890
F: +44 (171) 824 8892
E: trekforce@dial.pipex.com

The Wilderness Trust
The Oast House
Hankham
Pevensey
East Sussex BN24 5AP
T: +44 (1323) 461 730
F: +44 (1323) 761 913
E: wilderness@dial.pipex.com

The Trust takes people into wild areas on foot, vulnerable yet protected, guided and watched over, so that they achieve a profound closeness with the natural world... Participants return inspired to make the continued existence of wilderness a personal concern... Our journeys are usually conducted in a primitive and minimum impact way. That is to say, we take the minimum amount of equipment into the area: ie, no tents, everything, including food, is carried. Water is obtained on site. We insist on ensuring that as a result of our having passed through an area, nothing is left to mark our passage. We leave nothing but our footprints...'

Royal Geographical Society
1 Kensington Gore
London SW7 2AR
T: +44 (171) 591 3000
F: +44 (171) 591 3031
URL: www.rgs.org

RGS Expedition Advisory Centre
T: +44 (171) 591 3030
F: +44 (171) 591 3031

Royal Scottish Geographical Society
10 Randolph Crescent
Edinburgh EG3 7TU
Scotland
T: +44 (131) 225 3330

Contemporary expeditions, whether planned as exercises in scientific research, individual endeavour or personal development, or even as purely commercial enterprises, should ensure that their journeys are as environmentally sustainable as possible – regulating the numbers of people travelling, employing experienced local guides, minimising waste or the use of fuel, and so on. The Wiltshire-based Steppes East company, for example, introduced walking expeditions across the Pamir mountains region of the former Soviet Central Asia, with a policy of using local food rather than importing supplies from Britain, employing local staff and seeking to minimise cultural intrusions into remote communities, while at the same time offering medical and other assistance when called upon – thus helping to ensure its tours were seen as welcome expeditions rather than commercial intrusions.

The spiritual home in Britain for would-be expedition organisers is the Royal Geographical Society (RGS) in London, which offers a wide range of expertise and advice for the intending traveller. Its meetings, talks and conferences are invariably absorbing and well-attended, its publications stimulating and its library and map collection voluminous. The list of speakers at its meetings reads like a roll-call of environmental endeavour, in the steps of explorers past. The RGS – which is open to prospective members on application – also houses the Expedition Advisory Centre, which publishes an invaluable *Expedition Planners' Handbook* as well as issuing an excellent, detailed pamphlet, *Environmental Responsibility for Expeditions*, jointly published by the British Ecological Society and the Young Explorers' Trust. It can also supply a formidable body of literature on aspects of expedition organising ranging from insurance to the best way of taking zoological or botanical specimens. The Centre also maintains a register of expeditions that may need volunteers or additional members.

SPORTS AND ACTIVITY HOLIDAYS

On Firm Ground

Walking, Rambling, Trekking, Hostelling, Hill Walking – and Mud Walking

Walking holidays, weekends and days out are among the simplest ways of enjoying the countryside. Getting out of the car means not only are you not contributing to the pollution, congestion and general social and environmental degradation that motor traffic can cause, but you are no longer cut off by glass and metal from what it is you've come to see. But pedestrians have had a bad deal in many urban areas in recent years: along with public transport users, they have often suffered at the hands of planners and the continued growth of motor traffic.

Photo © Isle of Man Tourism

Walking companions enjoy a sunny weekend on the Isle of Man

Photo © The Ramblers' Association

A walk on the wild side – West Highland Way, Scotland

Walking is among the best forms of exercise, and walking in the countryside, on the hills or in more exotic environments abroad can be one of the cheapest, purest forms of pleasure you can take. Of course, there is a difference between half-an-hour's walk around the local park and three weeks spent back-packing in the Australian outback, or trekking in Nepal. But essentially, the elements remain the same; you and your route.

In the UK, long-distance walks have been developed for people who want to cross particular areas of the countryside at their own pace. The Pennine Way, the South Downs Way, the Devon Coastal Path – such walks take you over different terrain and through various wildlife habitats. Other longer-distance walks follow the routes of different modes of transport – canal paths are increasingly being valued as part of a network that can take walkers around the country (see section below on Canal Holidays). But probably the most used network of paths for walkers – other than the pavements in towns and cities – are Britain's footpaths, byways and bridle-ways, some 140,000 miles in England and Wales. The Ramblers' Association, Britain's largest organisation for walkers, is particularly concerned to campaign for the preservation and extension of such rights of way. It works with local authorities, landowners and other bodies to help maintain footpaths and keep them open, not always without some friction with farmers, landowners and other individuals – paths can cross agricultural land as well as coming close to people's homes. To help resolve such conflict, while protecting footpaths from closure, the 1990 Rights of Way Act provides means of preventing the illegal ploughing or blocking of footpaths. The Ramblers' Association has also long campaigned for a public right to roam – giving access to uncultivated open land (as well as forests and woodlands), a touchstone for many countryside walkers since the days of the 1930s when the mass trespass at Kinder Scout in the Peak District highlighted the issue. The Labour Party pledged its support for extending rights of access to open land before the 1997 election, and the government was considering its legislation as this guide went to press. Groups such as the Country Landowners Association argue that improved access for the public to open land is best left to local agreements. The Ramblers' Association and other groups insist that legislation is necessary if all such land is to be opened. More detailed information about local rights of way (the legal situation differs in Scotland from that in England and Wales) is available from the Ramblers' Association, as well as in various information produced by the Countryside Commission and local tourist boards. See also local authority maps showing rights of way, as well as the maps produced by the Ordnance Survey.

Pedestrians Association
126 Aldersgate Street
London EC1A 4JQ
T: +44 (171) 490 0750
F: +44 (171) 608 0353

The Ramblers'
Association
1–5 Wandsworth Road
London SW8 2XX
T: +44 (171) 339 8500
F: +44 (171) 339 8501
E: ramblers@london.
ramblers.org.uk
URL: www.ramblers.org.uk

Walking holidays are widely advertised in the publications of the Ramblers' Association and the Youth Hostels Association (YHA), which maintains a network of accommodation across the UK. (Membership of the YHA is open to adults over 18, incidentally!) Both organisations have increased their commitment to improved environmental standards; the YHA, for example, has introduced new policies at its hostels, designed to conserve water and energy, encourage recycling, the use of public transport, and – at some sites – the growing of fruit and vegetables for local consumption. For hostellers and for Cyclists Touring Club members, it may be possible in some parts of the country to organise transport for your luggage – it is taken ahead of you, while you walk or cycle during the day. In a recent development, it is now even possible to rent an entire YHA hostel for a group holiday. Both the Ramblers' Association and the YHA have links with walking and hostelling organisations overseas, and supply information on these, for anyone considering a holiday abroad. The Hostelling International logo is a mark of such accommodation.

Whether you are walking or hostelling in the UK or abroad, you have responsibilities as well as rights:

- Follow the Country Code: do not interfere with, or disturb, livestock; close gates behind you; don't pollute watercourses, don't drop litter or cause unnecessary noise; keep dogs under control. In summer or in dry weather, beware of the risk of fire, especially in grassland, woodland or on moors.
- Protect pathways; join or support organisations such as the Ramblers' Association, the YHA or the Pedestrians Association. Volunteers are always welcome to help clear pathways of obstructions. But remember to protect paths from careless walkers – don't erode damaged footpaths during dry or very wet

conditions. The tramp of thousands of feet can have its impact, too. Respect, too, the privacy of people who live near paths, and the livelihood of country workers: don't damage crops.

- Go properly equipped. A good pair of boots will help you cover the miles comfortably. If you are walking far from home or shelter, wear or carry adequate showerproof or rainproof clothing – modern walking gear (including boots) should allow your body to breathe while protecting you from the worst of the rain. If you are walking at night, carry a torch (and in remote areas a whistle, in case you need to attract help). If you are travelling far, or are walking in remote countryside in hot weather, take a water bottle, and sufficient food where necessary.
- On the subject of clothing, it is arguable that while walking in the countryside, aesthetic or conservation considerations should dictate that walking jackets and coats are natural colours – greens, browns and blues seem more appropriate than bright reds, yellows and pinks – but in some cases, bright colours can be useful for safety purposes, being more easily seen by rescue services. At least one company now makes walking or hiking 'fleeces' from recycled plastic bottles, which is a further gesture towards the environment.
- Take a map – in Britain, Ordnance Survey 1:25,000 Pathfinders (now being replaced by the Explorers series) and 1:50,000 Landranger maps are particularly helpful for walkers – and learn how to use it, both for navigating, following paths and rights of way, and for increasing your awareness of the countryside. In remoter areas, a compass will be extremely useful – again, learn how to use it.
- If you are walking in remote areas, or in poor weather conditions, tell someone where you are going, your route, and when you expect to arrive at your destination. Check in on your arrival.
- Don't disturb wildlife, especially during breeding seasons. Carry binoculars to enjoy wildlife watching at a distance. The Ramblers' Association recommends that walkers in moorland areas take care during game shooting seasons not to disturb shooting, nor put themselves at risk.
- Support local traders and farmers; stay at farms and local hostels, pubs or hotels, and eat local produce wherever possible.

British Orienteering
Federation
Riverdale
Dale Road North
Darley Dale
Matlock
Derbyshire DE4 2HX
T: +44 (1629) 734 042

The specialised sport of orienteering – where cross-country runners follow predetermined courses, using their skills at map-reading, compass use and navigation – has developed its own code of practice to ensure that orienteers conserve the countryside. It is available from the British Orienteering Federation.

Camping and Caravanning

Life under canvas is a popular option for holidaymakers of all ages. Whether you stay at a fixed camping site, staying in a tent maintained by the camp operators, or whether you travel with your tent loaded in your car, on your bicycle or even your back-pack, the attractions of tenting are many, not least its cheapness (compared to staying in a hotel or even hostel) and its closeness to nature. The YHA publishes several pamphlets on camping in Britain, including *Camping Barns in England*, an option which saves pitching a tent.

If you are camping away from a permanent camping site, it is important to realise that even a temporary camp can have an environmental impact. When choosing where to camp, therefore:

British Holidays and
Home Parks Association
Chichester House
6 Pullman Court
Great Western Road
Gloucester GL1 3ND
T: +44 (1452) 526 911
F: +44 (1452) 307 226

- Camp in an appropriate spot, where you are not damaging farmland or crops, or impacting on wildlife – check you are not camping on a wildlife route to a watering hole, for example (if the wildlife is on the large side, it might not be the animals that are disturbed).
- Wherever possible, camp away from livestock. It is unwise to camp in the same field as a bull...
- Camp on land designated for the purpose wherever possible. Where there are no designated camp sites, ask permission of a local farmer or landowner. Buy locally produced food wherever possible – it reduces packaging and the weight you are carrying, and also helps make for better relations locally.
- If you are staying in the same spot for more than a couple of days, move your tent, to prevent damage to the grass and ground beneath you.
- Protect water sources from pollution or contamination. If there are no toilet facilities, bury solid waste (don't just scrape some soil over it), well away from your camp. In arid zones, use well or spring water sparingly.
- Guard against fire. Especially in regions where firewood is scarce, or there is a danger of dry undergrowth catching fire, use gas or kerosene camping stoves. Store any fuel carefully, where it is safe from fire, or from the risk of polluting water courses.
- As always, do not leave litter behind you. If there are no litter facilities near your camp site, take your litter away with you. In remote regions where this may be impractical for logistical reasons, bury it, taking care it is away from water sources which could become contaminated.
- Keep noise levels low.
- Don't feed wild animals.
- When you strike camp, make sure you leave the site as you found it. Tidy up after you, covering any fire sites, etc. Make sure you remove any tent ropes, pegs and other equipment – not only will you need it when you next camp, but left behind it could be a risk for wildlife.

Caravan parks have been accused, often with much justification, of being blots on the rural landscape. At other occasions, it is difficult to avoid the feeling that some of the criticism is thinly veiled snobbery. But for every horror, with acres of caravans or trailers straddling hillsides scarred by car tracks, there are increasing examples of well-planned caravan camps designed to blend in with the environment, and to incorporate sensible, sustainable use of local resources.

David Bellamy, the indefatigable conservationist, believes that such sites can contribute to preserving wildlife and local habitats at the same time as bringing benefits to local economies. The economic contribution is a serious one: in 1996, holiday and 'home' parks, together with the touring caravan trade, accommodated 17.2 million tourist trips in Britain (around 18 per cent of the total), produced £200 million in foreign earnings from overseas visitors and supported more than a quarter of a million jobs. According to the British Holiday and Home Parks Association, 35 per cent of Britons holiday in caravan or chalet parks at some time. Professor Bellamy's enthusiasm for the conservation role of caravan parks is marked by an annual award scheme for those camps who are taking their environmental responsibilities seriously. 'They are unsung champions of conservation in the countryside,' he said at the 1997 awards ceremony. 'They are bursting with biodiversity, and many have created an absolute oasis for wildlife.'

Camping and
Caravanning Club
Greenfields House
Westfields Way
Coventry CV4 8JH
T: +44 (1203) 694 995
F: +44 (1203) 694 886

Caravan Codes

■ Follow the advice and environmental codes published by groups such as the Camping and Caravanning Club, and the camp rules where you take your caravan.
■ If you are towing a caravan on holiday, in addition to the normal road safety precautions, ensure that your load is as light as possible: extra weight means burning more fuel.
■ On the road, let following traffic overtake wherever possible, particularly in country areas where local people have a right to consideration.
■ Make sure your camp reaches the highest environmental standard, in terms of handling waste material, litter, use of energy and conservation of natural resources. Favour those camps who do well in environmental or conservation award schemes.

Trekking, Climbing and Mountaineering

Long-distance walking, especially in the world's more remote regions, particularly in mountains, has become increasingly popular. Mountains in many cultures represent something unattainable, mystical, and the isolation of mountain regions is part of their allure. The Inca Trail in the Andes, or various routes in Nepal, have in recent years become so well-trodden that serious environmental and social disturbance has been caused in some parts. Many trekking parties in the Himalayan regions have contributed to a fuel crisis in parts of Nepal by burning locally hewn wood (the resulting deforestation is believed to contribute to erosion and flooding further down river valleys, into India and beyond); while other tourists may alternately lavish money on some consumer goods or services, distorting local economies, or take advantage of traditional mountain community hospitality, taking portering, guide and other services cheaply. In 1997, there was understandable outrage when many newspapers and magazines reported on the piles of discarded rubbish left on the Himalayan slopes by several generations of mountaineering expeditions. Closer to home, the hiking magazine *TGO* (from *The Great Outdoors*) has drawn attention to the fetid state of some bothy lodges (built for overnighting climbers and other hill users) after thoughtless visitors have effectively used them as toilets. And elsewhere in the UK, mountaineers have been divided over such environmental issues as the use of fixed bolts – supports that are left embedded in the rock face after the climber moves on. The Earth's high places, source of wonder (and for many regions, the source of fresh water), can easily be defiled by unthinking travellers. Their attraction for holidaymakers, in all forms, is their beauty, isolation and spiritual significance. It is a test of our commitment to the environment that we preserve them.

The British Mountaineering Council, as well as the London-based organisation Tourism Concern, have both compiled codes of conduct for travellers in hill and mountain regions. They can well be adopted for domestic, as well as overseas high places. The Alpine Club, a membership-based organisation catering for those who climb in the Alps and the greater ranges of the world, also promotes a code of climbing ethics which seeks to protect mountains, mountain regions and their people from any harmful impact by climbers. The booklet, *Environmental Responsibility for Expeditions* (see section on Expeditions, above), is also full of useful advice.

Of specific interest in the Alpine region of Europe is Alp Action, an organisation set up by Prince Sadruddin Aga Khan, to help counter the myriad threats to the mountains and their inhabitants, from industrial pollution as well as the sometimes negative economic, social, cultural and environmental impacts of tourism.

British Mountaineering Council
177–179 Burton Road
West Didsbury
Manchester M20 2BB
T: +44 (161) 445 4747
F: +44 (161) 445 4500
URL: www.thebmc.co.uk

Alpine Club
55 Charlotte Road
London EC2A 3QT
T/F: +44 (171) 613 0755
URL: www.alpine-club.org.uk

Alp Action
20 Quai Gustave-ador
CH–1207 Geneva
Switzerland
T: +41 (22) 736 8181
F: +41 (22) 736 8060

BOX 2.1

HIGH LIFE IN THE BALANCE

'Thousands of tired, nerve-shaken, overcivilised people are beginning to find that going to the mountains is going home; that wilderness is a necessity; and that mountain parks and preservations are useful not only as fountains of timber and irrigating rivers, but as fountains of life.' So rhapsodised John Muir, the pioneer US conservationist, in 1898. A hundred years on, he may be regretting it from beyond the grave.

Since 1945, visits to the ten most popular mountainous National Parks in the US have increased at least twelvefold, from around 2 million to over 25 million a year. Mountain tourism has also skyrocketed in developing regions. The sixteenth century stronghold of the Incas, Machu Picchu in the Peruvian Andes, now attracts over 100,000 visitors a year. They leave behind them a trail of garbage, vandalised stonework and polluted streams. In the Gangotri region of India's Himalayas, more than 250,000 Hindu pilgrims a year visit the sacred source of the Ganges River, with similar consequences. Still more notorious is the impact of tourists embarking on trekking holidays in the Annapurna and Annapiral regions on the Nepal side of the range, who now number more than 50,000 a year. As 'adventure holiday' tourism grows, ever more infrastructure and creature comforts must be supplied, racking up environmental overload.

Tourism can have extraordinary bolstering effects on rural economies in mountain regions. Mass tourism in Europe's Alps is now a $52 billion a year business that yields 100 million visitor-days of tourism custom a year and creates 250,000 local jobs. In the Yellowstone region of the US, a recent study by the Wilderness Society showed that in the past 20 years, 96 per cent of new jobs and 89 per cent of growth in employment income came from tourism rather than oil or gas extraction, mining, logging or grazing. Ski resort construction in the Appalachians and other ranges is growing at up to triple the national average. Many ski resorts now consume massive amounts of water to make instant snow at the time of year when mountain water is least available. Pollution from tourist motor traffic adds significantly to a general rise in pollution levels in mountain regions. Each weekend on Switzerland's St Gotthard Pass, traffic deposits 30 tons of oxides of nitrogen, 25 tons of hydrocarbons and 75 kilograms of lead, often turning the snow black.

Around 8 per cent of the world's mountains are situated in officially protected areas, but coverage in some regions is patchy. Even where protection is adequate in terms of area cover, state budgets are becoming increasingly strained and standards of management are all too liable to slip. Pressures on endemic species of wildlife, which frequently abound in mountain ecosystems, arè increasing inside and outside protected areas. Out of 14 tropical 'hotspots' threatened with imminent ecological crisis, seven have at least half their total area in tropical

mountains. Like island wildife, mountain species are especially vulnerable to intro-
ductions: examples of harmful invasions include feral pigs in Hawaii and Costa
Rica, goats in Venezuela and foreign grass varieties in Puerto Rico. Rare mountain
life needs protection from pushy incomers of all descriptions!

The complex biological and climatic layering of mountain landscapes and
ecosystems has also nurtured spectacular cultural diversity. Small-scale farming
and pastoral societies abound in the mountains and uplands of China, Iran, Nepal,
Afghanistan, Pakistan and the central Asian states of the former Soviet Union. By
contrast with the sparsely populated mountain regions of many northern
countries, some tropical mountain ranges, such as the highlands of Papua New
Guinea and Rwanda's Virunga volcanic zone, support large concentrations of
people. In many regions, mountains attract major development investment in
hydropower and reservoir construction, often with highly disruptive consequences to local communities. Tourism can act as an antidote to destructive
development, but in many cases adds yet another item to the list of obstacles to
social justice and fair living standards faced by mountain people.

The best answer to these social and environmental dilemmas is to work with
local people to map out agreed strategies that integrate conservation of the wild
with economic and community development and environmental protection
measures. Working examples of such programmes are now emerging around the
world. In most cases, all-round benefits are being delivered, showing it *can* be
done. Travel and tourism often supply the 'missing link' that can make sustainable
development dreams a reality.

Sources: Brown, L et al (1995) *State of the World 1995*, Earthscan, London; and McNeely, J A et al
(1994) *Protecting Nature: Regional Reviews of Protected Areas* IUCN, Gland

Green Hints for Trekkers and Climbers

■ Leave the mountains as you would wish to find them. Reduce waste, recycle
materials wherever possible, remove litter (or bury it, away from any water courses,
if this is not possible). Some climbing codes discourage the habit of piling stones
as cairns, to mark your ascent or passage.

■ Respect local cultures and religious traditions, including mountain shrines.

■ Conserve fuels, including local wood supplies. Use kerosene or gas where possible (recycle cylinders).

■ Avoid polluting water courses.

■ Be careful of fire – in remote regions it can easily get out of control.

■ Mountain ecosystems can be particularly fragile – don't take plants or cuttings as
souvenirs, and avoid disturbing wildlife.

■ Take care to spread any economic benefits from your visits among local communities. Employ local guides, or porters, wherever practicable, and buy local
produce.

BOX 2.2

PROTECT AND RESPECT: TIPS FOR TREKKERS

- Limit deforestation – make no open fires and discourage others from doing so on your behalf. Where water is heated by scarce firewood, use as little as possible. If possible, choose accommodation that uses kerosene or fuel-efficient wood stoves.
- Remove litter, burn or bury paper and carry out all non-degradable litter. Graffiti often end up as permanent examples of environmental pollution.
- Keep local water clean and avoid using pollutants such as detergents in streams or springs. If no toilet facilities are available, make sure you are at least 30 metres away from water sources, and bury or cover wastes.
- Plants should be left to flourish in their natural environment – taking cuttings, seeds and roots is illegal in many parts of the Himalayas.
- Help your guides and porters to follow conservation measures.
- When taking photographs, ask permission first and use restraint.
- Respect holy places – preserve what you have come to see and never touch or remove religious objects. Shoes should be removed when visiting certain temples.
- Giving to children encourages begging. A donation to a project, health centre or school is a more constructive way to help.
- You will be accepted and welcomed if you follow local customs. Use only your right hand for eating and greeting. Do not share cutlery, cups and the like. It is polite to use both hands when giving or receiving gifts.
- Respect for local etiquette earns you respect. Loose, light-weight clothes are preferable to revealing shorts, skimpy tops and tight-fitting action-wear. Hand-holding or kissing in public are disliked by local people.
- Observe standard food and bed charges but do not condone overcharging. Remember when you're shopping that the bargains you buy may only be possible because of low income to others.
- Visitors who value local traditions encourage local pride and maintain local cultures. Please help local people gain a realistic view of life in Western countries.

Source: Tourism Concern

- Take advice on how to support local communities. For example, in some areas, rather than giving to beggars (save where this is a custom or religious observation), or handing out sweets to children, try to give money or contributions via local schools or community organisations.

Golf

Boosted by the rise of such new champions as Tiger Woods and Vijay Singh, golf is increasingly shedding its old image as essentially a white, middle-class sport (though some redoubts remain), and is now popular around the world – more than 50 million people play the game, and many more flock to watch major tournaments. In Europe alone there are 5,200 golf courses, covering 250,000 hectares. But such popularity has come at a cost. The drive to develop new golf courses in many parts of the world has often caused undesirable environmental impacts, and considerable social disruption.

In parts of South-East Asia, the spread of golf courses came partly as a result of the enthusiasm for the game in Japan, and the rising wealth of that country in the 1980s. In Thailand, businesses began to develop new golf courses to cater for the boom in golfing holidays for Japanese, Taiwanese and South Korean golfers – often amid accusations that local villagers and farmers were being forced off their land, and that planning laws were corrupted. In Hawaii, visiting American tourists also flocked to new courses, again against a background of complaints in some cases that traditional cultural sites had been lost, along with farmland and access to land and water.

Nor are critics of the golf boom confined to the Far East. In Britain, the Council for the Protection of Rural England (CPRE) has expressed concern that golf course development leads to unsuitable new building, together with its associated traffic, in the countryside. And in many parts of the country, the opening of new golf driving ranges, open at night, can lead to complaints that the ranges' floodlighting causes light pollution – obscuring the night sky.

Other environmental problems golf courses can cause include:

■ Water wastage and pollution. Spraying greens in summer can waste vast amounts of water, not just in the warmer climates of the Mediterranean and Far East. Pesticides and herbicides used on the greens and links can also pollute nearby water courses.
■ Wildlife can be adversely affected by the use of such chemicals.
■ Native species of plants and animals can be displaced by new courses built on their former habitats.
■ Traditional landscapes can disappear if new courses are developed unsympathetically.

More recently, golfers have begun to address some of these problems. In Europe, a leading role is being played by the European Golf Association (EGA), which has set

Golf and Tourism: A flourishing business with high environmental risks, by Anita Pleumarom, published by Tourism Concern, has a more detailed account of the controversial development of golf courses in Thailand in the 1980s and early 1990s.

up its own ecology unit, while in the US, the conservation organisation Audubon International has done pioneering work alongside golf authorities to encourage improvements.

European Golf
Association
Ecology Unit
51 South Street
Dorking
Surrey RH4 2JX
T: +44 (1306) 743288
F: +44 (1306) 742496
E: ega.golf.ecology@
dial.pipex.com
URL: www.golf
ecology.com

In 1997, the EGA Ecology Unit launched a new campaign, 'Committed to Green', aimed at encouraging environmental improvements in the game. The campaign was launched during the Ryder Cup tournament at Valderrama in Spain by Jacques Santer, president of the European Commission, who remarked:

'Respect for the environment goes hand in hand with human well-being and, indeed, sporting excellence. This is certainly true for golf, in which harmony with nature is part of the game's heritage and its enjoyment.'

David Stubbs, executive director of the EGA Ecology Unit, notes that:

'The game still faces many environmental challenges – we have to be good conservationists; we need to address water resource and pest management issues; we want to ensure that greenkeepers receive appropriate training in ecological management; and we must communicate these points throughout the golf industry and to the golfing public.'

According to the *Committed to Green Handbook*, 'golf courses serve a broader function than simply as a particular type of sports ground. In a wider context they can provide important areas of green space in urban areas, they can be buffers between natural areas and developed land, they can provide valuable wildlife habitat in their own right, and they also have the opportunity to conserve and enhance water resources – turfgrass is a highly effective biological filter, capable of improving water quality.' To help achieve these ends, the EGA Ecology Unit has drawn up an environmental strategy for Europe's golf courses, and publishes guidelines for new course development. The 'Committed to Green' campaign suggests that golf courses can follow some or all of the following policies:

Wetland habitat created at the golf course at San Lorenzo, Portugal, is now home to a population of the rare purple gallinule (Porphyrio porphyrio).

■ **Encourage wildlife**, by identifying and preserving areas as wildlife sanctuaries; developing wildlife corridors such as hedges, tree lines, ditches or uncut grass strips; allowing vegetation to grow along the edges of water courses; putting up nesting boxes for birds and bats.

■ *Respect the landscape and cultural heritage* of the area where a golf course is built, by using local natural materials where possible for buildings, bunkers and paths; planting trees and shrubs that are complementary to existing, indigenous vegetation; placing signs, litter bins, ball-washers and other features where they do not protrude above the skyline; and survey and preserve archaeological sites and historic landscape features.

The Royal St Davids golf course at Harlech is one of two clubs undertaking an environmental review in a Welsh Golfing Union pilot project.

■ *Conserve water.* Assess the grass on the fairways and greens, and use the species best adapted for the local climate. Repair leaking water pipes, don't over-water greens, monitor water use and conserve the quality of water courses by better use of vegetation, reducing chemical use and run-off and by monitoring the health of pond and stream life.

■ *Improve the management of the turf grass*, planting appropriate grass species, using slow-release or natural, organic fertilisers and by choosing the least toxic pest controls.

■ *Reduce and control waste*: reducing the use of toxic chemicals, preventing leaks and improving the handling of waste water, grass clippings – not dumping them in water courses or wildlife habitat areas – and recycling materials such as paper, tins, bottles, plastics and metals.

■ *Increase energy efficiency.* Golf courses can improve by taking simple steps. For example, the Ljunghusens golf club in Sweden provides extra golf bag storage space during the school holidays, so young players can simply cycle to the course rather than have to use their – or their parents' – cars. Using electric golf trolleys rather than petrol powered vehicles is also less polluting, and a saving of energy.

■ *Improve training and communication.* Golf course personnel, including greenkeepers, and ordinary club members, can be encouraged to be more environmentally aware. The handbook suggests, among other steps, producing leaflets or erecting signs drawing attention to the wildlife around a golf course, to enhance conservation awareness.

Green travellers can improve their golf by persuading their clubs and those they visit on holiday to adopt the EGA's campaign, and – wherever possible – choose courses that are already committed to good environmental practice.

Cycling and Mountain Biking

The bicycle is often held up as the perfect example of individual green transport – pollution free (apart from the process of producing the metal and rubber parts, and possibly excluding the more garish of modern day lycra cycling clothes), relatively cheap, simple and easily maintained, using little if any fossil fuels (lubricating oils apart), and capable of helping to keep the user healthy (if they survive modern traffic). In normal, flat conditions in towns, a bike is perhaps the best mode of transport for journeys of up to two or three miles. For holiday touring, it is among the more satisfying modes of travel – the very phrase, 'free-wheeling' summons up moments of relaxed, effortless passage.

In spite of its advantages, however, much modern traffic planning, particularly in the UK, has militated against cycling. Even in The Netherlands, cycling has declined, relatively, as a favoured mode of transport. This is largely because of the growth in motor traffic, both in popularity and its impact on the roads. Without adequate protection, whether by provision of cycle lanes or better traffic management, cyclists have a hard time of it in most modern towns and cities. In the UK, the privatisation of the railways has left a bewildering muddle of some train companies doing more to encourage cyclists to use their services, and others their apparent best to discourage them.

Even so, conditions are improving – slowly in some towns. Cities such as York, for example, are pushing ahead with plans designed to increase cycle use. Organisations such as the Bristol-based Sustrans, have been pioneering new cross-country cycle routes – in 1995, it won an International Tourism for Tomorrow award for its coast-to-coast cycle path across northern England. And as a means of getting around on holiday, particularly in the countryside, the bike is still hard to beat if you want to be in touch with your surroundings. In Jersey, collaboration between a local pressure group and Jersey Tourism has led to the development of a 96-mile rural cyle network (see The Channel Islands, page 116).

The Youth Hostels network provides accommodation for travellers whether on foot or cycle, but it is the cycling organisations themselves who are, understandably, some of the best sources of information for ideas about holidays on two wheels. The Cyclists' Touring Club (CTC), the largest such group, was – when this Guide went to press – in discussion with two other groupings, the London Cycling Campaign and the Welsh Cycling Union, with a view to joining forces. The CTC currently issues information about train, bus, air and ferry services that take bicycles, both in the UK and in continental Europe, as well as issuing advice for cycle tourists. Its literature, including a magazine, *Cycling*, regularly reviews new machines and equipment as well as suggesting touring routes for two-wheeled holidaymakers, in the UK and abroad. CTC issues information booklets for its members, on cycle touring, camping, mountain areas, desig-

British Cycling Federation
National Cycling Centre
Stuart Street
Manchester M11 4DQ
T: +44 (161) 230 2301
F: +44 (161) 231 0591
URL: www.bcf.uk.com

Cyclists' Touring Club
Cotterell House
69 Meadrow
Godalming
Surrey GU7 3HS
T: +44 (1483) 417 217
F: +44 (1483) 426 994
E: cycling@ctc.org.uk
URL: www.ctc.org.uk

London Cycling
Campaign
Unit 228
30 Great Guildford
Street
London SE1 0HS
T: +44 (171) 928 7220
F: +44 (171) 928 2318

Sustrans
35 King Street
Bristol BS1 4DZ
T: +44 (117) 929 0888
F: +44 (117) 929 4173
URL: www.sustrans.org.uk

Photo © Steve Patterson/Sustrans

A well-deserved rest for riders on the Sustrans Kingfisher Trail, Co Fermanagh,
Northern Ireland

nated cycle routes, off-road riding, cycle hire, airport access for cyclists at several UK and European air hubs, information on which London Underground lines and overground train services carry bicycles, as well as similar details for the rail services in Europe. It is also campaigning for greater access to rights of way for cyclists, including to the estimated 10,000 currently unclassified, unsurfaced roads in the country. By contrast, the London Cycling Campaign has a more radical edge and character, pushing for better facilities for bikes in the capital, and a cross-city network of routes. Sustrans, meanwhile, is continuing to establish cycle-routes across the country, and currently offers more than 140 maps and guides to those already established. For those cyclists who want to race or join other sporting events, the British Cycling Federation is the sport's governing body in Britain.

One of the major developments in cycling in recent years has been the arrival of the mountain bike, rugged enough to enable off-road riding. Though most now seem to be used by city cyclists – in part a reflection of the pot-holed condition of many of our roads – others reflect a more pugnacious attitude towards cycling. Off-road, however, the mountain bike enables the cyclist to move across country.

Green Hints for Cyclists

■ Learn to ride a bike properly – cyclists have as many responsibilities as rights on the road. Keep your bike well maintained, and wear safety equipment when necessary (sadly, this means a safety helmet on most occasions, and always lights and reflective equipment at night).

- Join and support cycling organisations and other transport lobby groups in campaigning for better provisions for cyclists – not just on the roads, but on the railways and in connection with bus services, as part of an integrated transport system.
- Apart from following the Country Code in the normal way, cyclists should give way to walkers and horse riders on bridleways and byways. On most upland, moorland and farmland, cyclists normally do not have automatic right of access – consult the landowner.
- If you are riding off-road, think about your own safety, as well as that of others, and that of the environment. For yourself, carry identification, lights for night riding, and a first aid kit in remoter regions (where it is usually safer to cycle in company).
- Keep to hard tracks and paths, and don't take shortcuts that can lead to ground being eroded, wildlife being disturbed and vegetation destroyed. Over very soft ground – walk, don't cut it up with your tyres. It is usually better to avoid sensitive terrain, such as mountain tops and plateaus, unless there are established cycle routes – bicycles can help degrade some habitats. When cycling downhill off-road, avoid excessive braking or skidding which can damage path surfaces.
- Show consideration to other country users, giving way to horse riders and pedestrians, farm and forestry workers. Sound your bell rather than coming up silently behind walkers or horse riders – a horse could be startled by your sudden appearance.
- Take care not to disturb livestock cycling off-road.

Horse and Pony Riding, Trekking, Trail-riding and Caravanning

British Horse Society
Stoneleigh Deer Park
Kenilworth
Warwickshire CV8 2XZ
T: +44 (1926) 707700
F: +44 (1926) 707800
E: enquiry@bhs.org.uk
URL: www.bhs.org.uk

The Wales Trekking &
Riding Association
Standby House
9 Nevill Street
Abergavenny
Gwent NP7 5AA
T/F: +44 (1873)
858717

If walking or cycling are among the greenest forms of travelling on land, then horse riding must be a close rival. Though the Thelwell cartoons of young misses on ponyback seem to harken back to a world of gymkhanas as a middle-class preserve, many more people are now taking to riding, either as horse owners themselves or as an activity during holidays or weekends.

Nichola Gregory, spokeswoman for the British Horse Society (BHS) remarks:

'Horse riding could make a claim to be even more environmentally friendly than cycling or walking, in some senses. Certainly, if you are riding in the countryside you seem less likely to disturb wildlife than you would do on foot or on a bicycle. Wild animals seem not to be so disturbed by the sight, sound or scent of a horse. And of course, on horseback, you can see over hedges and rather further than you can on foot or on a bike.'

Photo © British Horse Society

Riding in the countryside affords a good view over hedgerows and is unlikely to disturb the wildlife

Long-distance trail-riding holidays are now offered in many parts of the world – the US-based Equitours company, for example, organises such events from India to the Andes, using BHS-approved facilities en route. In choosing such holidays, whether at home or abroad, check beforehand to ensure that horses, equipment and facilities are approved by the BHS or other appropriate national body. The national tourist boards of England, Wales, Scotland and Northern Ireland can also supply details of possibilities for horse riding and pony trekking holidays for people with varying levels of equestrian experience. In Ireland, horse-drawn caravan holidays are another recent reworking of a traditional way of life. The BHS issues a series of guides to horse riding and routes in many of the English counties, together with a booklet, *Bed and Breakfast for Horses*, which lists more than 300 venues around the country which offer accommodation for both horse and rider. Some also offer horses for hire, or the services of a trail guide.

Whether you ride for an hour or two at the weekend or during an otherwise conventional holiday, or for greater periods of time and distance, the attraction is of being closer to nature, and of working with an animal that has changed little over the centuries.

Riding for the Disabled Association
National Agricultural Association
Avenue R
Kenilworth
Warwickshire CV8 2LY
T: +44 (1203) 696510

The Trekking & Riding Society of Scotland
Boreland
Fearnan
by Aberfeldy
Perthshire PH15 2PG
T: +44 (1887) 830274
F: +44 (1887) 830606

Green Hints for Riders

- Ride safely: learn to ride with professional tuition, wear an approved riding hat or safety helmet. If you are transporting a horse in a horsebox, make sure you comply with the Ministry of Agriculture Certificate of Competence required by the Welfare of Animals Transport Order.

The BHS has its own code for riding and carriage-driving responsibly. Follow it:

- Care for the land. Do not stray off the line of the path; do not damage timber or hedgerows by jumping; remember that horses' hooves can damage surfaces in bad weather; pay particular attention to protected areas that have significant historical and/or biological value.
- Show courtesy to other travellers. Remember that walkers, cyclists and other riders may be elderly, disabled, children or simply frightened of horses. Wherever possible, acknowledge courtesy shown by drivers of motor vehicles.
- Show consideration for the farmer. Shut gates behind you; ride slowly past livestock; don't ride on cultivated land unless the right of way crosses it. Remember, dogs are seldom welcome on farmland or moorland unless on a lead or under close control.
- Observe local bylaws.
- Ride or drive with care on the roads. Take the BHS Riding and Road Safety Test. Always make sure you can be seen at night or in bad visibility – wear the right kind of reflective or fluorescent aids.
- Take care riding in groups. Groups from riding establishments should contain reasonable numbers, for reasons of both safety and amenity. They should never exceed 20 in total, including the relevant number of escorts. Rides should not deviate from the right of way or permitted route and regard must be shown at all times for growing crops; shutting and securing of gates and the consideration and courtesy due to others.
- Follow the Country Code. Enjoy the countryside and respect its life and work. Guard against risk of fire. Fasten all gates. Keep dogs under close control. Keep to public paths across farmland. Use gates and stiles to cross fences, hedges and walls. Leave livestock, crops and machinery alone. Take your litter home. Help keep water clean. Protect wildlife, plants and trees. Take special care on country roads. Make no unnecessary noise.

Snow and Ice

Skiing and snow-boarding

Once the province of a small minority of (usually rich) enthusiasts, winter sports such as skiing are now increasingly popular, and for every upmarket, exclusive ski resort, peopled by the chic and exclusive ski set, there are now many more catering for thousands of ordinary skiers. Ice and snow sports suggest a clean, pristine environment – the sharp tang of fresh air, the hiss of skis upon the sparkling snow. But the explosion of interest in winter sports – world-wide, as well as in Europe – has had its environmental down-side. In many Alpine districts, the boom in skiing – and more recently, off-shoot sports such as snow-boarding – has added to the pressure on local environments. Mountain regions do not normally support large human populations, but now face an annual winter influx of tens of thousands. Just as Alpine Europe has begun in the last decade to show the effects of more generalised pollution – acid rain, the impact of drier, warmer climates – so the extra demands made by a tourist economy have also begun to show. The development of new ski runs has led to further loss of tree cover, in a region where tree health has already suffered from pollution and climate change. At times of no or little snow (itself a possible consequence of climate change), snow-making machinery is now routinely employed, with consequent increased pressure on water supplies, together with chemical and power use. The building of new roads to new resorts, with new hotels, restaurants and chalets, has impacted on mountain environments. There have also been social consequences. A once largely agricultural mountain community is now predominantly tourism-oriented. As a result, many towns and villages in skiing areas are largely depopulated during the summer, with migrant workers flocking back during the winter months. This in turn has led to other groups leaving the mountains for year-round work in the cities of Alpine Switzerland, Italy, France, Austria and Germany.

This is not to suggest a process that is irreversible. In Switzerland, for example, local authorities are now taking more proactive steps to ensure that new ski slopes do not proliferate in areas where they could be environmentally damaging. The Swiss people have also become more vociferous in calling for curbs on road traffic in mountain regions. And in the UK, arguments about tourism development in the Cairngorms has led to further studies of ways in which the fragile mountain environment can be preserved, while allowing local communities to develop economically. Winter sports enthusiasts can help contribute to this process:

- As with any activity, be fit for the slopes, and learn your winter sport from approved instructors. You'll stay safe on the slopes, and so will other slope-users around you.
- If you are skiing off-piste, or taking part in cross-country skiing, learn survival techniques, including mountain navigation and avalanche awareness. The Ski Club of Great Britain runs specific courses. Many experts recommend carrying a transceiver – a radio device that pinpoints your position if you are caught up in an avalanche.
- Take public transport wherever possible to ski resorts. This reduces the impact of the car in mountain areas. From Britain, it is now possible to take Eurostar and connecting train services to some of the Alpine resorts rather than flying.
- Watch out for mountain wildlife, particularly if skiing off-piste.

- Heli-skiing – taking a helicopter to more remote slopes beyond the range of ski-lifts – must be considered an indulgence environmentally.
- Litter and waste are even more apparent on snowy slopes than elsewhere. Take rubbish back with you.

On and In the Water

From Space, the Earth is a blue, rather than green, planet. The oceans that cover more than half the surface of our globe are, traditionally, a source of life. And along with the atmosphere, earth and forests, the seas – as well as inland waterways – are indicators of the planet's environmental health. Meanwhile, the various means of enjoying the sea, our coasts and inland waterways – swimming, sailing and other forms of navigation – have become increasingly popular forms of recreation. This means that water-users have a real responsibility – as well as an incentive – to ensure that the seas and inland waters are preserved in a healthy state.

Swimming in clean water is one of the most enjoyable forms of exercise. Yet, as swimmers, surfers, canoeists and other water-users discover all too often, our bathing waters – whether at sea or inland – are often at risk from pollution. In the UK, the last Conservative government privatised the water industry, arguing that this would stimulate the vast amount of investment – £37 billion was the estimate – needed to improve infrastructure and treatment techniques, including ending the simple pumping of untreated sewage out to sea. The Labour government elected in 1997 has brought additional pressure on the privatised water industry to improve its performance, with extra investment. In 1998, the Government launched a new consultation document warning the privatised water industry that it intends to take a tougher line on those who damage waterways through over-abstraction or pollution. Even so, environmental critics note that while there has been a distinct improvement in the quality of the UK's coastal and inland waterways, much remains to be done. Too few beaches, rivers and other waters meet EU standards.

For swimmers and holidaymakers generally, good indications of the general state of beaches and bathing waters can be found in the reports of the Department of the Environment, Transport and the Regions, or more specific publications such as the *Good Beach Guide*, compiled each year by the Marine Conservation Society (MCS) and sponsored last year by *The Reader's Digest*.[1]

1 At the time this Guide was going to press, it was uncertain whether *The Reader's Digest* would continue to sponsor the guide: the 1998 details were published on the web sites of *The Reader's Digest* – www.readers-digest.co.uk – and the Marine Conservation Society – www.mcsuk.mcmail.com – which compiles it.

The best qualify for the European Blue Flag award, made after water quality is inspected, and other beach facilities, including general cleanliness, are regularly assessed. More information is usually available from local authorities, tourist boards or other agencies.

Depressingly, the number of UK beaches recommended as safe for bathing by the *Good Beach Guide* in 1998 was down by 8 per cent on the previous year. Some 755 beaches were scientifically monitored for water quality by statutory bodies in 1997. Only 125 of them met the stringent criteria for clean bathing water required by the Marine Conservation Society, however. Of these, 52 were in south western England; 20 were in the south east; five on the east coast; 24 in Wales; two in Scotland; five in Northern Ireland and 17 in the Channel Isles. None of the beaches on the Isle of Man or in the north west of England met the criteria. However, it should be noted that the MCS's standards demand that bathing water is not affected by any sewage outfall unless the discharge is treated to at least secondary level, as well as conforming to the microbiological standards established in the EU's Bathing Water Directive, now some 23 years old. The MCS insists upon a higher standard than that required by the law. Clearly, though UK bathing water standards are improving, there is still some way to go.

Marine Conservation
Society
9 Gloucester Road
Ross-on-Wye
Herefordshire HR9 5BU
T: +44 (1989) 566 017
T: +44 (1989) 567 815
URL:
www.mcsuk.mcmail.com

Green Hints for Water-Users

- *If you can't swim – learn.* Swimming is great exercise; knowing how to swim not only adds to your enjoyment of the environment, it adds to your safety, and that of others.
- *Learn your water sports properly.* Whatever water sport you're planning to take up, from sailing to sub-aqua, learn with an appropriate, qualified instructor.
- *Don't pollute the water.* Whether you're simply on the beach for an afternoon, taking a canal cruise or a sailing holiday, don't foul the marine environment. Take litter home, and ensure that you don't cause pollution, whether it is from a boat engine, waste food, the cleaner you use on your yacht-hull or a discarded fishing line.
- *Keep your noise down.* Whether it is your voice, your radio, or your boat engine, noise travels widely over water. Keep it down.
- *Safeguard water wildlife.* Avoid sensitive wildlife sites, such as areas where birds may be nesting or feeding.
- *Preserve the water environment.* Report pollution and other environmental hazards to the appropriate authority (The Environment Agency hotline: 0800 80 70 60). It's worth remembering that your health can be a barometer of the state of

the water. Whenever you are in or on the water, keep wounds clean and covered. If you are ill after being in or on the water, see a doctor – you might have caught a water-borne disease.

Sailing, Boating, Water-skiing and Jet-skiing

The UK is traditionally an island nation, with a history of famous navigators. In this century, popular interest in 'messing about in boats' has increased – the annual London Boat Show draws thousands of would-be sailors each year. The attraction of sailing, whether inshore or in coastal waters, is that it is financially accessible for many people – a rich man's yacht may be just that, but it is still possible to own and sail a small dinghy relatively cheaply. The popularity of power-boating, water-skiing and – more recently – jet-skiing has also grown, particularly as holidaymakers who have developed a taste for these sports bring it back home with them.

This increase in popularity in all areas of sailing and boating has resulted in a number of environmental problems. We can all understand the environmental impact of a large oil slick, but the cumulative effect of many small incidents of pollution caused by private yachts or motor boats can be locally serious. Pollution can be caused through poorly maintained engines leaking fuel, through the discarding of litter or waste into the water, even through the use of anti-fouling paints – some types of which have been shown to have a serious effect on marine life, affecting the reproductive health of some invertebrate species. On inland waterways, the wash generated by fast, powerful motor boats can cause damage to river and canal banks. Large powerboats, driven at speed, can also inflict serious damage on some marine

Photo © British Marine Industries Federation

Sailing holidays have become increasingly popular this century

Meet the challenge, experience the Difference!

Have you ever dreamed of standing at the helm of a tall ship as she glides gracefully across a sparkling sea – a certain dignity, a certain romance, a definite thrill of adventure?

The Jubilee Sailing Trust offers you the opportunity to realise your dream on board its award winning tall ship, the LORD NELSON. The LORD NELSON is the only tall ship in the world which enables both physically disabled and able bodied people to share the challenge of crewing a tall ship at sea.

A varied programme of 4 - 10 day long adventure sailing holidays sees the LORD NELSON sailing in British waters during the summer months and the Canary Islands during the winter. This year, there is also a special Millennium Voyage, taking place in the sun-soaked beauty of the Canary Islands – your opportunity to escape!

JUBILEE SAILING TRUST LIMITED

To find out more about your voyage of a lifetime, please contact the Jubilee Sailing Trust at

Jubilee Yard, Hazel Road, Woolston, Southampton SO19 7GB
Tel: (01703) 449138   Fax: (01703) 449145
eMail: jst@jst.org.uk   website: http://www.jst.org.uk
(Reg Charity No 286487)

British Marine Industries
Federation
Meadlake Place
Thorpe Lea Road
Egham
Surrey TW20 8HE
T: +44 (1784) 473 377
F: +44 (1784) 439 678

National Federation of
Sea Schools
Purlins
159 Woodlands Road
Woodlands
Southampton
Hampshire SO40 7GL
T/F: +44 (1703) 293 822
URL: www.nfss.co.uk

Navigate with Nature
UK CEED
Suite E
3 King's Parade
Cambridge CB2 1YA
T: +44 (1223) 367 799

Royal Yachting
Association
RYA House
Romsey Road
Eastleigh
Hampshire SO50 9YA
T: +44 (1703) 627 400
F: +44 (1703) 629 924
URL: www.rya.org.uk

life – off the coast of Florida, the 'Miami Vice' popularity of such craft is held by ecologists to have been responsible over the last decade for numerous injuries, often fatal, to the slow-moving manatees that are now endangered over much of their range. Closer to home, restrictions have now been introduced on power boating in parts of the Lake District, after complaints that the vessels' engine noise was disturbing other visitors' quiet enjoyment of the region.

Several sailing or marine organisations have produced excellent guidelines for people who want to enjoy the water while protecting the environment at the same time. The Royal Yachting Association (RYA), for example, publishes a helpful leaflet, *Tide Lines*, listing hints on dealing with waste and protecting wildlife species and habitats. The British Marine Industries Federation has produced voluminous advice, particularly on the various chemicals used to clean and maintain boats, and in partnership with the UK Centre for Economic and Environmental Development (and with additional support from the Department of the Environment, Transport and the Regions), publish a series of *Navigate with Nature* leaflets. From all these sources, several points emerge, particularly useful for coastal and inland water sailors. While there are anti-dumping laws, for example, boat users can help protect the marine environment by sensible self-regulation:

- Know your boat and your craft. Learn to sail or water ski with an appropriate, recognised instructor (the RYA or the National Federation of Sea Schools can advise you).
- Don't throw your waste food or operational waste – plastic, glass, metal or paper packaging, cleaning rags and materials, rope, line or netting – overboard. Bring it back to shore and dispose of it properly, recycling where possible. Keep some suitable bags or other containers for your waste on board.
- Don't dump food waste within three miles of shore – 12 miles if in the North Sea or English Channel.
- When you are at a mooring, avoid discharging all except washing-up water.
- Don't discharge any oil, fuel or similarly harmful or toxic substance into the sea or inland waterways. Keep your boat well maintained – fuel lines and seals in good condition – to minimise the risk of accidental leaks and discharges. A well-tuned engine cuts down on exhaust emissions.

- Use unleaded petrol and biodegradable oils where possible.
- If oil or other fuels leak, try to clear them up with absorbent pads, and dispose of them – appropriately – onshore.
- Don't discharge sewage where it will affect local water quality, especially in inland, non-tidal or weak tidal bathing waters, near beaches, moorings or commercial shell-fish beds. Instead, fit and use sewage holding tanks on your boat. Don't empty chemical toilets into the sea or inland waters.
- Sailors seem to spend as much time cleaning or maintaining their boat as sailing it. But again, this is a time to remember the environment. Keep toxic materials out of the water. Use anti-fouling paint with the least possible toxicity – manufacturers and suppliers can advise – to prevent the release of chemicals that can harm wildlife. Carry out anti-fouling work with the boat out of the water whenever possible, using sheeting to prevent scrapings blowing away into the environment. Minimise the amount of detergents you use, and try to choose those which are biodegradable, and free of phosphates and chlorine.
- Store paints, cleaners and other toxic materials carefully, to avoid leaks.
- If your local mooring or marina doesn't have adequate facilities for waste storage and disposal, encourage it to install them.
- At sea, or on the water, watch out for wildlife. In shallow or inland waters, keep your speed and noise down (on some waters, the Norfolk Broads, for example, there are set speed limits) to avoid wash damaging the banks or reed beds, or endangering nesting birds or marine mammals. Check with local regulations on water-skiing or power boating. Jet-skis can be fun to ride – but they can be infuriating to listen to! Don't use them in restricted areas (but be careful if you head further out to sea).
- When anchoring, be careful not to damage coral reefs, shell-fish beds or other habitats (eel-grass, for example). When mooring or going ashore, use recognised landing places and avoid damaging nesting sites or disturbing wildlife – basking or breeding seals, birds or other animals.
- If you come across any threat to the environment, inform the appropriate authorities. The Environment Agency has an emergency hotline – 0800 80 70 60 – on which you can report such episodes as chemical pollution, damage to waterways or large-scale fish deaths that could indicate water poisoning.

Canoeing, Kayaking, White-water Rafting

In Britain, sports canoeing dates from the mid-19th century. An engaging history produced by the British Canoe Union records how John MacGregor, 'a London Scot of very great energy', got the boatbuilders Searle's of Lambeth to build him a 'Rob Roy' boat in 1865, inspired by craft that he had seen in North America and Kamschatka. They were all-purpose vessels, propelled by double-bladed paddles, but with the possibility of carrying a small lugsail. Enthusiasts joined MacGregor in taking up the sport, and the Canoe Club was formed in 1866, becoming the Royal Canoe Club in 1873 after the Prince of Wales (later Edward VII) joined in 1867. Now canoe-

British Canoe Union
John Dudderidge House
Adbolton Lane
West Bridgford
Nottingham NG2 5AS
T: +44 (115) 982 1100
F: +44 (115) 982 1797
URL: www.bcu.org.uk

Welsh Canoeing
Association
Canolfan Tryweryn
Frongoch
Bala
Gwynedd LL23 7NU
T: +44 (1678) 521 276
F: +44 (1678) 521 158

Scottish Canoe
Association
Caledonia House
South Gyle
Edinburgh EH12 9DG
T/F: +44 (131) 317 7314
URL: www.scot-canoe.org

Canoe Association of
Northern Ireland
c/o The House of Sport
Upper Malone Road
Belfast BT9 5LA
T: +44 (1247) 469 907

ing has various branches, both for sport and recreation, and there are many differing types of design, using differing materials. River and sea conditions also vary – sea kayaking differs widely from canoeing, and the latter varies from the strenuous, fast-moving sport in upland regions to the more placid waters of the lowlands. But being close to the water allows a privileged access to wildlife and the surrounding environment. The British Canoe Union (BCU) and its related national organisations also encourage river clean-up events, when members and supporters help clear litter and other debris from rivers and riverbanks.

Access rights to waterways in the UK differ around the country: on tidal rivers, there is generally public right of access, but harbour authorities may exercise varying degrees of control. Large non-tidal rivers – and most canals in England and Wales – are managed by navigation authorities, which normally require canoes to have a licence. Licence fees go towards maintaining locks, canal and riverside facilities. Smaller rivers may be subject to access agreements with local landowners – it is always a good idea to find out just what you are entitled to do, to prevent arguments over trespass. The British Canoe Union can provide information to members on access rights to waterways, as does British Waterways and the Environment Agency. (Information on the National Navigation Network is available on 0891 546 555.) The BCU campaigns for better access to waterways for canoeists; in the long-term by changes in the law, in the short-term by seeking local agreements with riparian landowners and other water users.

The BCU, together with the Environment Agency and British Waterways, lays great stress on environmental awareness by those who use rivers, canals and lakes for sport or recreation. Among the guidelines worth following are the following:

■ Before taking to the water, learn how to swim. The BCU says that even in the easiest waters, canoeists should be able to swim at least 50 metres in their canoeing clothing. Follow approved safety codes, including wearing helmets and buoyancy aids wherever they are appropriate, especially in rapid or whitewater, estuaries or coastal waters where special care is needed. Take care against waterborne diseases such as Leptospirosis and Weil's Disease. Consult a doctor if you feel ill after using waterways.

- Join the BCU, or the equivalent national organisation, and support their work on the environment and access.
- Observe local access rules.
- Be friendly and polite to local residents as well as other water users, including anglers (keep clear of fishing lines) and other craft.
- Use recognised access and exit points entering and leaving the water. Avoid unnecessary disturbance to the bankside and its vegetation.
- On the water, avoid disturbing wildlife, especially nesting birds. Gravel beds are often used by fish for spawning, and should not be disturbed at certain times of the year.
- Keep your noise down – noise travels widely over water.
- Don't leave litter, or pollute the waterways. Follow the Country Code.
- Report pollution, poaching, flooding, damage or danger to rivers, lakes and coastal waters.

Canoe Camping Club
25 Waverley Road
South Norwood
London SE25 4HT
T: +44 (181) 654 1835

Some people enjoy a waterborne camping holiday. The Canoe Camping Club can offer more information on this.

Canal Holidays

Once used for commercial and industrial traffic at the onset of the Industrial Revolution, the UK's canal system is now, after years of decline, being revived. Canals can be green corridors – both for wildlife and for the people who enjoy watching it – in towns and cities, while stretching further out into the countryside. Canal wildlife can

Photo © Julia Bayne/Sustrans

Slow down the pace – canal boats in Birmingham

British Waterways
Willow Grange
Church Road
Watford
Herts WD1 3QA
T: +44 (1923) 201 120
F: +44 (1923) 201 300
E: info@canalshq.
demon.co.uk
URL: www.british
waterways.co.uk

Drifters Narrowboat
Holidays
T: +44 (1905) 721 300
URL: www.drifters.co.uk

*To report environmental
problems on canals dial
100 and ask for
Freephone Canals – if
you are using a mobile
'phone, dial 01384
215785.*

include such birds as herons, kingfishers and moor hens, fish species including pike and perch, dragonflies and butterflies among the insects, and a variety of mammals using the banksides, from water voles to badgers. The diversity of canal life is due not only to their being less used by human traffic these days; much of their wildlife value is due to the combination of differing habitats within a narrow strip of land.

At their best, canals are quiet, calm places amid the bustle of metropolitan areas, or – if you are actually on the water – a means of seeing the world, in town or country, from a new perspective. Canals can be walked or cycled – where the tow-path permits – or enjoyed by boat. In recent years, British Waterways, the official body responsible for more than 2000 miles of canals and river navigations, has increased its attempts to make the canals more accessible and enjoyable, as well as restoring and repairing them. It publishes guides to canal walks – longer routes such as the 83 miles between Oxford and Coventry, or the 145 miles along the Grand Union Canal between Birmingham and London, for the determined walkers, for example – as well as shorter excursions, and illustrated guides for others who want to use the canals as the routes for holidays. Mooring a narrowboat overnight, and walking to a nearby pub or restaurant, theatre or concert hall, then travelling on the next day to a new environment, is the essence of canal holidaying. In one scheme, a consortium of seven independent companies organised as Drifters Narrowboat Holidays, in partnership with British Waterways, offers canal craft for hire. Other people may own their pleasure craft, or even live on a narrowboat – in which home becomes a means of travelling, too. Abroad, canal holidays are also being developed. France, Germany, Belgium and The Netherlands, all have canal traditions now being turned to modern holidaymaking, either for individual families or – on larger vessels – for bigger groups.

British Waterways also produce codes of conduct for canal users which include environmental guidelines, for example:

- Never dump rubbish, sewage, or oily bilge water into the canal or onto the bank.
- Clean up after your dog, and keep it under control.
- Don't light fires.
- Report any potential environmental danger, such as damage to a bank, or a leaking canal.
- For details on any licences required for boating, fishing or cycling on canals, telephone 01923 201 120.

- If you are boating on canals, stick to any speed limit (usually 4mph or less), and avoid creating a wash that could damage the bank, or injure wildlife or the occupants of moored vessels. Don't run a propeller while moored. Learn and follow the rules of navigation, signalling and lock operation on the canals. Many canals prohibit passing through locks at night – carelessly secured gates or paddles can lead to water losses. When you are moored, ensure that mooring ropes and pins are not a danger to other canal bank users.

- If you are fishing, don't discard hooks, lines, netting, bottles or tins. Respect the privacy of people living on the canal, don't block the towpaths – and watch out both for passing boats and for overhead power lines!

- If you are cycling along canal paths, avoid damaging the path or verges, especially in wet weather. Take special care cycling at night, when passing through bridges, or at bends.

- Canal pubs can be great places. But – as with any way of spending time on or by the water – don't drink to the extent that alcohol can endanger your safety. In particularly hot weather, the cold water of a canal can also be dangerous for the unwary swimmer – sober or not.

For a variation on a canal holiday, why not join one of the volunteer canal camps run by the Waterway Recovery Group, who repair and restore neglected canals? See Conservation Holidays in Chapter 2.

Cruising

Once the preserve of the wealthy, cruising has suffered from an image problem in recent years, with television documentaries presenting a picture of shiploads of holiday makers either bent on on-board romance or round the clock hedonism, indifferent to the ports and people they pass on their voyage. Environmentally, cruising has also attracted critics. While cruises do offer the environmental advantages of people holidaying in a relatively confined – and hence potentially manageable – environment, there are many ways in which they can have a negative impact. At their worst, cruise ships (as opposed to smaller, privately-owned yachts) isolate holiday makers from the communities they visit – the cruise ship docks and disgorges a few hundred tourists, who venture a few hundred yards and then spend a few dollars on souvenirs from a few shops or restaurants before

retreating to their floating home. But the effect on small island communities can be economically disruptive – a few locals benefit from the cruise ships' arrival, but most do not. Again, studies in the Caribbean have shown that in the past, many cruise ships were responsible for dumping waste at sea, profligate in their use of water (often in short supply on islands and among coastal communities) and energy, and sometimes responsible for damage to coral reefs and other local marine life habitats, with careless anchoring mostly responsible. Polly Pattullo's study, *Last Resorts* (Latin America Bureau with Cassell, 1996), is a useful description of this process.

In recent years, a number of cruise lines have made considerable strides in altering not only the emphasis of their holidays, but also in greening their operations. In the Caribbean, for example, the Carnival Corporation, which runs many cruise ships in the region, won a special long-haul Tourism for Tomorrow award in 1995 for its record in pre-treating waste paper, plastic, aluminium, glass and cardboard for recycling; for changing its refrigeration units to non-CFC versions, sourcing its new decking wood from 'replenishable forests' and using desalination units for most fresh water requirements. The Princess Line of cruise ships has publically proclaimed a 'zero discharge' policy of ensuring that all waste is removed to shore rather than being dumped at sea. Another leading cruise operator, Orient Lines, which cruises to Antarctica, claims it too has introduced a number of environmental measures on its ship: a biological waste treatment plant with liquid waste disposal system; refuse sorting, pulping and incineration; and water treatment plant. As cruise lines seek to add value to the holidays they offer, many are now cooperating with other organisations to provide educational, arts or heritage cruises, where holidaymakers can combine an interest – painting, photography, classical art or architecture, for example – with a sea voyage.

Green Hints for Cruises

■ When you book, ask about any environmental policies the cruise line may have. Support the company you think is doing the most – even the very act of asking the questions starts a process whereby companies must provide more information, and change their own policies.

■ Learn at least a little about the ports your cruise will visit. Plan to use your time there so that you can get away from the usual tourist 'strip', thus spreading the economic benefits your visit can bring.

■ As on any holiday, be careful when buying souvenirs that you are not buying anything produced from wildlife species that may be endangered. Remember, you may also be committing an offence under the CITES treaty on the international trade in wildlife products, and your purchase could be confiscated by Customs on your return home. If in doubt, ask your tour guide, or refer to the section on CITES, TRAFFIC and wildlife products in this book.

■ If your cruise allows you to swim, snorkel or dive, ensure that you don't damage the marine environment, particularly coral reefs or other wildlife habitats. (See the section on snorkelling and sub-aqua.)

■ Messages in bottles belong in cartoon strips – don't throw waste overboard.

Surfing, Sail-boarding, Snorkelling and Sub-aqua

Surfing or swimming in clean water is among the most enjoyable forms of exercise, sport or recreation. As a pamphlet produced by the British Sub-Aqua Club puts it, describing a diver's experience:

> 'Shoals of fish flash by, their iridescent bodies caught in shafts of sunlight...banks of coral sway in the myriad currents, extraordinary sea creatures living in their midst... This is soul-time... One-on-one with nature... Environmentally tuned in as you wind down...'

Surfing has also acquired its own ethos, a major part of which is being part of the environment, riding the waves. Not surprising, then, that surfers and divers have been among

the more vocal groups demanding better environmental standards for waters around the world. In the UK, the group Surfers Against Sewage has fought a long campaign to raise the quality of water treatment around the coast, often employing imaginative, headline-grabbing tactics to persuade government authorities, town councils and water companies alike of the need to improve the condition of sewage and waste-water treatment. Its magazine, *Pipeline News*, is a sparky, combative combination of campaigning and celebration of the surfing life.

Of course, the growth of modern tourism has in many instances contributed to the degradation of the marine environment. The growth of large coastal resorts, in the UK and around the world, for example, in many cases led to the discharge of virtually untreated sewage and waste water into the sea. This has created health hazards for bathers, as well as damaging marine life, including coral reefs. But individual swimmers can also cause their own environmental damage. Coral reefs, for example, can be damaged by carelessly placed boats' anchors, discharged waste, by people walking over them at low tide, or by swimmers touching or kicking them violently (of course, swimmers can also be damaged by such encounters – some corals can be poisonous if you cut yourself, and some coral reef marine life can also be a threat). Global warming, and the rise in sea temperature, are also

Surfers Against Sewage
Unit 2 Workshops
Wheal Kitty
St Agnes
Cornwall TR5 0RD
T: +44 (1872) 553 001
F: +44 (1872) 552 615
URL: www.sas.org.uk

believed to be causing coral death, while explosive-fishing, used in some parts of the world, can be very destructive.

If you are surfing, snorkelling or diving, or want to enjoy these sports:

■ Learn with an appropriate organisation or club. The British Sub-Aqua Club, for example, is the world's largest diving club, and governing body of the sport in the UK. It has many branches and instruction schools, including recognised institutions around the world, at which you can learn or improve your diving, or snorkelling, as well as such skills as underwater photography, marine life identification and ecology, rescue and safety procedures, life saving and boat handling.

■ Whether surfing, snorkelling or diving, don't litter the sea or the beach.

■ Protect coral reefs – be careful where you anchor, if diving or snorkelling from a boat. Don't walk over coral at low tide, or break off a piece of coral as a souvenir.

■ Spear fishing is best left to those fishing for food, not sport.

■ Support environmental campaigns by surfing or diving organisations. For one way of combining a sub-aqua holiday with practical conservation work, see the entry on Coral Cay Conservation in the section on conservation holidays.

The British Sub-Aqua Club
Telford's Quay
Ellesmere Port
South Wirral
Cheshire L65 4FY
T: +44 (0) 151 350 6200
F: +44 (0) 151 350 6215
URL: www.bsac.com

Up in the Air

There are some parts of southwestern England where, every summer weekend, the sky seems to contain at least one hot-air balloon, such is the popularity of the sport. Similarly in some hilly regions we see enthusiasts taking to the airwaves on hang-gliders, defying gravity on a frame of fabric and light metal. Flying, ballooning, gliding, hang-gliding, micro-light flying and parachuting may be minority sports, but they can be remarkably visible. The travel trade has begun to pick up on what have hitherto been individual pastimes: it is now possible to go on balloon safaris in East Africa (opinions are divided on how much a low-flying balloon can 'spook' wildlife). The sports do throw up environmental arguments, however, as can be discerned from the letters columns of some of the hang-gliding magazines, for example.

While most of these sports are obviously less polluting than conventional, fixed-wing, fossil fuel-burning aeronautics, enthusiasts – and most of the clubs involved – stress the need to observe reasonably sensible conduct.

Balloon Club of Great Britain
Montgolfier House
Fairoaks Airport
Chobham
Surrey GU24 8HU

British Parachute Association
5 Wharf Way
Glen Parva
Leicester LE2 9TF
T: +44 (116) 278 5271
F: +44 (116) 247 7662
E: skydive@bpa.org.uk
URL: www.bpa.org.uk

British Hang-Gliding and
Paragliding Association
The Old Schoolroom
Loughborough Road
Leicester LE4 5PJ
T: +44 (116) 261 1322
F: +44 (116) 261 1323

- Any flying that involves the use of fuel means you need to avoid polluting the ground, or water courses, from accidental leaks or discharges.
- Hot-air balloonists should be on guard against any fire risk when using their burners.
- Whether you are ballooning, hang gliding or parachuting, be careful where you take off or land. Wherever possible, seek permission of the landowner, or farmer. Avoid any damage to crops or disturbance to livestock or wildlife.
- If you are driving to your take-off point, be careful not to damage verges when parking. Avoid leaving any litter or other detritus.

Hunting and Fishing

The arguments over foxhunting in the UK continue to rage. In 1997, a Private Member's Bill to ban hunting with hounds was introduced by the Labour MP for Worcester, Michael Foster. Although it gained a large majority in the Commons, it subsequently failed for lack of parliamentary time, the government declining to intervene. At the same time, supporters of hunting, under the umbrella organisation of the Countryside Alliance group, organised two publicity-catching events: a Hyde Park rally and a 'Countryside March' through the capital, to show their opposition to the Foster Bill. The issue of hunting has increasingly been involved with other debates, on animal rights as well as the principles of conservation. Advocates of hunting argue that it is necessary to control an agricultural pest, and that together with game bird shooting and angling, it helps preserve the shape of the countryside, as well as the rural economy. Their opponents maintain that there are more humane means of controlling foxes, if this is necessary, and argue against the morality of hunting animals for sport rather than from any need for food.

Certainly, anglers have an interest in ensuring the health of rivers (though some are less than keen to share the waters with cormorants, an increasingly common fish-eating bird in some areas). Again, some moorlands have been preserved in their present form because of the income from grouse shooting, though again there are now disputes as to whether this has been done at the cost of poisoning or trapping birds of prey.

Abroad, shooting and fishing holidays are offered by a small number of travel firms. In parts of Africa, there is continuing debate about the economic importance of hunting. In both East and Southern Africa, there are countries which permit limited hunting for trophy animals (almost always species not considered to be regionally endangered), where the revenue from such activities is seen as helping local communities that otherwise might see wildlife as simply a threat to crops or personal safety.

BACK TO THE LAND – FARM AND FOOD HOLIDAYS

It is possible to stay on a farm in most areas of the UK, and in many overseas countries now, as farmers increasingly turn to tourism and bed and breakfast accommodation as a means of diversifying their income. In the UK, the economic crisis of 1998 in most sections of agriculture highlighted the inadequacy of many purely agricultural incomes. Most tourist boards now offer lists of farms offering bed and breakfast accommodation. So too does the Farm Holiday Bureau, which is attached to the National Agricultural Centre, and which produces an annual guide, *Stay on a Farm*, listing bed and breakfast or self-catering accommodation available in more than 1000 farms around the country. Some farm holidays offer riding lessons, private fishing or other additional attractions, others simply the chance to relax in the countryside while being part of a working farm.

The recent growth of interest in environmental issues has increased support for organic farming and produce. The Soil Association, which is responsible for certifying organic produce, is also keen to encourage visitors to organic farms, especially those who want to learn more about this means of food production – many people are now using organic methods to grow food at home, or subscribing to organic food box distribution systems. The European Centre for Eco-Agro Tourism, set up by the Soil Association, can offer extensive lists of such farms. But for those who don't just want to learn by observation, the enthusiastic organisation, Willing Workers On Organic Farms, established in 1971, welcomes people who want to spend their time working. Meals and accommodation are offered in return for work – 'not holidays' – which may be for a few days or longer, in the UK or abroad. In return for your work, you get a holiday and the chance to learn some of the techniques of organic farming, and the satisfaction of helping to expand an environmentally sustainable form of modern agriculture, now slowly making headway against the more conventional high-tech intensive agribusiness. This movement is also helping spread an awareness of the importance, environmentally, of preserving and encouraging local distinctiveness. Organisations such as Common Ground, which helps

Farm Holiday Bureau
National Agricultural Centre
Stoneleigh Park
Warwickshire CV8 2LZ
T: +44 (1203) 696 909
F: +44 (1203) 696 630
URL:
www.webscape.co.uk/
farmaccom

The Soil Association
Bristol House
40–56 Victoria Street
Bristol BS1 6BY
T: +44 (117) 929 0661
F: +44 (117) 925 2504
E: soilassoc@gn.apc.org

Willing Workers on
Organic Farms
PO Box 2675
Lewes
Sussex BN7 1RB
T/F: +44 (1273) 476 286

promote the annual Apple Day celebrations, emphasise how important it is to preserve local recipes and locally-grown produce. While it is beyond the scope of this book, food and drink societies and magazines now encourage holidays spent sampling local wines, cheese and other food in the regions where they are produced; a welcome trend, especially where such agriculture is environmentally sustainable. You could do worse than to start with an Apple Day celebration (washed down with cider, or perhaps even a glass of Somerset Cider Brandy, naturally enough).

On-the-Farm Hints for Green Travellers

- Check whether dogs are allowed before you take them. Keep them under control, especially around livestock.
- Farms – organic or otherwise – are working places. Respect people's livelihoods as well as their privacy. Don't damage crops or machinery. Similarly, if you are on a working holiday, be aware you know how to handle machinery, equipment or materials.
- At times – fortunately they are rare – agricultural pests or diseases can threaten epidemics. Take advice on how to avoid spreading them from farm to farm.
- Support local agriculture by enjoying locally produced food and drink.

Vegetarian Holidays

The Vegetarian Society
Parkdale
Dunham Road
Altrincham
Cheshire WA14 4QG
T: +44 (161) 928 0793
F: +44 (161) 926 9182

For vegetarians, dietary requirements can usually be met on most conventional holidays with increasing ease as the popularity of vegetarianism increases. The Vegetarian Society offers information not only on how to enjoy holidays which cater for vegetarians, but also on a number of holiday opportunities with vegetarians specifically in mind.

LEARNING HOLIDAYS AND ENVIRONMENTAL EDUCATION

Continuing education is no longer the preserve of those who have retired from full-time work, as the success of the Open University and almost every local authority evening class shows. Similarly, many people now take holidays which are about new types of learning. It may be a course on an academic subject, with two weeks' accommodation in an Oxbridge college, or studying art in an Italian Renaissance city, or exploring the history of the Mediterranean on a cultural study cruise. Environmental education is another new way of using holidays. The explosion of interest in environmental issues has led to a corresponding increase in courses ranging from discussions on the meaning of sustainable development, to practical nature conservation.

Some institutions have concentrated specifically on such green themes. Near the Devon town of Totnes, Schumacher College was founded in 1991 and takes its name from E F Schumacher, the author of *Small is Beautiful*. It now occupies a site based around a medieval house in the Dartington Hall estate – it is part of the Dartington Hall Trust established in 1925 by Dorothy and Leonard Elmhirst, inspired by the ideas of the Indian poet, educationalist and social reformer, Rabindranath Tagore. While Dartington College offers degree courses in Theatre, Music and Visual Performance, Dartington Hall provides short courses, as does Schumacher College. In the 1998–99 programme, for example, Schumacher College has offered two-to-three-week courses led by internationally-known experts on such topics as 'Deep Ecology', 'Natural Capitalism', 'Beyond an Economy of Work and Spend' as well as 'Acting for the Earth', an examination of various strategies for environmental activism. Dartington Hall's programme is usually of shorter courses, around a weekend, and including practical activities, such as (in Autumn 1998) calligraphy, printmaking and animal sculpture as well as topics such as 'Changing Self – Changing Society' or 'The Psychology of Awakening'.

A long-standing focus of technological innovation, the Centre for Alternative Technology has blossomed on the site of an old quarry in Wales to become a regular attraction for visitors who spend hours learning about the practical details of solar and water power, wind turbines and how to improve the insulation and energy efficiency of their own homes. The centre is now seeking to build an Autonomous Environmental Information Centre, a £544,000 project to be housed in a low-energy building using rammed earth and sheep's wool insulation. Since 1975, the centre has grown to the point where it is now acknowledged as one of Europe's leading eco-centres, and attracts more than 80,000 visitors a year. Meanwhile, in northern England, the Earth Centre, near Doncaster, which has been taking shape in the last two years at a reclaimed industrial site in a former mining area of Yorkshire, is also developing exhibits designed to focus on environmental possibilities. With a date in April 1999 set for

Schumacher College
The Old Postern
Dartington
Totnes
Devon TQ9 6EA
T: +44 (1803) 865 934
F: +44 (1803) 866 899
E: schumcoll@gn.apc.org
URL: www.gn.apc.org/
schumachercollege/

Dartington Hall
Programme
Totnes
Devon TQ9 6EL
T: +44 (1803) 866 688
F: +44 (1803) 865 551
E: dart.hall.prog@
dartingtonhall.org.uk

Centre for Alternative
Technology
Llwyngwern Quarry
Machynlleth
Powys SY20 9AZ
Wales
T: +44 (1654) 702 400
F: +44 (1654) 702 782
URL: www.cat.org.uk

The Earth Centre
Kilner's Bridge
Doncaster Road
Denaby Main
South Yorks DN12 4DY
T: +44 (1709) 512 000

Photo © Julian Cremona/Field Studies Council

Nature photography run by the Field Studies Council in Shropshire – take photos, not plant cuttings!

its opening to the public, the Earth Centre is designed to offer insights into various means of ensuring a sustainable future – including water features, a series of gardens, pavilions and other exhibits.

Perhaps the widest range of courses for those with general environmental interests, however, are those run by the Field Studies Council (FSC), an educational charity which sets out to promote a better understanding of the environment. It has a network of residential and day centres, including 12 field centres in England and Wales, often in converted historic buildings. The courses are usually linked in some way with their locality – at Flatford Mill, in 'Constable country', there are a range of art courses geared to those interested in portraying landscapes. Other courses are more directly environmental: for example, walking, exploring and natural history topics are offered at the centres in the Lake District, the Yorkshire Dales and Snowdonia, with the emphasis divided between learning about the landscape and enjoying it on foot. The FSC runs many courses, running from weekends to longer, on various aspects of natural history, as well as other courses on ecology and conservation, gardens and gardening, geology, history and archaeology, and artistic skills such as photography, creative writing and craftwork.

Field Studies Council
Preston Montford Hall
Montford Bridge
Shrewsbury
Shropshire SY4 1HW
T: +44 (1743) 850 674
F: +44 (1743) 850 178
E: fsc.headoffice@
ukonline.co.uk
URL: www.field-studies-
council.org

Some of the larger environmental groups, such as Friends of the Earth or Greenpeace, carry listings of environmental education courses in their membership magazines. Non members can find out more in such magazines as *Resurgence*, edited by the indefatigable Satish Kumar; *The Ecologist* and – with a more left-of-centre political alignment – *Red Pepper*. The annual *Green Guide for London*, which lists numerous environmental services and activities in and around the capital, is also a useful source of information. Local education authorities, schools and colleges may also offer details of courses, evening classes, day and weekend schools.

RETREATS, PILGRIMAGES, SPIRITUAL, HEALING AND HOLISTIC HOLIDAYS

Retreats

Just as the origins of the word holiday are to be found in the phrase, Holy Day, so some of the first holiday makers were the people in early societies who celebrated significant religious or cultural dates in their calendar. Whether the celebration was that of an equinox, to mark the passage of the year or the seasons, or whether it was to observe a particular saint's day, the early holy days could either be occasions for solemn religious observation, or less restrained forms of enjoyment – or sometimes a combination of the two. In a development of the idea of holy days, spiritual journeys were often undertaken by pilgrims as a mark of devotion. Just as in Chaucer's *Canterbury Tales*, so pilgrims travelling to the site of religious observation would be making a journey that was both physical and spiritual. And of course, the pilgrims would require many of the same comforts *en route* that today's holidaymakers enjoy – accommodation, food, drink and entertainment. Even so, their journey was essentially an internal one; a spiritual quest, and a retreat from the everyday world.

Today, religious pilgrimages are still common. Devout Muslims try to make the journey to Mecca, in performance of the *haj*, at least once in their life. Many Catholics follow the route of mediaeval pilgrims from Belgium to the cathedral church of Santiago de Compostella in northern Spain. Others make the journey to the Vatican in Rome. Each year, walkers climb to the summit of the holy mountain of Ireland, Croagh Patrick, many remaining in prayer overnight. Each faith has its own traditional pilgrimages.

National Retreat Association
Central Hall
256 Bermondsey Street
London SE1 3UJ
T: +44 (171) 357 7736
F: +44 (171) 357 7724

British Buddhist Association
11 Biddulph Road
London W9 1JA
T: +44 (171) 286 5575

The Buddhist Society
58 Ecclestone Square
London SW1V 1PH
T: +44 (171) 834 5858
F: +44 (171) 976 5238

The Buddhist Centre
51 Roman Road
London E2 0HU
T: +44 (171) 834 5858

Meanwhile, just as pilgrimages survive, so an increasing number of people are taking retreats as a form of break from their everyday lives. By contrast to the consumerist holidays, spent overindulging on food, drink, sunbathing and shopping, retreats are an opportunity to reflect and meditate. Many retreat houses in Britain are run by religious orders, but equally a large number cater for visitors from other faiths, or those who have no formal spiritual affiliation.

The Islamic Centre of
England
140 Maida Vale
London W9 1QB
T: +44 (171) 258 0526
*Offers advice on pilgrim-
ages for Muslims.*

The Pagan Federation
BM Box 7097
London WC1N 3XX
*Can offer local contacts
for those interested in
other traditions.*

'There is an enormous interest in retreats from people who simply want to go to an environment in which they can be quiet, and in which they feel safe, secluded and protected, in order to spend time in a way which is not normally open to them in their everyday lives,' says Paddy Lane, of the National Retreat Association, which publishes an annual magazine, *Retreats*, which this year includes listings of more than 200 retreat houses in Britain. 'Often, they appeal to people who feel stressed by their job or domestic lives, and need to reflect on the paths their lives – spiritual as well as secular – are taking. Most retreats offer you not just the basics of food and your own room – they offer you a sense of calm. People won't come up to you for a casual chat, which can be an enormous relief, though if you need it, many retreats will have people who are there to listen and counsel, if you need that help.'

Most retreats take visitors for anything from a few hours in some cases – some have begun to cater for people taking a brief break from caring for a relative – with the usual length of stay being anything from a day to more than a week. 'At most retreats, you can be by yourself, being silent, or join in communal activities, such as painting, sculpture or group meditation,' Paddy Lane says.

Prices vary greatly between various retreat centres. Some houses will ask merely for a donation, others will suggest a figure that covers the cost of your accommodation. An organised weekend retreat might cost £60–80; an individual going on a private retreat could pay a day rate of £30. Other retreats could be more expensive – and the standards of accommodation do vary. 'Some retreat houses have rooms with en suite bathrooms, just as a standard hotel. Others stress a more basic simplicity, such as you associate with a convent or monastery, which many people are seeking as a change from their home lives,' Paddy Lane says. 'But all will be clean and warm, even if they are not lavishly decorated.'

The National Retreat Association links a number of Christian retreat groups, including the Association for Promoting Retreats (mainly Anglican); the National Retreat Movement (mostly Roman Catholic); the Methodist Retreat Group; the

Baptist Union Retreat Group; the Quaker Retreat Group and the United Reformed Church Silence & Retreat Network. It publishes an annual magazine, *Retreats*, each December.

Some retreat houses are run by ecumenical or non-Christian faiths or groups. Within the UK, in particular, there are many Buddhist retreat centres or meditation centres, a number of which also cater for non-Buddhists. Besides offering opportunities for quiet reflection and spiritual contemplation, an increasing number of retreats offer treatments in alternative or complementary medicines and therapies, such as aromatherapy, acupuncture or massage. 'For many people, a concern about their physical health is leading to concern for their psychological as well as spiritual well being,' Paddy Lane observes. 'We have noticed that when magazines that run health columns or features carry articles about retreats and mention us, we get inundated with requests for more information.'

The growing interest in yoga, meditation, holistic exercises and physical/spiritual disciplines, as well as in complementary or alternative forms of medicine and New Age teachings has been paralleled by an increase in the numbers of centres offering courses of varying duration. If you are already practising any of these, your teacher or healer will probably be able to advise you on them. Alternatively, information is usually available from local complementary medicine centres, health clubs, meditation centres and other sources. It is always advisable to seek advice on what sort of retreat or course would suit you before you make a booking – the national bodies of most holistic disciplines usually issue such information. In the case of finding out more about some of the newer religious groups, it may also be worth contacting INFORM, an independent charity based at the London School of Economics, which can call upon a network of academics and others with experience of such groups.

More extensive information about retreats is also available in *The Good Retreat Guide*, by Stafford Whiteaker (Rider, £12.99). *The Buddhist Directory*, published by the Buddhist Society, also lists many local groups and centres offering advice on retreats and courses.

Holistic holidays

The Skyros Centre, which advertises itself as the 'world leader in alternative holidays', has for two decades offered courses in personal growth and development subjects ranging from music, painting and creative writing to windsurfing, massage, yoga and T'ai Chi on the Greek island of Skyros. The founders of Skyros, Dr Dina Glouberman and Dr Yannis Andricopoulous, described their aim as to create a 'life-enhancing experience which can be integrated into people's everyday realities', and to varying degrees it is arguable that the pattern has been repeated elsewhere. The

Skyros
92 Prince of Wales Road
London NW5 3NE
T: +44 (171) 267 4424
or 284 3065
F: +44 (171) 284 3063
E: skyros@easynet.co.uk
URL: www.skyros.com/

effect is to combine ideas of holistic disciplines and pursuits with the attractions of a Mediterranean holiday. Prices for two-week courses in the 1998 programme ranged from £495 to £945, with some discounts available. More recently, a Skyros programme has also been established on the Caribbean island of Tobago. Perhaps inevitably, the Skyros Centre is advertising an £895 Millennium event, described as 'a two-week celebration of life, to honour the past, relish the present and commit ourselves to a safer and happier world'.

Complementary Medicines and Healing Holidays

It is almost impossible to list all the organisations, centres and individuals involved with the various forms of complementary medicine and other forms of healing. But more information may be obtained from some of the following national organisations, including details of courses, workshops and individual practitioners. NB some organisations may make a small charge for distributing information, or request a stamped, addressed envelope. Remember also that both in Britain and abroad (Hungary is a notable example) spa resorts have long been popular with visitors taking the waters for health reasons, as well as for recreation.

Umbrella Organisations

British Complementary Medicine
Association
249 Fosse Road South
Leicester LE3 1AE
T: +44 (116) 282 5511
F: +44 (116) 282 5611

Council for Complementary and
Alternative Medicine
Suite D
Park House
206–208 Latimer Road
London W10 6RE
T: +44 (181) 968 3862

Institute for Complementary Medicine
PO Box 194
London SE16 1QZ
T: +44 (171) 237 5165

Professional Practitioner Organisations

Acupuncture
British Acupuncture Council
206–208 Latimer Road
London W10 6RE
T: +44 (1881) 964 0222

Alexander Technique
Society of Teachers of Alexander
Technique
20 London House
266 Fulham Road
London SW10 9EL
T: +44 (171) 351 0828

Aromatherapy
Aromatherapy Organisations Council
3 Latymer Close
Braybrooke
Market Harborough
Leicestershire LE16 8LN
T: +44 (1858) 434 242

Astrology
Astrology Panel on Astrological
Education
396 Caledonian Road
London N1 1DN

Bach Flower Therapy
Dr Edward Bach Foundation
Mount Vernon
Sotwell
Wallingford
Oxfordshire OX10 0PZ
T: +44 (1491) 834 678

Chiropractic
British Association for Applied
Chiropractic
The Old Post Office
Cherry Street
Stratton Audley
Oxfordshire OX6 9BA
T: +44 (1869) 277 111

British Chiropractic Association
Equity House
29 Whitley Street
Reading
Berkshire RG2 0EG
T: +44 (1734) 757 557 or
0800 212 618

Colonic Hydrotherapy
Colonic International Association
16 Englands Lane
London NW3 4TG
T: +44 (171) 483 1595

Colour Healing
International Association for Colour
Therapy
PO Box 3
Darkes Lane
Potters Bar
Hertfordshire EN6 3ET

Counselling
British Association for Counselling
1 Regent Place
Rugby CV21 2PJ
T: +44 (1788) 578 328

Cranio-Sacral Therapy
Cranio-Sacral Therapy Association
Monomark House
27 Old Gloucester Street
London WC1N 3XX
T: +44 (1886) 884 121

Cranial Osteopathic Association
478 Baker Street
Enfield
Middlesex EN1 3QS
T: +44 (181) 367 5561

Crystal Therapy
Affiliation of Crystal Healing
Organisations
46 Lower Green Road
Esher
Surrey KT10 8HD
T: +44 (181) 398 7252

Healing
Confederation of Healing Organisations
113 High Street
Berkhampstead
Hertfordshire HP4 2DG
T: +44 (1442) 870 660

National Federation of Spiritual Healers
Old Manor Farm Studio
Church Street
Sunbury on Thames
Middlesex TW6 6RG
T: +44 (1932) 783 164

British Alliance of Healing Associations
3 Sandy Lane
Giselham
Lowestoft
Norfolk NR33 8EQ
T: +44 (1502) 742 224

International Self-Realisation Healing
Association
1 Hamlyn Road
Glastonbury
Somerset BA6 8HS
T: +44 (1458) 831 353

Reiki Association
68 Howard Road
Westbury Park
Bristol BS6 7UX
T: +44 (1981) 550 829

Homeopathy
British Homeopathic Association
27a Devonshire Street
London W1N 1RJ
T: +44 (171) 935 2163

Society of Homeopaths
2 Aratizan Road
Northampton NN1 4HU
T: +44 (1604) 21400

Homeopathic Trust
Hahnemann House
2 Powis Place
Great Ormond Street
London WC1N 3HT
T: +44 (171) 837 9469

UK Homeopathy Medical Association
6 Livingstone Road
Gravesend
Kent DA12 5DZ
T: +44 (1474) 560 366

Hypnotherapy
National Register of Hypnotherapists
and Psychotherapists
12 Cross Street
Nelson
Lancashire BB9 7EN
T: +44 (1282) 699 378

National Council for Hypnotherapy
Hazelwood
Broadmead
Sway
Lymington SO41 6DH
T: +44 (1590) 683 770

Massage
British Massage Therapy Council
Greenbank House
65a Adelphi Street
Preston
Lancashire PR1 7BH
T: +44 (1772) 881 063

Medical Herbalism
General Council and Register of
Consultant Herbalists
32 King Edward Road
Swansea SA1 4LL
T: +44 (1792) 655 886

National Institute of Medical Herbalists
56 Longbrook Street
Exeter
Devon EX4 6AH
T: +44 (1392) 426 022

Naturopathy
General Council and Register of
Naturopaths
Goswell House
Goswell Road
Somerset BA16 0JG
T: +44 (1458) 840 072

Osteopathy
Osteopathic Information Service
PO Box 2074
Reading
Berkshire RG1 4YR
T: +44 (1734) 512 051

Psychotherapy
UK Council for Psychotherapy
167 Great Portland Street
London W1N 5FB
T: +44 (171) 436 3002

National Council of Psychotherapists
Hazelwood
Broadmead
Sway
Lymington SO41 6DH
T: +44 (1590) 683 770

Qigong
Dao Hua Qigong School
Chinese Heritage
15 Dawson Place
London W2 4TH
T: +44 (171) 229 7187

Reflexology
Association of Reflexologists
27 Old Gloucester Street
London WC1N 3XX
T: +44 (1935) 817 617

International Federation of
Reflexologists
76–78 Eldridge Road
Croydon
Surrey CR0 1EF
T: +44 (181) 667 9458

British Reflexology Association
Monks Orchard
Whitbourne
Worcester WR6 5RB
T: (1886) 821 207

Shiatsu
Shiatsu Society of Great Britain
Interchange Studios
Dalby Street
London NW5 3NQ
T: +44 (171) 813 7772

Yoga
British Wheel of Yoga
1 Hamilton Place
Boston Road
Sleaford
Lincolnshire NG34 7ES
T: +44 (1529) 306 851

SECTION TWO
POINTS ON THE
GREEN COMPASS

CHAPTER 3
CLOSE TO HOME

BRITAIN

For the British green traveller, holidaying in Britain has many attractions. Remaining closer to home should have environmental benefits: you are travelling less far afield, and using fewer resources. There are also many positive reasons for staying in Britain, a fact that many have already discovered for themselves: out of 54 million holidays of four nights or more taken by Britons in 1996, 57 per cent were spent in the country. In addition to a wealth of beautiful landscapes, historic towns and villages, the environment of the British Isles is our most immediate. The dictum 'think globally, act locally' applies most readily here: if we learn to understand and appreciate our local environment, we are more likely to protect it. Having done that, we will be more ready to maintain greener standards elsewhere.

Travelling closer to home means that the normal considerations of transport can be reversed. Walk first, or cycle. Take a bus or a train. Use a car sparingly. However, despite many encouraging local initiatives, it has become progressively harder to use greener modes of transport. Although the newly privatised railway companies in England, Scotland and Wales have pledged to make significant new investment in track and rolling stock, their first few years have been more notable for cancelled or reduced services. Hopefully, as investment begins to take effect, and with the hint of

stronger regulation from the Labour government elected in May 1997, public transport will improve, both on rail and road. And, lest it be forgotten, international travel from Britain can have environmental impacts at home and abroad: there has been long-running opposition from many green groups to the plans for a new, fifth terminal at London's Heathrow Airport, and a new runway at Manchester's Ringway.

In the British countryside, farming practices encouraged by the European Union's unreformed Common Agricultural Policy have slowed, but not stopped, the loss of hedgerows, the less-than-discriminate use of agrochemicals, pollution of water courses or the loss or degradation of sites of special scientific interest (SSSIs).

Britons continue to seek out the countryside, however, and this love affair brings its own problems. One is planners' projections that by early next century some 4.4 million new homes will be needed in Britain, of which many are likely to be built on greenfield sites. Another is the pressure on parts of the countryside most popular with tourists and those wanting to live there – particularly from traffic and the trend towards second-home buying. On a more basic level, access to open space, especially in the country, continues to be a sensitive issue. At the same time, public space continues to be lost in towns, a point recently taken up by radical environmentalists such as The Land Is Ours group. To meet these challenges, as well as Britain's international environmental commitments, is a daunting challenge for the government.

Britain's countryside may be increasingly suburbanised but, at its best, each county, indeed each village, retains something of its own local characteristics, its sense of place and belonging, whether reflected in distinctive building styles, local food and drinks or traditional games and customs. The creative environmental group Common Ground has long campaigned to highlight and preserve local distinctiveness, most notably through their annual 'Apple Day' celebrations. The Campaign for Real Ale publishes its *Good Beer Guide*, including a list of pubs and hotels that could form a local distinctiveness itinerary in itself (of course, indistinctiveness might set in a few pints later).

Britain has much to offer the green traveller, whether home-grown holidaymaker or overseas visitor. How and where you spend your time is up to you, but the opportunities are remarkably varied. Walking or cycling holidays, or simply taking off for a few days, can be the best way to see Britain at your own pace (see under Sports and Activity Holidays in Chapter 2 for details). Sadly, the ability to take a bicycle on a train has been reduced in recent years but, where possible, it is a good combination.

A series of long-range walks have been established in recent years, covering different types of countryside, and enticing for walkers whether they want to cover several hundred miles in a couple of weeks, or simply take a weekend break. They range from the Highland Way in the north of Scotland, the Pennine Way in northern England and the Scottish Borders, Offa's Dyke Path in Wales, the Icknield Way in the east of England and the South West Coastal Path, running from Somerset around the Cornish peninsula to Dorset.

Cyclists can explore Britain along those canal paths which remain open, or follow some of the tracks being opened up by such organisations as Sustrans, whose coast-to-coast cycle path across northern England, using a variety of minor roads, bridleways and former railway lines, won the global prize in the Tourism for Tomorrow awards, sponsored by British Airways, in 1995. Of course, it is also possible to combine modes of transport. Walking or cycle tours of the Scottish Islands, for example, will almost certainly involve using ferries that are part of the pleasure, while some of the smaller Welsh valley railway lines are a delight to travel.

Britain's coastline, rivers and canals also provide routes for those wanting to take to the water whether under sail, by narrow boat or even canoeing. Horse riding and caravanning holidays are increasingly popular, with the former offering the opportunity to leave the tarmac behind for gentler, less crowded bridleways. As for accommodation, that can range from camping out, staying at a youth hostel or a bed and breakfast hotel to enjoying five-star luxury. This book can obviously only hint at the range of possibilities for a British holiday for the environmentally minded. Otherwise, the various tourist boards can provide information on what to see and do in a particular region. See also Chapter 2 for hints on how to enjoy your holiday while also helping protect the environment in Britain, just as you would abroad.

Less of a joy are some of Britain's beaches. The number of beaches recommended as safe for bathing in *The Reader's Digest Good Beach Guide 1998*, was down 8 per cent on the previous year, while only 125 out of the 755 monitored beaches met the Marine Conservation Society's guideline standards. MCS standards for inclusion in the guide require that a beach does not have inadequately treated sewage routinely discharged within its vicinity, as well as conforming to the highest microbiological standards based on the European Community's Bathing Water Directive. It should be pointed out that the society's criteria insist on a higher degree of water cleanliness than the EC directive (see On and In the Water in Chapter 2 for further details).

Compared to elsewhere in Europe, Britain's wildlife reflects an island landscape that has been largely dictated by human settlement, agriculture and industry over many centuries. The once-native wolf and beaver have long been extinct, and reintroduced 'wild' boar are confined to farms. But for all that, naturalists can enjoy themselves in Britain. Most obvious are the tens of thousands of bird watchers who daily and weekly train their lenses on species ranging from commonly found garden visitors to rare species in remote places – red kites in the Welsh Hills, golden eagles and ospreys in Scotland or migratory waders at numerous wildlife reserves across the country. The RSPB can offer information on bird watching holidays.

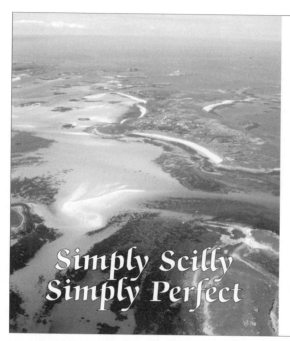

Supporting those aspects of the tourism industry that encourage more environmental awareness is a good way of contributing to practical conservation and sustainable development. In recent years, both the government and the tourism industry have begun to question the environmental sustainability of tourism. The British Tourist Authority (BTA) and the English Tourist Board (ETB) have both supported such efforts as promoting guidelines for 'sustainable rural tourism', initiating or supporting award schemes, helping to identify and develop visitor-management techniques and other methods that 'combine sound business practice with good "green" principles'. Both organisations have developed marketing and promotional schemes to further 'sustainable' tourism, particularly to stimulate low-season travel and to 'effect wider tourist dispersal, to ease congestion where it is environmentally damaging and spread tourism to areas where it is appropriate and acceptable'.

In November 1995, the ETB published an advisory manual, *Sustainable Rural Tourism: Opportunities for Local Action*, designed for local councils and others in the business of promoting or supplying tourism. In March 1996, the ETB began to distribute a 'green audit kit' to help small businesses improve their environmental performance. This and other activities by tourist boards in Scotland, Wales and Northern Ireland followed a period of growing recognition that tourism pressures were having a serious impact on the environment. In 1990 Michael Howard, the then Environment Secretary, set up a taskforce to report on the issue. Its findings were delivered the next year under the title, *Tourism and the Environment: Maintaining the Balance* (also published by the English Tourist Board). 'Problems arise from visitor pressure when the relationship between the visitor, the place and the host community is not kept in harmony,' the report concluded. These problems, it said, were principally:

- overcrowding, resulting in an unpleasant experience for the visitor, increased risk of damage to the resource and extra pressure on the host community;
- traffic overload from out-of-place cars and buses;
- extra wear and tear on the place's physical fabric;
- intrusive development which spoils the setting;
- alienating local communities through noise, unruly behaviour or a change in the character of the place.

'The scale of these problems varies widely from place to place,' the report argued, going on to suggest that 'they occur in a severe form at relatively few locations and where they do exist are often concentrated at particular points and specific times'. It concluded that many of the problems could be resolved by better management. But looking ahead, the report sounded a warning. 'Although techniques to tackle most of the problems can be found, action needs to be taken if unacceptable damage is to be avoided,' it conceded. The fact that some action is being taken by a wide range of organisations in Britain is evidenced by the large number of awards made in recent years by the Tourism for Tomorrow scheme. These are detailed at the end of this chapter.

IRELAND

The very name 'Emerald Isle' evokes an image that should appeal to the green traveller: the Ireland (for the purpose of this book, the Irish Republic and Northern Ireland) of green hills and largely deserted beaches, wide rivers and rugged coasts. Ironic, then, that one of the most intense of environmental controversies in recent years, only recently resolved, has been about the impact of tourism. For much of the mid-1990s, a proposal to build an interpretative centre in the heart of the Burren region of County Clare, a district of exposed limestone cliffs and pavements which supports a rich and rare variety of plant life, was argued over fiercely. Though the scheme was supported by the European Commission, and some local authorities, as a means of boosting local employment and adding to tourists' appreciation of a unique habitat, it was fiercely opposed by environmental and conservationist groups before it was finally withdrawn.

Similarly, environmental problems of a more familiar kind are not unknown across Ireland. Dublin, once one of the finest Georgian cities, permitted much of its period architecture to be despoiled in the 1970s, and has suffered from both air and water pollution in recent decades, though these have both been targeted in recent clean-up drives (coincidentally, the city became one of the first world capitals to elect a Green Party mayor). Over-fishing off the south west coast is thought to have endangered stocks of the rare basking shark, pursued for its high-quality oil. And rashes of caravan parks or holiday cottages can be found dotted over landscapes that call out for solitary appreciation.

BOX 3.1

TOURISM IN BRITAIN: SOME OFFICIAL
FACTS AND FIGURES

Tourism is one of Britain's largest industries, and one of the leaders in the international market. According to the British Tourist Authority, overseas visits to Britain and domestic tourism are worth more than £37 billion each year, including £15 billion in foreign exchange earnings, and five per cent of Britain's GDP. Directly or indirectly, tourism employs 1.7 million Britons, some seven per cent of those in work.

In 1996, Britain was fifth among the world's most popular tourist destinations, after the US, Spain, France, and Italy. That year, according to the BTA, there were 3 million visitors* to Britain from the United States, 3.7 million from France, 3 million from Germany, 2 million from the Irish Republic and 1.5 million from the Netherlands. But tourists from Eastern Europe are increasing in number. In 1996, there were 858,000 visitors from Eastern Europe spending £400 million, double the figure of 1993.

Holidays accounted for 44 per cent of trips to Britain, with the remainder being mostly for business (25 per cent), visits to friends or relations (19 per cent) and study (3 per cent).

Top Ten Towns and Gardens

The ten leading town or city attractions for foreign visitors in 1997 (after London) were Edinburgh, Glasgow, Birmingham, Manchester, Oxford, York/Cambridge (equal 7th), Bath, Inverness/ Brighton with Hove (equal 10th). The top ten garden attractions (1996 figures) were Hampton Court (London), Kew Gardens (London), Tropical World (Leeds), Royal Botanic Gardens (Edinburgh), Wisley Gardens (Surrey), Botanic Gardens (Belfast), Botanic Gardens (Glasgow), University Botanic Garden (Oxford), Sir Thomas and Lady Dixon Park (Belfast) and the Arboretum Illuminations, Walsall.

Britons who stay in the country for a holiday of four nights or more outnumber their compatriots who go abroad. In 1996, out of 54 million holidays of four nights or more taken by Britons, more than 57 per cent were spent in the country.

In 1995, in terms of volume, England received 82 per cent of UK travellers, Scotland 8 per cent, Wales 8.6 per cent. Britons spent 39 per cent of their holiday trips that year at the English seaside. Blackpool and Brighton headed the list of seaside pier and pleasure beach attractions in 1996.

Visits to free tourist attractions grew by 4 per cent in 1996, while those charging admission clocked a 2 per cent growth in numbers. Industrial heritage sites and purpose-designed visitor centres such as Cadbury World in Bourneville,

Birmingham, were major growth areas. Steam railways, historic monuments, gardens and buildings all showed a rise but country parks showed a 1 per cent drop on record figures recorded in the previous year.

Top of the league table for all UK attractions charging admission were the Alton Towers leisure park (Staffordshire), Madame Tussaud's waxworks (London), the Tower of London, Canterbury Cathedral, Chessington World of Adventures, London's Natural History Museum and Science Museum, Legoland (Windsor), Windsor Castle and Blackpool Tower.

Source: British Tourist Authority 1998
* The BTA figures are technically for visits rather than visitors – some travellers may visit more than once in a year.

For all that, Ireland remains a magnet for travellers who want to savour the quiet enjoyment of the countryside. Both tourists boards of Ireland and Northern Ireland have been actively promoting various forms of 'green' holidays, even if one of Ireland's major passions, golf, is not always highest on the list of environmentally sensitive sports. Riding and horse-drawn caravanning, cycling, walking, sailing, canoeing and fishing are all widely marketed, as are bird-watching and botanical holidays. The authorities have also been keen to improve the environment in a way that both encourages tourism as well as regenerating local economies. Two award-winning schemes in the Tourism for Tomorrow scheme are worth mentioning in this context: the water treatment scheme in Newcastle, County Down; and the regeneration of the Temple Bar district of Dublin. Guided town walks are offered by students of Trinity College, worth a visit in its own right for its architectural splendour as well as its displays of Celtic history and culture.

The 150th anniversary of the Irish Famine, arguably modern Europe's greatest environmental disaster, has already been the subject of intense historical and political debate. Between 1845 and 1850, when the Irish potato crop was hit by a new form of blight, probably imported from the US via Belgium, the population of Ireland fell by at least a quarter. According to some estimates, well over two million people died of starvation or were driven to emigrate. The continuing controversy, which still divides politicians as well as historians, is to what extent the British Government and landlords reinforced the effects of the collapse of the staple food of most of the population. For the traveller, however, the Famine has still left its mark on the land. Especially in the West, one can still come across the remains of abandoned villages, complete with the still-visible outlines of the 'lazy beds' potato fields. At Strokestown, in County Roscommon, a permanent museum not only recalls the events of the period, but places the Famine in the context of present-day environmental or social 'disasters'. It is a moving and thought- provoking presentation, well worth the visit.

ISLE OF MAN

Part of neither the UK nor of the European Union – though a member of the Commonwealth – the Isle of Man is steeped in history and folklore, a reflection of its often turbulent past fashioned, by virtue of its position in the Irish Sea, by both Viking and Celtic cultures. The island's governing body, Tynwald, bears the distinction of being the oldest parliament in continuous existence in the world: a fact which the Manx people proudly marked with their own Millennium Celebration in 1979.

Although perhaps better known for its less-than-environmentally sensitive motorcycle road racing events – the Tourist Trophy (TT) races have been held in the island since 1907 – the island offers many environmentally friendly features which the green traveller can enjoy and support with enthusiasm. Greener transport is provided by the horse-drawn trams – 'toastracks' – which have plied the three-mile sweep of Douglas Bay since the Victorian era; the Manx Electric Railway which runs a regular coastal route from Douglas to Ramsey in the north; and the Snaefell Mountain Railway, also electrically powered. Both rail systems still use some original tram cars built at the turn of the century. It is also easy to get to the island by sea from ports in Ireland and Britain; a choice made by 50 per cent of the island's 300,000 visitors in 1997. Less green but a draw for rail buffs, the Isle of Man Steam Railway still operates about 15 miles of narrow gauge line in the south of the island, using locomotives which date back to 1873 and are maintained in part by equipment and workshops from the same era.

Photo © Isle of Man Tourism

The scenic route of the Manx Electric Railway on the Isle of Man

As half of the island's population live in or around Douglas, the capital, more than 60 per cent of the island is unpopulated, providing a rare tranquillity for walking, horse-riding, cycling, bird watching, or swimming in the many tiny secluded coves which fringe the coastline. For a small island – little more than 400 square miles – the landscape is remarkably varied, ranging from sand dunes and marshes, wild flower meadows and old woodlands, to blanket bog, heath moorland, and lichen bryophyte heath (the Ayres in the northern tip of the island). To enable visitors and locals alike to appreciate this rich diversity, the island's authorities have established a network of wildlife and landscape walking routes ranging in length from the four-mile stroll through Tholt-y-Will glen, or the 28-mile Millennium Way which follows the route of Manx kings and their entourages 600 years ago, to the 95-mile Raad ny Foillan (Road of the Gull) which goes around the coastline.

BOX 3.2

SHARKS BASKING IN THE LIMELIGHT

The Isle of Man, better known for a fish of the smoked variety – the Manx kipper – has gained a fresher notoriety recently for a rather larger species, the basking shark. The basking shark, the second largest fish in the world, is an endangered species, yet is still pursued in some areas of the world for the high quality of its oil, and for the Japanese delicacy, shark fin soup. 'Nations like Iceland have realised there is more money in live animals which keep returning than killing the animals and only receiving one payment from them,' Ken Watterson, Director of the Island's Basking Shark Society, explained. 'I believe the future of the basking shark lies in the eco-tourism industry'.

Although the Isle of Man is perhaps better known as a holiday destination for its beaches, its largely unspoilt countryside and its less environmentally friendly Tourist Trophy motor cycle racing, during the last four years increasing numbers of tourists have been coming to the island to see the sharks. Basking sharks can grow to 35 feet in length but are known for their gentle behaviour. They can live for as long as 20 years and return every year to the same feeding grounds. A tour company called Wild Oceans is offering 'the Basking Shark Experience' – a weekend break which includes an opportunity to snorkel alongside the sharks and observe them feeding, as well as to observe whales, dolphins and seals. Ken Watterson acts as guide for the groups, which are limited to 12 participants.

Wild Oceans
The Saltmarsh
Partnership
55/56 St Martin's Lane
London WC2N 4EA
T: +44 (171) 240 1940
F: +44 (171) 240 4454

Source: Isle of Man Department of Tourism and Leisure; *Isle of Man Times* 1998

Apart from a plethora of both land and sea bird species, and grey seals off the northern coast, notable among the wildlife to be seen is the rare basking shark. Mention should also be made of two indigenous domesticated species, the tail-less Manx cat and the four-horned Loughtan sheep. The need for cultural awareness and sensitivity to local customs is pointed out in several places in this guide; visitors to the Isle of Man should respect the island's 'little folk,' and greet them courteously, especially when passing over Ballaugh Bridge ('Fairy Bridge'), along the road south from Douglas.

THE CHANNEL ISLANDS

The Channel Islands, about 100 miles south of mainland Britain and some 14 miles west of France, are perhaps best known as tax havens for off-shore financial dealings. But this proximity yet isolation has been attractive also to the political exile – notably Victor Hugo, who lived in Guernsey for 15 years at the time of the French Revolution; to the German army of occupation during the Second World War and, more recently, to tourists drawn by the islands' rich cultural heritage and mild climate. The Channel Islands are not part of the UK nor of the European Union, but comprise two independent nations, the States of Jersey and the States of Guernsey, which include also the tiny islands of Sark and Herm, and Alderney, the most northerly of the islands.

Jersey has the honour of being the world's first tourist destination to receive the Green Globe destination status award, made by the World Travel and Tourism Council (WTTC), in 1996. In the same year it won the Silver Unicorn Award from the Guild of Travel Writers. It is also proud of the fact that 12 of its beaches have received the highest award for water cleanliness from the Marine Conservation Society. But for green travellers who prefer the joys of horse riding, walking and cycling over those of the sea, the highlight of Jersey is its Green Lanes, first started in the Parish of St Peter in 1986. This 40-mile network of quiet country lanes now extends throughout the island, linking nine of Jersey's twelve parishes. Priority is given to pedestrians, cyclists and horse riders because of a 15 mph speed limit on the few motorised vehicles which use these routes. The network is not yet quite complete – three parish assemblies are still debating the issue but it is to be hoped that they will soon join in the scheme. A more recent project is a 96-mile rural cycle network which also makes use of Green Lanes, and has been developed by Jersey Tourism in close cooperation with the Jersey Cycle Group – a local pressure group which has contributed to the island's new Transport Strategy, giving more credence to walkers and cyclists. Further encourage-

For information about

Jersey Cycle Group and

tours contact:

Jersey Cycle Tours,

2 La Hougue Mauger,

St Mary, Jersey

T: +44 (1534) 482898

F: +44 (1534) 484060

ment is given to the 'environmentally friendly' visitor by free guided cycle tours offered four times a week from May to September, led by qualified cycle tour guides.

Jersey's numerous inland, coastal and cliff-top paths give access to an amazing diversity of habitats. Of particular interest in the autumn and winter are migrant birds en route from northern Europe to warmer climes – snow and Lapland buntings and ring ouzels are seen on the heathland of Les Landes, and in the reed beds of St Ouen's sedge warblers and occasionally hoopoes are sighted. Although wild flowers are everywhere in this 'garden island', the rare sand crocus and various species of orchid are of particular interest to botanists. Equally accessible are prehistoric and heritage sites including a massive Neolithic mound and passage grave in La Hougue Bie dating from 3800 BC; the 16th century Elizabeth Castle in St Aubin's Bay and, marking more recent history, the German Underground Hospital at St Lawrence. Despite the ease of access around the island, and a range of accommodation types, from small family guest houses to five-star hotels, disappointingly Jersey lacks any youth hostels.

'... to the rock of hospitality, to this corner of old Norman land where resides the noble little people of the sea, to the Island of Guernsey, severe and yet gentle...'
Victor Hugo

Despite its green image, Jersey is not free from environmental problems, to some extent created by its own success. While the island's bus company, JerseyBus, runs a regular service to all points, such that a green traveller has no real need for a car, many residents are less conscientious. Jersey is a relatively affluent society and has a very high rate of car ownership. As a consequence, in St Helier both traffic congestion and air pollution from vehicle emissions are causing concern, a problem which the new Transport Strategy, released for public debate in the latter half of 1998, is designed in part to resolve.

During Victor Hugo's exile at Hauteville House in Guernsey – the house is now a museum and makes a fascinating visit – he continued to publish major works including *Toilers of the Sea*, which he dedicated to the island; and it is to the sea, and especially to sailing, that many of the island's visitors are drawn. But for sea watchers, and bird watchers, there is a network of coastal walks and nature trails, in fact the whole south coast cliff area has been designated since 1989 as a Site of Nature Conservation Importance (equivalent to the UK's SSSI), although at present this provides no legal protection.

Guernsey, like so many other holiday islands, promotes cycling as a green activity for visitors and has recently published a sturdy and shower-proof ring-bound booklet of maps and descriptions of cycle routes around the island. Green lanes, however, are less well developed as an environmental concept than in neighbouring Jersey. Since 1992, however, the Guernsey Branch of Friends of the Earth has been organising monthly walks as part of a 'Reclaim the Green Lanes' campaign to raise public awareness. Many of the quiet country lanes that criss-cross Guernsey are not signposted as paths accessible to the public, and some have disappeared completely from maps of the island. Over the years some lanes have been turned into tarmac roads while building development has obscured others, so that there is no longer a connected network. The campaign publishes a booklet of green lanes and encourages walkers to use the paths in order to maintain public access; a contribution which green-minded visitors can pleasurably make to the island's environment.

In general, Guernsey's beaches fare better and several have appeared in the *Reader's Digest Good Beach Guide*; awards have also been made by the Marine Conservation Society and the Blue Flag scheme. But the point is clear, that even in destinations with a well-founded green image, constant vigilance is necessary to maintain high standards of environmental awareness, and the green traveller has an important role to play in that process.

TOURISM FOR TOMORROW AWARDS

Rhondda Heritage Park, South Wales

Lewis Merthyr Colliery
Coecae Road
Tremafod
Rhondda Cynon Taff
South Wales CF37 7NP
T: +44 (1443) 682036
F: +44 (1443) 687420

Highly Commended: UK 1997

The project regenerated the economy of this traditional coal mining area by reclaiming derelict mining land and establishing a heritage park to draw visitors to the area. Local jobs have been created to run the model town, which depicts traditional mining life, the visitor centre, shops, museum and displays. Underground tours of the mines are also available. The area receives about 76,000 visitors each year.

Farm Diversification, Llangorse, Wales

Gilfach Farm
Llangorse
Brecon
Powys LD3 7UH
T: +44 (1874) 658272
F: +44 (1874) 658280

Highly Commended: UK 1997

A family farm project which enhances the surrounding environment and supplements declining income from agriculture by providing a range of tourism facilities. Some 40km of walking/horse trails have been constructed, and old farm buildings have been converted to centres which bring outdoor activities (abseiling, rock climbing) inside. New forms of land-use have reduced the amount of pesticides and other chemicals applied to the land, and no fossil fuels are used on the site.

Festival of the Countryside, Wales

Highly Commended: Europe Special 1998

This year-long annual festival of over 1500 events encourages environmentally sound activities that incorporate the community. Over 40 managed and protected sites are listed in a manual to encourage their several million visitors to sample a wider range of attractions in rural Wales. The festival has spread out the tourism load to inland as well as coastal areas, and extended economic benefits throughout the year.

Frolic House
23 Frolic Street
Newtown
Powys S716 1AP
T: +44 (1686) 625384
F: +44 (1686) 622955

Sea Life Surveys: Mull, Scotland

Highly Commended: UK 1994

The first whale-watching and research centre in the UK, operating around the Isle of Mull. Land-based facilities include accommodation for visitors, a book and video library and a display centre. Leisure tourism is combined with a working holiday, collecting useful data from a 12-berth research vessel on behalf of the Tobermory-based Hebridean Whale and Dolphin Trust. The centre also won a Green Globe award for environmental achievements in 1996.

Sea Life Surveys
Dervaig
Isle of Mull,
Argyll PA75 6QL
T: +44 (1688) 400223
F: +44 (1688) 400383

Tourism and Environment Initiative: Scotland

Highly Commended: UK 1996

The Initiative's mission is 'to promote sustainable use of Scotland's world-class natural and built environment in order to maximise the wealth of opportunities for the Scottish tourism industry'. Among steps taken towards this goal are the establishment of 13 strategically-sited Tourism Management Programmes, involving around 70 small tourist projects, in areas where tourism development may conflict with environmental concerns or has not yet realised its potential.

Tourism and Environment
Bridge House
20 Bridge Street
Inverness IV1 1QR
Scotland
T: +44 (1463) 244435
F: +44 (1463) 244241

The Green Tourism Business Scheme, Scotland

Green Tourism Business
Scheme
c/o Highlands and
Islands Enterprise
20 Bridge Street
Inverness IV1 2QR
T: +44 (1463) 244435
F: +44 (1463) 244241

Highly Commended: UK 1998

The scheme aims to encourage accommodation providers to reduce environmental impacts while reducing operating costs. Standards (gold, silver, bronze) are set for specific areas of concern; waste, energy, water and effluents, suppliers and sub-contractors, staff, storage, noise, and wildlife opportunities. Independent inspectors monitor annually. One 70 bed hotel saved nearly £40,000 in water and waste costs.

Shannon-Erne Waterway: Ireland

Shannon-Erne Waterway
Golf Links Road
Ballinamore
Co Leitrim
Ireland
T: +353 (78) 44855
F: +353 (78) 44856

Highly Commended: Europe 1995

The Ballinamore to Ballyconnell Canal, closed since 1869, has been restored to new use as a leisure resource linking the river Shannon in the Republic of Ireland to Lough Erne in Northern Ireland. Native fish and waterfowl stocks have been increased and wildlife habitats (including artificial otter holts) have been created to lure in wild visitors. Facilities include luxury hotels, guest houses, bed and breakfast hostelries and self-catering accommodation, boat and cycle hire, and pony trekking.

Restoration of Ardagh, Ireland

Ardagh Village
County Longford
Ireland
T: +353 (43) 75277
F: +353 (43) 75278

Winner: Europe 1997

A community project which restores and sensitively enhances the village of Ardagh in County Longford, to promote quality tourism and generate income for the surrounding area. Through local fund-raising efforts and local government funds, telephone cables have been put underground, gardens planted and old buildings restored. A special tourism group has formed to promote agri-tourism. Ardagh has previously won Best Village in Ireland awards, and the Entente Florale (a Europe-wide competition) for its use of flowers and gardens.

Temple Bar Development: Dublin, Ireland

Winner: Europe 1995

'A leading example of sensitive and community based regeneration … of a derelict area of historical and archaeological importance in a large city popular with tourists and businesses', noted the award citation. An arts centre, housing, restaurants and cafés, together with many new offices and shops, have offered new benefits and options to residents of a previously neglected urban quarter, while enhancing the experience of large numbers of tourists who flock all year round to sample Dublin's distinctive cultural heritage.

Temple Bar Properties
Ltd
18 Eustace Street
Temple Bar
Dublin 2
Ireland
T: +353 (1) 677 2255
F: +353 (1) 677 2525

British Waterways: Sustainable Tourism and Environmental Conservation

Highly Commended: UK 1995

British Waterways developed an integrated strategy for managing boating, angling and other recreational uses of the towpath along Britain's intricate network of inland waterways, tied in with visitor attractions, education, access and information programmes. Cycleways, nature trails, canal restoration and studies of boat and pedestrian traffic, are part of the package. Conservation measures include introduction of grass carp to curb plagues of water weed, and replanting of reed beds.

British Waterways
Willow Grange
Church Road
Watford
Herts
WD1 3QA
T: +44 (1923) 201356
F: +44 (1923) 201300

Birmingham's Waterfront, British Waterways

Winner: UK 1997

The major re-generation of derelict and underused canals has diversified the economy and provided a focus for the promotion of the city as a tourist destination. Eighteenth century architecture has been refurbished and guidelines laid down to ensure new buildings maintain the historical character of the area. With improved quality of water, canals have been re-stocked with fish and indigenous species of reeds. An education programme, rubbish-recycling, pedestrian links and guided walks involve the community for long term sustainability of the area which receives 2 million visitors each year.

British Waterways
Willow Grange
Church Road
Watford, Hertfordshire,
WD1 3QA
T: +44 (1923) 201356
F: +44 (1923) 201300

Lake District Tourism Conservation Partnership Ltd

Highly Commended: Europe Special 1997

Brocknole
National Park Visitor
Centre
Windermere, Cumbria
LA23 1LJ
T: +44 (153) 9446601
F: +44 (153) 9445555

A joint action project between commercial and conservation interests to benefit the environment, the local community and the quality of visitor experience in the Lake District National Park. Over 100 key tourism and government agencies in the Partnership provide funds for projects such as footpaths and restoration of foreshore, which also create jobs and strengthen relationships between tourism and the community.

New Forest Badger Watch: Hampshire, UK

Highly Commended: UK 1995

New Forest Badger Watch
PO Box 2297
Ringwood
Hampshire BH24 4YH
T/F: +44 (1425)
403412

In a weatherproof hide, up to 22 people nightly from March to October can observe wild badgers from a few feet away without intrusion, through a one-way screen split above and below ground level. The observation chambers and linking tunnels were artificially created, but local badgers have dug their own connections to the site from their natural set nearby. Visitors receive instruction on the badgers and the correct way to watch without creating disturbance.

Saltburn-by-the Sea: Regeneration of a Victorian seaside resort, England

Highly Commended: UK 1994

Dept. of Leisure and
Tourism
Cargo Fleet Offices
Middlesborough Road
PO Box South Bank 20
Cleveland TS6 6EL
T: +44 (1642) 231212

Situated on the north east coast of England, this town prospered for over a century as a typical seaside resort on traditional lines but in recent years it has (like many others of its kind) suffered a dramatic slump in visitor numbers. The project was launched to revitalise the resort without destructive redevelopment by refurbishing historic buildings and various other distinctive features of the town. As a result Saltburn has been able to market itself anew as a Victorian resort.

Lakeland Country Breaks: County Fermanagh, Northern Ireland

Winner: UK 1996

Investment in rural tourism is the focus of this programme, run by a consortium of official and grassroots groups intent on developing sustainable 'niche tourism' in this unspoilt and secluded corner of Ireland. Holiday facilities are on offer in 13 participating villages, including accommodation, special events and guided trips into the countryside, famed for its lakes and natural habitats. Without building a single new development, the scheme has drawn visitors into the community for holidays with human contact as well as ancient heritage and music pubs. The response has been an estimated 234 per cent growth in tourist visits to the area since the scheme began.

Lakeland Country Breaks
Tourist Information
Centre
Wellington Road
Enniskillen
Co Fermanagh
Northern Ireland
T: +44 (1365) 327205
F: +44 (1365) 325511

Dales EnviroNet, Yorkshire Dales Millennium Trust

Winner: Europe Special 1998

Focused on landscape, wildlife and cultural heritage, the Trust has begun the first phase of a four-year project by setting up Dales EnviroNet and implementing over 100 environment and community schemes. The Trust provides grants of up to 50 per cent for local projects, ranging from village hall improvements and rebuilding drystone walls to regeneration of old native woodland and restoration of historic sites. Nature conservation schemes have reintroduced otters to some rivers and enhanced heather moorland and upland grasses. Facilities have also been improved for the eight million annual visitors to the Dales.

Yorkshire Dales
Millennium Trust
Beckside Barn
Church Avenue
Clapham
North Yorks LA2 8EQ
T: +44 (15242) 51002
F: +44 (15242) 51150

Sea to Sea (C2C) Cycle Route: Sustrans, UK

Global Winner 1995

Sustrans
35 King Street
Bristol BS1 4DZ

T: +44 (117) 926 8893
F: +44 (117) 929 4173

A nationwide pathfinder project for future travel and tourism initiatives. Sustrans works with local authorities and other partners to develop a 6500-mile National Cycle Network, a Millennium Project. The Network links disused railway lines, forest tracks and minor country lanes as well as side roads linking town centres. The C2C route runs 140 miles across 14 rural districts in the North of England, passing through many scenic areas of the Pennines and Lake District. An information pack is available, including maps and a guide to shops and lodgings along the cycleway.

Museum of Science and Industry, Manchester

Museum of Science and
Industry
Liverpool Road
Castlefield
Manchester M3 4FP

T: +44 (161) 8322244
F: +44 (161) 8332184

Highly Commended: UK and Europe Special 1998

Threatened historic railway buildings were restored and transformed into one of the top science museums in the world. The initiative stimulated regeneration of the surrounding area whilst maintaining authenticity of buildings. The museum also uses water and energy conservation systems, low-pollution heating and paper re-cycling.

Budget Rent A Car Eco-friendly Strategy

Winner: UK 1998

Budget Rent a Car
41 Marlowes
Hemel Hempstead
Hertfordshire HP1 1XJ

T: +44 (1442) 276000
F: +44 (1442) 276041

Budget Rent a Car received this award for being one of the first vehicle rental firms to develop environment-friendly transport options for travellers in the UK and Europe. In the UK 50 liquid petroleum gas (LPG)-fuelled cars and 10 transit vans, and in France 150 LPG vehicles and over 100 electric cars are available for hire. LPG vehicles emit 80 per cent less carbon monoxide and 50 per cent less carbon dioxide than petrol vehicles. Budget has also started a national bike hire service; over 150 21-gear folding mountain bikes are available for hire at 31 locations across the UK.

Conservation Working Holidays: British Trust for Conservation Volunteers

Highly Commended: UK 1996

BTCV's global working holidays scheme helps set up locally-run practical conservation programmes around the world, then provides opportunities for visiting participants to combine overseas travel with hands-on involvement in implementing them together with local volunteers. By 1996, more than 60 projects were under way in 21 countries. Current projects include improving footpaths in Iceland, managing wetlands in Japan, conserving orchids in Canada and monitoring turtles in Turkey (see under Conservation Holidays in Chapter 2).

BTCV
36 St Mary's Street
Wallingford
Oxon OX10 0EU
T: +44 (1491) 839766
F: +44(1419) 839646

Bellozanne Treatment Plant for Ultra-Violet Disinfection of Effluent: Jersey

Winner: UK 1995

Tourism is Jersey's main industry and the island's population of around 80,000 increases by over 25 per cent in the summer months. It was recognised that clean beaches and bathing water were essential to keeping this thriving commerce alive. A new ultra-violet effluent treatment system has resulted in highly satisfactory water quality standards. The project is praised in the Tourism for Tomorrow citation as an example to other tourist destinations and a good case of 'a combination of skills brought to bear on a real issue'

PSD
PO Box 412
South Hill
St Helier
Jersey JE2 4UY
T: +44 (1534) 601690
F: +44 (1534) 33578

CHAPTER 4
EUROPE

WESTERN EUROPE

The opening of the Channel Tunnel has increased the accessibility of many parts of Northern and Western Europe to many British travellers. It has also increased the opportunity to travel by public transport. Environmentally, that should be counted as an advance, though there are many who would argue that this could be offset by the increase in numbers of travellers as well as the local impact of building the Tunnel on the south east of England, let alone those working on cross-Channel ferries who have felt the impact of increased competition on the route. Whatever the analysis, the attractions of Britain's nearest continental neighbours are likely to become more apparent, and, in Northern Europe especially, public transport (notably the railways) is an efficient means of getting around.

Environmentally, the countries of Western Europe have all felt the impact of tourism, arguably as much as those of many other industries. The Mediterranean coast, in particular, suffered in the mid-1960s as developers capitalised on the boom in the package holiday market. Along the Mediterranean coasts of Spain, France and Italy, poorly planned hotels and housing sprang up. The scarcely regulated influx of tourists led to pollution of the sea from untreated sewage and casually dumped litter, while growing numbers of coach parties and other traffic generated congestion and

EXPERIENCE

...which covers 30 years. Since our first safari in 1962 we have grown to become one of the Worlds most experienced travel companies. And with that experience comes compassion, and a deep understanding of our World and its precarious future. For a brochure on Europe, a new continent, call Abercrombie & Kent.

UK 0171 730 9600   US 800 323 7308.

noise that disturbed the peace of mediaeval town and rural hamlet alike. In Switzerland, where increasing numbers of British tourists began taking holidays in the mid-19th century (in part as a result of Thomas Cook's pioneering developments as a tour operator), modern tourism shares the blame for the denuding of some of the upland areas, as trees make way for ski runs, and traffic-generated pollution adds to the stress on fauna and flora.

Social life can also be disrupted by tourism as much in Europe as in developing countries. In Switzerland, many former agricultural villages have become tourist resorts, busy only during the winter months. With so many local people migrating to the cities, the tourists are mostly serviced by migrant workers. Groups such as the Geneva-based Alp Action, set up by Prince Sadruddin Aga Khan, are now working to support local cultural traditions, conserve wildlife (a recent triumph was the successful wild breeding of an alpine vulture for the first time in a century) and encourage a more sustainable approach to tourism development. Both environmental and social impacts of tourism are being addressed in many holiday areas of Europe as a matter of urgency. In the last few years more than 20 such projects have been recognised with various awards by the Tourism for Tomorrow scheme (see listings at the end of this chapter).While mentioning the social drawbacks of tourism it is, of course, only fair to point out that Europe has been criss-crossed by travellers for centuries – ancient pilgrimage and trade routes were in some cases the forerunners of those taken by modern tourists – and that tourism has in many cases been welcomed by both locals and visitors alike.

France, by virtue of being the UK's nearest neighbour, is a popular destination for British travellers. The French railway, including the TGV high-speed train system, is extensive enough to ensure that most travellers need not think about driving the length of the country. That is important, as more holidaymakers are discovering that, away from the Mediterranean or Atlantic coasts, one of the more enjoyable ways of holidaying in France is by staying in a *gîte*. These converted farm buildings reflect a general drift away from the land in recent decades, partly due to the increased mechanisation of French agriculture, but also because of the move towards more urban jobs. Although it is debatable that some *gîtes* may reflect a loss of local housing and employment opportunities – a reflection of the arguments over second homes in

127

Britain's rural areas – their supporters argue that instead they are helping put back investment into countryside economies. The recent revival of interest in the country's canal system has sparked moves to promote canal boat holidays; a leisurely way of seeing the countryside. France also scores particularly highly with its many camping sites, together with a network of shelters and *gîtes d'étape* for hill climbers and walkers. Given the geographical diversity of France, it is not surprising that all the most popular activity holidays are possible in one part of the country or another. More surprising, perhaps, are those not generally connected with the country: surfing along the Atlantic coast, in the Biarritz region, for example. France draws much of its electricity from nuclear power – while not contributing to greenhouse gas emissions, this has long worried environmental groups, on both sides of the Channel.

Spain was long associated with the first wave of the European package holiday boom, and the results can still be seen along the various costas: sprawling development, concrete and breeze-block canyons that reflect the market among Northern Europeans for a cheap week or two in the Mediterranean sun. In neighbouring **Portugal**, the Algarve region has also been developed along the coast, with numerous golf courses being built to accommodate the interest in the sport and at the same time contributing to the strains on water supply. In parts of southern Spain the market for holiday homes continues to grow, particularly since a recent relaxation in property and finance laws. The result, particularly in the southern province of Andalusia, for example, has been double-edged: some empty properties have been renovated, bringing investment and (some) employment, but with resulting changes in local demography.

Both countries of the Iberian peninsula can offer many attractions to the green traveller, particularly in the northern less visited regions. In northern Portugal, the Peneda-Geres national park is a magnet for walkers; Spain's verdant Galicia region is now beginning to draw visitors to enjoy its hills and coastline; the Moorish remains of Granada and other towns are increasingly recognised for the architectural gems they are; Barcelona's artistic and civic regeneration is making a city break there highly fashionable; and long-distance walking holidays in Spain have as much romance now as in the days of the young Laurie Lee. It is also worth mentioning the work being done by both Portuguese and Spanish agencies and environment groups in the Extramadura region that straddles the two countries, around the Tagus river and Alcantra dam. In a project that was a finalist in the 1993 Ford European Conservation Awards scheme, work has been done to safeguard local flora and fauna from, among other things, unregulated tourism, including motor boating and illegal hunting. The aim is to create an International Tagus Park. Meanwhile, to show that even areas that have suffered from unregulated tourism can begin the process of regeneration, back at the coast, some resorts, such as Benidorm, and places along the Algarve, have begun to insist on higher environmental standards, in an attempt to keep their tourist trade.

Of the four Balearic Islands – Majorca, Minorca, Ibiza and Formentera – Majorca and Ibiza have dominated recent press accounts of the impact that tourism can have on island environments and communities. Majorca, and especially the coastal strip

around the capital, Palma, became for a while synonymous with the cheap package holiday and with the rash of development that sprawled along the coast to accommodate the plane-loads of (mostly) British and German tourists arriving for a fortnight's sand, sea and sin. More recently, the island's authorities have begun to take steps to ameliorate the worst of the excesses. Particularly notable has been an ongoing award-winning project in Palma itself, reducing the permitted height of new hotel buildings, cleaning up and regenerating the sea-front area, and improving sanitation so as to reduce the pollution of the sea.

At the same time, tourists have begun to explore the wildlife-attractive northern coasts of Majorca, presenting new environmental problems and challenges. As golf courses and other new developments proliferate, water shortage is seen as a serious problem. Parts of Majorca are also experiencing the holiday home phenomenon – but with a difference. Though German and other visitors have begun to spend heavily on old farm cottages and townhouses in parts of the island, the increasing prosperity of the Majorcan economy means that some local people are now able to afford to return to the remote villages that they once left for jobs in Palma or on the Spanish mainland. Equally, some villages are now reasserting their desire for development, but on their terms, not the tourists'. Two recent case studies illustrate the point. In 1996 the British entrepreneur Richard Branson's plans to develop a hotel in the village of Banyalbufar aroused concerted reaction from some locals, concerned that it could stretch already limited water supplies, while failing to significantly stimulate local employment. And in the nearby village of Deya, made famous as the long-time home of the British poet Robert Graves and subsequent artistic 'colonists', the (resident) anthropologist Jacqueline Waldren, in her book *Insiders and Outsiders: Paradise and Reality in Mallorca*, has documented how local people have increasingly sought to ensure that tourism and tourism-related development occur on their terms.

In **Italy** a new stress is being placed on greener holidays, such as walking and wildlife watching in national parks, away from the traditional honeypot cities such as Florence and Venice, and from parts of the Adriatic (where sea pollution is still a problem). In **Greece** too, much effort is now being put into local sanitation schemes in an attempt to preserve bays and coastal inlets from sewage, while in Athens the local authorities now regularly ban private motor vehicles (usually on a rota basis) to try to cut the air pollution that endangers health and historic architecture alike. Perhaps the most widely publicised environmental initiative directly connected to tourism has been the lengthy campaign by the Greek Sea Turtle Protection Society to protect the loggerhead turtle colonies on the island of Zakynthos. Increases in both tourism and shipping had been threatening the turtles. The noise and disturbance from tourist resorts was particularly intrusive, discouraging the animals from nesting. Campaigning by NGOs brought the issue to European-wide prominence, and the Greek government was forced to promise action, but only continued pressure will ensure protection for the species. As desperately competing holiday companies see profit margins cut to the bone, the downside of tourism in Greece remains an illustration that cheap holidays can carry an expensive environmental cost.

Beset by economic, social and political turmoil in recent years, **Albania**, the former staunchly independent Communist state of the days of Enver Hoxha, has been slowly opening up to Western travellers since the early 1990s. A legacy of widespread industrial pollution in some areas is matched by the fragility of some of its largely unvisited archaeological sites, such as the astonishing remains of the Roman city of Butrint. Unthinking tourism development could do enormous harm here.

The Radisson SAS Bay Point Resort Malta
Perfect for mixing business with pleasure

Situated in quiet St George's Bay, overlooking the Mediterranean, this de luxe resort hotel is the ideal location for meetings, seminars, or just for pure relaxation. All our 252 spacious air-conditioned rooms and suites have balconies with panoramic sea views and our conference department can host a wide range of events for up to 2,000 guests. A diving centre, 4 pools, a children's area, gymnasium and a variety of restaurants and bars mean that you won't want to settle for anything less. Experience the Radisson SAS Bay Point Resort for yourself and discover how we make your pleasure our business.

Radisson /// SAS
BAY POINT RESORT MALTA

St George's Bay, St Julian's STJ 02, Malta. Tel: (356) 374 894. Fax: (356) 374 895.
Url: http://www.islandhotels.com e-mail: wjzahra@islandhotels.com

CENTRAL AND NORTHERN EUROPE

The traditional 'clean' tourist image presented by such countries as **Austria**, **Switzerland** and **Germany** is a key factor in attracting visitors. Of course, the reality is not always as straightforward. In the Alpine region (the same holds true for those parts of Alpine France and Italy), tourism has brought its own problems, as we have already seen, together with recent initiatives to restore the natural and social environment. In Austria, the Tyrolean Tourist Board has, since the mid-1990s, developed an environmental 'Seal of Quality' scheme which is intended to cover all accommodation and catering establishments in the country's most intensive tourist province. The economic importance of tourism to the region is overwhelming: with a resident population of 640,000, the Tyrol has some 45 million 'overnights' by visitors each year. The annually reviewed scheme is designed to encourage and reward initiatives to avoid or reduce waste and noise, conserve water and energy, and improve the impact of transport on the mountain region. In 1993, the Tyrol also won second prize in the Ford European Conservation Awards, while a Green Village scheme, which invoved village communities in improving and monitoring the sustainability of tourism as a part of rural development, won the European regional award from Tourism for Tomorrow.

SCANDINAVIA

The Scandinavian countries of **Denmark**, **Norway**, **Sweden** and **Finland** are generally held to be good examples of nations that in recent decades have displayed a strong sense of concern for the environment and civil rights. Of course, the true picture is rather more complex: just as it has recently emerged that traditionally 'progressive' Sweden had engaged in a disturbing programme of hidden eugenics, in an attempt to eliminate those with 'undesirable' features, so too the environmental record of some of the Scandinavian nations has come in for closer scrutiny. Norway, for example, which under the leadership of prime minister Gro Harlem Brundtland had a reputation for leadership in international issues of environment and development, found itself at odds with many green groups in the late 1980s and early 1990s for its continuing support for whaling. Denmark, with its keen advocacy for countering the pollution of the North Sea, has been accused of endangering one of the same sea's most important sources of food for birds by its policy of industrial fishing for sandeels. Finland's extensive forestry and paper industry has been the subject of debate over how environmentally sustainable it is.

Nevertheless, the Scandinavian countries do have undoubted attractions for the visitor concerned for the natural environment. Not least is its apparent emptiness: in an otherwise crowded continent, Scandinavia offers vast expanses of barely populated countryside. This is a particular boon for anyone who likes hiking, walking, long-distance cycling, kayaking, climbing or many other outdoor activities, while winter sports, such as skiing, cross-country skiing, skating and outdoor ice hockey are all highly popular.

Access to most of the countryside, particularly in Sweden and Finland, is also more open than in much of Britain; a fact which has led the Ramblers' Association to advocate that reforms to British access legislation should learn from Scandinavian experience.

Given the size of the three northernmost Scandinavian countries, transport considerations are important for the green traveller. Thankfully, rail, bus and ferry services are good examples of how public transport can work, while provisions for cyclists are equally enlightened.

Denmark, the smallest of the Scandinavian states, may have less topographical variety than its northern neighbours but by compensation offers a rich sense of local place, and an equally rich history still evident in its towns and villages. You don't have to recall Hamlet to be impressed by the country's castles and other ancient buildings; and a mixture of cycling and walking can be an enjoyable way of seeing much of the country. Copenhagen, inevitably, is the city that draws most visitors with its range of historic buildings, museums, restaurants and other attractions (including the Carlsberg brewery), but some of the country's smaller towns deserve to become better known. So, too, do Denmark's various small islands and coastal villages and resorts. Within Denmark, an independent nation, the remote seafaring community of the Faroe Islands, is located several hundred miles north of the British Isles. Off the normal tourist map, it is a quiet haven for the small number of visitors, particularly ornithologists, who take boat trips to see cliff colonies of thousands of sea birds. More vocal, however, have been the various conservation groups who continue to protest at the regular killing of pilot whales, which are harpooned and hacked to death after being netted in shallow waters. The Faroese defend the practice as an integral part of their economic and cultural existence.

Norway enjoys a spectacular coastline that stretches north into the Arctic Circle. Perhaps one of the best ways to appreciate it is by taking one of the many ferries or cruise ships that ply the routes north. Apart from the dramatic scenery, the wildlife is also of keen interest; orcas regularly visit some of the fjords, and sea-eagles dominate the skies. Against a backdrop of greens and greys, the wooden buildings of many Norwegian towns, villages and hamlets resonate with their richly painted colours in an atmosphere that is as clear as any in the world. Ancient settlements, such as the beautiful Old Town district of Bergen, reflect the country's maritime heritage. Cross-country trekking (and skiing during the winter) is a popular pastime for Norwegians as well as visitors, while sailing and kayaking are also popular along coastline and rivers.

Sweden, like Norway, has an outdoors tradition which encourages the walker, hiker and other countryside lovers. The country's Baltic coastline, together with tens of thousands of lakes, provides ample opportunities for water sports. Indeed, each summer, the Swedish capital hosts the annual Stockholm water festival and conference which culminates with a vast fireworks display in the middle of the city's harbour. As elsewhere in Scandinavia, the many well-preserved buildings dating back to the period of Sweden's days as a great European power are evidence of a strong conservationist tradition. Sweden was also one of the first European countries to develop a system of national parks: they remain strongholds for much of the country's wildlife, though some species, such as the wolf, survive in only very small numbers; bears and lynx are slightly more common. Fish are rather more numerous, to the delight of many anglers who have begun to visit the country. Partly because of a tradition of living off the land, and partly because of Sweden's strong social democrat traditions, access to the countryside is legally guaranteed by the *allemansrätt* system, which allows walkers much wider rights than in Britain.

Finland, long perched uneasily between East and West during the days of the Cold War, is now beginning to promote its tourist attractions more widely. It shares with Sweden a geography in which the countryside is dotted with numerous lakes and other waterways, as well as extensive forested areas, a source for the country's economically important timber and paper industries. The Finnish government has been anxious that they present an improving environmental image, particularly since the country voted to join the European Union. Though much old-growth forest has been cleared, a large amount of reforestation has taken place (not always monocrop, either) and forays into the woods to pick fruit, nuts and mushrooms are traditional activities during the Finnish holiday seasons.

The Lapland region of northern Finland culturally extends into Swedish latitudes. The Saami people are one of Europe's last partly nomadic ethnic groups, though reindeer herding is increasingly carried out from established settlements. The Saami culture has, inevitably, begun to be seen as a tourist attraction, which has brought some economic benefits.

EASTERN EUROPE

With the end of the Cold War, the break-up of the Soviet Union and the reunification of Germany, Central and Eastern Europe have seen slow but steady increases in the number of Western tourists making the journey east – as well as the beginnings of a tourist flow in the opposite direction. The attractions for Westerners, other than relative novelty, are many: historic cities such as Prague, capital of the **Czech Republic**, have already become hip venues for Americans and Western Europeans, and in **Hungary**, Budapest is acquiring a similar reputation.

The region has had, and continues to have, its share of environmental problems, however. In some countries, the withdrawal of the Soviet Army left a legacy of polluted sites. Old industrial practices have contaminated underground and surface water sources, as well as contributing to a high level of air pollution in places. Yet some of the countryside in parts of Eastern Europe is as unspoiled as any across the continent, with a wide range of wildlife. Hungary, for example, has a diverse geography, including the massive Lake Balaton, the great plains that separate the Danube from Romania, and forested mountain ranges, with a series of national parks offering some conservation protection. Although Lake Balaton has suffered from agricultural pollution in recent decades, some of Hungary's underground spa waters remain a singular tourist attraction – hot baths that can be enjoyed for their therapeutic qualities or simply for relaxation.

While the fighting that convulsed much of former **Yugoslavia** in the early 1990s made conventional travel in parts of the region difficult, the Dalmatian coast is slowly beginning to revive as a tourist destination, though it will undoubtedly take many years before it recovers to the levels of the early 1980s. A different prospect awaits those who go north to the Baltic states of **Estonia**, **Latvia** and **Lithuania**. Reassertion of independence from the Soviet Union has been followed by varying degrees of economic success, but the ancient Baltic towns are beginning to draw curious travellers. The Baltic countryside is also being touted – rather like parts of **Poland** and the **Ukraine** – as some of the wilder and more mediaeval in the continent.

RUSSIA

Spanning such a vast geographical area, **Russia** has traditionally evoked a sense of mystery for the Western traveller. Since the epoch-making changes initiated by Mikhail Gorbachev in the late 1980s, access has become easier, at least in theory. But the new breed of visitor has discovered two Russias: the traditional landscape of ancient, domed architecture and vast countryside existing alongside areas that have been seriously damaged by decades of polluting industry or military activity. Socially too the divide between the entrenched poor and the newly rich business class is growing wider – a gulf accentuated by the economic crisis of 1998. Despite economic difficulties, conservation work is restoring some of the treasures of the country; some of the buildings of St Petersburg, for example, are returning to their original 18th and 19th century splendour. Efforts are also being made to stem the assaults on wildlife that accompanied the economic and political difficulties of the last decade. In Siberia, for example, there is some evidence that an international campaign to protect the dwindling numbers of Siberian tigers from poaching for the Chinese medicine trade is beginning to reap results.

Western travel companies are slowly moving into the Russian market. Smaller firms have been leading the way since the days of 1980s perestroika. It is now possible to go trekking in the Caucasus mountains, by the border with Georgia, or fishing in Siberia. The route of the Trans-Siberian Express remains one of the great railway journeys of the world. Yet there is some evidence already that tourism needs to be managed if it is not to have a damaging environmental impact. One example of an initiative to encourage sustainable tourism has come in the Sudzal natural and cultural park region, possibly the oldest cultural centre in Russia, with more than 150 important monuments, including four World Heritage sites in and around the ancient city of Sudzal. Here the Centre for Independent Ecological Programmes, together with Moscow University and local workers, are developing sustainable tourism programmes designed to help restore and conserve historic buildings and promote ecologically sound agriculture. The scheme, unprecedented in Russia, won the 1993 Ford European Conservation Award.

TOURISM FOR TOMORROW AWARDS

Gîtes de France Holiday Concept: France

Winner: Europe Special 1995

Gîtes de France

178 Piccadilly

London W1V 9DB

T: +44 (171) 4933480

Set up in 1954 under the auspices of France's Ministries of Tourism and Agriculture, to counter the effects of post-war migration from the countryside to the towns and cities, and subsequent dereliction of many rural dwellings. By 1995, there were more than 32,000 Gîtes de France, owned by country dwellers and farmers in roughly equal numbers, offering accommodation with a bed capacity of more than 285,000. Most visitors are city-dwellers intent on family holidays, 29 per cent are from abroad. Traditional buildings have been sensitively restored and owners have gained by a huge boost in capital investment, while farmers have been able to diversify their livelihoods without encroachment on regular farming activities.

National Park Ticket: Bavaria, Germany

Highly Commended: Europe 1996

The oldest National Park in Germany, the Bavarian Forest National Park attracts over a million tourists a year. Some 80 per cent travel by car. The exhausts cause photochemical pollution and acidification which has led to widespread environmental damage. In May 1996 a clean alternative transportation system was introduced for a six year trial period. Buses running on natural gas shuttle visitors from parking lots at the perimeter to main points of interest, at half-hour intervals.

Nationalparkverwaltung
Bayerischer Wald
Freyunger Str.2
D–94481 Grafenau
Bavaria
Germany
T: +49 (8552) 9600
F: +49 (8552) 1394

Nature and Culture Project: Hindelang, Germany

Winner: Europe 1996

Hindelang is one of the chief tourist regions in Germany's Bavarian Alps, attracting some 100,000 visitors each year. It is famed for its ecological diversity, fruit of the labours of generations of local farming people. But traditional farming has been declining. The Hindelang Nature and Culture Association was formed in 1992 by a group of local farmers in collaboration with tourism entrepreneurs, public authorities and communities of the area. The farmers have pledged to favour low-density herding, locally-sourced animal feeds, small field size, and exclusive use of organic fertilisers. The purpose is to safeguard the region's historical and biological riches and to nurture tourism, the community's main source of income.

Kurverwaltung Hindelang
Markstrasse 9
D–87541 Hindelang
Germany
T: +49 (8324) 8920
F: +49 (8324) 8055

Umweltsiegel Tyrol: Tyrolean Environmental Seal of Quality Scheme, Austria

Winner: Europe 1994

Umweltsiegel Tyrol

Tirol Werbung

A–6010 Innsbruck

Bozner Platz 6

Austria

T: +43 (512) 5320133

F: +43 (512) 5320150

The green labelling scheme offers incentives towards better environmental practice for hotel and catering businesses in Austria's prime Alpine region and most intensively visited province, the Tyrol. Its target is to create ecologically sound tourism facilities and improve quality and standards in the region's built and natural surroundings. Some 40 to 50 environmental criteria are set, depending on the type of establishment applying for the seal. These criteria include waste and effluent management standards and water and energy saving.

Nature and Life – Bregenzerwald, Austria

Highly Commended: Europe 1998

Bregenzerwald

6863 Egg

Austria

T: +43 (5512) 2365

F: +43 (5512) 3010

In this traditional farming area, tourism is becoming increasingly significant in the local economy. The local tourism industry, planning association, and local people have set up their own programme to promote tourism through joint efforts while controlling environmental impact. For example they have initiated special promotions such as the Cheese Route, and confined potentially damaging sports such as skiing and mountain biking to designated areas.

Urdaibai Biosphere Reserve Project: Spain

Highly Commended: Europe 1996

Tourism and Consumer

Affairs

Adriano IV 14–16

01008 Vitoria Gasteiz

Spain

T: +34 (451) 89952

F: +34 (451) 89931

Over 200,000 tourists visit this reserve in the Basque country each year. The reserve was designated by UNESCO in 1994 and has also been declared of special interest for its birdlife by the Ramsar Convention and Natura 2000 Network. Local authorities and community groups have created an integrated environment and education project. 'Farm schools', youth hostels and special observation areas cater for environment-conscious visitors, while safeguarding natural heritage, and traditional lifestyles and quality of life.

S'Albufera Natural Park for Conservation, Birds and Tourism: Mallorca, Spain

Special Award: Europe 1996

Located in the north east corner of the largest of the Balearic Islands, S'Albufera is a 1300-hectare wetland important as a feeding and breeding ground for waterfowl and rich in other wildlife and habitats. Care and restoration of these features is blended with education and research activities and with ecologically aware tourism that adds value to the Park for the local economy and community. A professional management team deals with such tasks as keeping open waters clear of weed infestations, re-introducing depleted species and improving access and interpretation facilities for the 100,000 tourists who visit the Park each year.

Parc Natural de
S'Albufera
Lista de Correus
07458 Can Picafort
Mallorca
Balearic Islands
T: +34 (71) 892250
F: +34 (71) 892158

The Calalfell Iberian Citadel Project, Spain

Highly Commended: Europe 1997

Opened in 1995, this archaeological site was partially reconstructed using traditional materials and techniques to give visitors an historical perspective of the area. A picnic area, reception and shop are provided. The small size of the site prohibits large numbers of visitors, but it attracts local school groups and enhances local understanding of cultural heritage.

Calalfell Iberian Citadel
Project
Sant Pere, 29–31
43820 Calalfell
(Tarragone)
Spain
T: +34 (77) 692981
F: +34 (77) 692981

Parque Natural da Ria Formosa: Algarve, Portugal

Highly Commended: Europe 1994

The Ria Formosa lagoon is a complex of islands, swamps, channels and mudflats abounding in wildlife, extending 60 kilometres along the coast of the Algarve. The coast's many fine beaches have also made the area a favourite haunt for tourists. The area was designated a Nature Park in 1987, since when a comprehensive scheme of environmental care and of wildlife research and monitoring has been integrated with steps to upgrade tourism facilities and to 'enhance the educational experience' for summer visitors.

Parque Natural da Ria
Formosa
Quinta de Marim
8700 Olhão
Portual
T: +351 (89) 704134
F: +351 (89) 704165

Vilamoura, Portugal

Winner: Europe Special 1997

Aparto 501
Vilamoura
8125 Quartiera
Agarve
Portugal
T: +352 89 380088
F: +352 89 315934

Until 1996, this tourist resort on the Algarve paid little heed to environmental issues, but the new management has joined Green Globe and over the last 12 months has been implementing an action plan to reverse previous neglect. Improvements include a sewage treatment plant, regular cleaning of the beach and marina, and recycling. New buildings are designed to minimise environmental and visual impact, and tourists are encouraged to walk or cycle in preference to motor vehicles. The company is also investing in a local nature conservation project as it strives for Green Globe Destination status.

Vale do Lima, Portugal

Highly Commended: Europe 1998

Praca Da Republica
4990 Ponte De Lima
Portugal
T: +351 58 741417
F: +351 58 741418

In the Lima Valley, a programme of restoration of built and cultural heritage was initiated by a consortium of government agencies, tourism associations and local communities. In a small village in the Peneda Geres National Park, for example, old villas were restored using traditional methods which provided employment for local craftsmen while increasing tourism accommodation.

Conservation in Southern Dodecanese Islands: Laskarina Holidays, Greece

Highly Commended: Europe 1995

Laskarina Holidays
St Mary's Gate
Wirksworth
Derbyshire DE4 4DQ
UK
T: +44 (0)1629 824881
F: +44 (0) 1629 822205

Laskarina Holidays, an international tour operator, has encouraged the local authorities on the islands of the Dodecanese archipelago to adopt a programme of renovation and restoration to boost the islands' appeal as a tourist destination. Included in the conservation programme are restoration of traditional buildings, restriction of through traffic in conservation areas, anti-litter campaigns, water conservation initiatives, dealing with stray animals and planting of shade trees and flower beds.

The Cyprus Agrotourism Programme, Cyprus

Winner: Europe 1998

In rural areas of Cyprus, government and private sector funds are being used to restore old buildings and convert them to tourist accommodation as a more reliable source of income than farming. So far over 60 buildings have been restored, providing 300 beds. Village squares and cobbled streets are also being restored, and nature trails constructed. The programme encourages tourists away from traditional coastal beach resorts and enables rural populations in the interior to benefit from small-scale tourism development. In 1997, 7000 visitors stayed in agrotourist accommodation.

PO Box 4535
CY–1390 Nicosia
Cyprus
T: + 357 2 337715
F: +357 2 339723

Hotel Renaissance Waste Management Programme: Prague, Czech Republic

Highly Commended: Europe 1996

In 1994, the 309-room Renaissance Prague Hotel set up an Environmental Committee to oversee improvements in all aspects of running the hotel. Hotel guests and local people participate in an environmental awareness and outreach campaign tied in with the in-house programme. With the National Federation of Hotels and Restaurants, the hotel co-sponsored publication of a Green Management Book of guidelines for better practice. Media campaigns were organised and co-operation was sought with environmental groups and committees active in Prague.

Hotel Renaissance
V Celnici 7
PO Box 726
Czech Republic

On the Trail of the Wolf, Poland

Highly Commended: Europe 1997

The On The Trail of the Wolf project was set up to manage and research wildlife, particularly the wolf, in the Bialoweiza Primeval Forest, which is a World Heritage Site. The project is managed by The British Trust for Conservation Volunteers who organise 60 volunteers a year who work in the area in small groups. They also fund the project.

On The Trail of the Wolf Project
36 St Mary's Street
Wallingford OX10 0EU
T: +44 (1491) 839766
F: +44 (1491) 839646

Inter-Continental Hotels and Resorts: Environmental Targets (Europe)

Highly Commended: Europe Special 1995

Inter-Continental Hotels
and Resorts
Devonshire House
Mayfair Place
London W1X 5FH
T: +44 (171) 355 6586
F: +44 (171) 355 6592

Inter-Continental has 60 hotels in 27 countries throughout Europe, employing 22,000 people and catering to an average three million guests each year. The chain has significantly exceeded the original goals of a seven-year programme of environmental improvements such as replacing solid-fuel heating systems with gas-fired boilers, and upgrading waste recovery, pollution prevention and recycling processes. Showcase examples include the group's hotels in Zagreb and Vienna.

CHAPTER 5
THE MIDDLE EAST

The countries generally lumped together under the generic heading of the 'Middle East' are in fact as diverse as any, in terms of culture, politics and environment. Some would even disagree that they were Middle Eastern: most recent governments in **Turkey**, for example, have been arguing for admission to the European Union, while countries such as **Egypt** are as much part of Africa as any other region. And while some have a regular and developed tourist industry (**Israel**, for example), others, such as **Iraq** or **Saudi Arabia**, can be difficult for the tourist to access easily. But there are some things they share. With the exception of Israel and **Lebanon**, all are Islamic nations to varying degrees. This means, as elsewhere, that the traveller must be mindful of local customs and sensitivities. Tourism can itself be vulnerable to other issues in the Middle East: in November 1997, more than 50 Western tourists were killed in a massacre near Luxor as part of attempts to destabilise the country's government and economy in pursuit of political change. As recent events in Yemen show, with any area subject to intermittent conflict, it is advisable to check on the security situation before travelling.

Turkey has become a destination for increasing numbers of British tourists as the travel industry has presented it as a relatively cheap, unspoiled holiday spot for sun-seekers, whether along its Mediterranean, Aegean or Black Sea coasts. Environmental impacts are already evident. Already there are fierce debates within the country, as well as those involving environmental groups from abroad, about the spread of tourist development in some new resorts, particularly where new building has put wildlife or archaeological remains at risk. The Black Sea, meanwhile, is already suffering from over-fishing and pollution from its surrounding states; one recent report predicted it could be the first sea to 'die' ecologically. And – ironically, given its role as host for the last United Nations Habitat summit conference on the future of cities – Istanbul, the Turkish capital, and one of the great tourist cities of the world, has annual episodes of air pollution, partly from domestic fuel burning, partly from its congested traffic. Turkey, like some other states in the region, has attracted strong criticism for aspects of its human rights policies, particularly towards the Kurdish minority.

Turkey's attractions are manifold, however. In addition to the coasts, the cultural heritage of the country is extraordinarily rich, while inland, the scenery can be spectacular, although travel in the east of the country can be difficult (and not without its risks at times). Along the coasts, Turkey offers good swimming and diving, as well as sailing and canoe holidays. Wildlife watching is also possible in the less populous areas. Turkish cuisine, together with that of Lebanon, is among the most diverse in the region.

Lebanon itself is emerging tentatively from the chaos of war and civil war after it became inextricably involved in the Arab–Israeli conflicts that have scarred the region. Indeed, for some travellers, Beirut is the height of chic once more. Even so, much remains to be done; only a comprehensive settlement of the conflict is likely to bring continued peace to the south of Lebanon. Yet holiday activities have returned: Lebanon is one of those countries where you can swim or sail then ski in the same day, trek or camp. The cedar trees of Lebanon were a biblical byword for natural beauty, although recent reports suggest that many stands have suffered from neglect.

Israel has within its borders some of the holiest sites of three religions: its landscape is inextricably linked to Biblical history. Yet it is also rich in its natural environment with diverse wildlife (Israel is on a significant bird migration route) and geography: there are several hundred nature reserves in the country. In some respects, the environment may also hold a key to the conflict that has gripped the region: in the opinion of many commentators, any eventual settlement will depend on resolving the question of access to the water of the River Jordan. Israeli environment groups are currently campaigning for limits to hotel development around the Dead Sea, and

along the shore of the Red Sea where there have been reports of damage to the coral reefs from boat anchors and discharged pollution. The Red Sea remains a favourite for divers, however; the undersea life is rich and colourful, with species including dolphins and sharks.Sailing and windsurfing are also popular. A tradition of holiday working on a kibbutz community farm in Israel has begun to wane, but many people still visit Israel for this purpose.

Egypt is trying to develop its Red Sea resorts for both economic as well as political reasons. Towns such as Hurghada have expanded, and swimming, snorkelling, scuba-diving, sailing and windsurfing are popular activities with visitors who these days include an increasing number of young Russians – a legacy of the recent history of both countries. For many people, however, the main attraction of Egypt is its land and culture, together with its extraordinarily rich archaeological remains. Tourism pressure can be heavy in parts of Cairo (including around the Pyramids) and – before the 1997 massacre – Luxor; timing your visit carefully (remembering how hot Egypt can be in high summer) may enable you to enjoy it more. Some tour operators include visits to the camps of nomadic Bedouin – although you may wish to check beforehand that the Bedouin you are visiting are treated with respect and not just as tourist objects. In some cases, local people can successfully take the initiative in tourism development. The villagers of Tayeth in Jordan were Global Winners in the Tourism for Tomorrow scheme in 1996 with their project which converted an old abandoned village near the ancient ruins of Petra into a tourist village and rural resort.

TOURISM FOR TOMORROW AWARDS

Wind, Sand & Stars: Sinai Desert, Egypt

Highly Commended: Southern Region 1996

Run by a small specialist tour company, the Wind, Sand & Stars project aims to provide a sustainable and high-quality travel experience and to generate income for the Bedouin people of the area, while enabling them to maintain traditional lifestyles and livelihoods as their relations with the outside world undergo inevitable processes of change. Travellers learn to understand the impact of modern life on traditional cultures and to value local control over tourism management.

Wind, Sand & Stars Ltd
2 Arkwright Road
London NW3 6AD
T: +44 (171) 4333684
F: +44 (171) 4313247
E: office@windsandstars.
co.uk

Experience the *tranquillity* and *luxury* of Al Maha.

AL MAHA
AN EMIRATES GROUP HOTEL

Al Maha, named after the Arabian oryx, offers exclusivity and luxury
to those who seek tranquillity and a taste of Arabia.
Cradled within a sweeping desert savannah stretching towards
the majestic Hajar Mountains, Al Maha combines 29 tastefully designed individual suites
with panoramic views and exceptional personal service.
Al Maha lies within easy reach of the vibrant, cosmopolitan city of Dubai
in the United Arab Emirates.
Enjoy the living legend of Al Maha - an experience never to be forgotten.

Opening March 1999.

Al Maha, P.O. Box 7631, Dubai, United Arab Emirates.
Tel: +971 4 343 9595, Fax: +971 4 343 9696
E-mail: almaha@emirates.com   On the web at http://www.al-maha.com/

Taybet Zaman Village Hotel and Resort, Jordan

Winner: Global and Southern Region 1996

Villagers of Taybeh, in Southern Jordan, have joined forces with Jordan Tourism Investments to convert an abandoned village quarter of 100-year-old semi-ruins into a tourist village and rural resort. Located close to the historic city of Petra, the site now offers visitors a unique experience of traditional buildings, local craft skills and rural lifestyle alongside modern comforts such as a restaurant, swimming pool, fitness centre, Turkish baths, museum, handicraft souk and accommodation in 105 converted cottages for up to 60,000 guests a year. Some 17,000 day trippers also visit the site each year as a side-excursion from Petra.

Jordan Tourism
Investments
PO Box 811640
Amman 11180
Jordan
T: +962 (6) 5537677
F: +962 (6) 5526785

Iberotel Sarigerme Park: Hotel 2000, Turkey

Highly Commended: Europe 1994

A pilot project developed to optimise environmental care in a modern hotel operation, with a view to expanding similar programmes of environmental management throughout a chain of at least 100 hotels. Aspects of environmental management embraced by the scheme include water and waste treatment, energy saving and sustainable transport.

Iberotel Sarigerme Park
Ortaca Postanesi PK1
TR–48600 Ortaca
Turkey
T: +90 (252) 2868031
F: +90 (252) 2868043

CHAPTER 6
AFRICA

Of all the world's continents, Africa is probably most commonly perceived by travellers and tourists as home to the most spectacular wildlife. On one level this perception is true enough, but it can also mislead. At best it sees the continent in just one dimension. Africa's cultural diversity is equally well worth experiencing and understanding better. At worst, thinking solely in terms of its wildlife is to relegate its human inhabitants to the status of walk-on parts. This view possibly explains why many in the global North still see Africa as the 'Dark Continent'; backward, primitive and somehow untamable, with all the prejudicial intellectual baggage that such imagery carries with it.

That said, many holiday makers visit Africa – and especially East and southern Africa – with the intention of seeing wildlife as the top priority of their trip. And while the beaches of **Kenya**, South Africa, the Red Sea or the North African shores of the Mediterranean attract holiday makers happy to spend their holiday relaxing, an increasing number of others are using them for sailing or diving holidays, or going inland on safaris, ballooning expeditions, river trips or hill or forest trekking as well as journeying further afield as independent travellers.

Some years ago, a leaked memo from a senior official in the White House complained that Africa was 'underpolluted'. Though the subsequent (and embarrassed) explanation was that these were unofficial musings on the possibility of American companies paying African countries for 'tradeable permits' in pollution emissions (in other words, allowing the US firms to use a notional African quota for industrial emissions or waste), it was also significant in reflecting a view that Africa has escaped the environmental degradation of more industrialised, developed regions. That is not so. However, like many other destinations, Africa bears its share of environmental ills, some at least part imposed by the nations of the North. As tourism develops, it too runs the risk of destroying habitats, wildlife and social cultures, unless it is managed sustainably.

Some environmental historians see this process beginning with the Roman occupation of North Africa, when the widespread felling of trees, so as to supply Rome with timber, coupled with the introduction of new agricultural techniques and species, helped spread deforestation and increased soil erosion along some parts of the Mediterranean coastline. In this century, the adoption of some Western agricultural practices, often ignoring or denigrating traditional local farming methods, is believed by some researchers to have proved equally problematic. More recently, a number of African countries have begun to switch agriculture from production to meet local food needs to the growing of cash crops for the European or American markets. This may help meet the crippling burden of multilateral debts owed by some of Africa's poorest countries, but it can also lead to both short- and long-term environmental problems, while local African communities are no longer self-sufficient, and at the mercy of international commodity price fluctuations.

In the 1980s, certain European companies sought to dispose of their toxic waste by shipping it to West Africa, where it was simply dumped in Nigeria, a trade exposed by Friends of the Earth campaigners led by Andrew Lees. Lees died in January 1991 while investigating a proposed RTZ mining scheme in the forests of Madagascar. Environmental issues have also become attached to widespread political protest in the Ogoniland region of Nigeria, where oil companies have been accused of widespread pollution and where the writer and environmental activist Ken Saro-Wiwa and eight of his colleagues were executed in 1995, sparking international protests.

European logging companies operating in West Africa have also contributed to an increase in the trade in 'bush meat', endangering some of the ape populations in the region, while European Union fishing fleets, having acquired the rights to fish off the coasts of countries such as Senegal, are reported by the London-based Panos Institute to be seriously depleting stocks and contributing to the decline of local fishing communities. Most immediately destructive, however, and with incalculable long-term consequences, are the violent upheavals which, exacerbated in some cases by the legacy of colonialism or long-seated ethnic or sectarian divisions, or present-day corruption, continue to rack some African nations. In some recently war-torn nations, such as Mozambique, an unlooked-for environmental consequence was the laying of hundreds of thousands of landmines which still continue to claim the innocent.

Sad to report, tourism, while contributing to national economies, is adding to some of these problems in parts of the continent. Some of the problems are common to other regions of the world: litter, the heavy use of water supplies in drought-prone areas by Western tourist hotels, a trade in wildlife and wildlife products that endangers some species, wildlife parks rutted and ploughed by too many vehicles. Other impacts are more specific. In some cases, anthropologists and others have warned that tourism is dislocating local cultures and economies. More controversially (in parts of Kenya and Tanzania, for example), pastoral peoples such as the Maasai have been barred from some of their traditional grazing grounds as they are designated for national parks or game reserves which are seen as an important focus for the tourist trade and the foreign currency it earns.

The Kenya Wildlife Service is now having to reach new relations with people living around its parks and reserves, after years in which they feel their interests (and sometimes lives) have been deemed secondary to the interests of wildlife. And wildlife, too, has suffered from tourist pressures in places: in the late 1980s and early 1990s, to take a notorious example, it was not unknown for safari minibus drivers in some Kenyan wildlife parks to chase after cheetahs, in order to get better photo opportunities for their tourist customers – a practice now firmly discouraged.

Wildlife remains, however, the major attraction for many visitors to Africa. Kenya, a popular destination for British and other European travellers and holiday makers, sees wildlife as central to its tourist economy, a fundamental part of national revenues. When ivory poaching in the late 1980s threatened African elephant populations across much of the continent, President Daniel arap Moi of Kenya appointed the anthropologist and naturalist Richard Leakey to head and reform the country's wildlife service (responsible for the National Parks), with a brief to beat the poachers. Helped by a campaign that in 1989 led to a world ban in international ivory trading, Leakey succeeded in beating the poachers and transforming the fortunes of the parks.

Whether it is the Nairobi National Park, on the very doorstep of the capital, the vast stretches of Tsavo or the rolling landscapes of Amboseli or the Maasai Mara, Kenya's wildlife reserves offer the visitor a chance of seeing a wide range of animals and an even wider choice of options for safaris. The same can be said for a number of other African countries including **Tanzania** (whose attractions include the awesome Ngorogoro volcanic crater and the Serengeti plains), **South Africa**, **Botswana**, **Lesotho**, **Malawi**, **Namibia**, **Uganda**, **Swaziland**, **Zambia**, and **Zimbabwe**. A more exotic, recent development has been the advent of balloon safaris. Environmentally, the silence of a balloon is preferable to the noise of light aircraft or helicopter, but a low-level approach may still startle wildlife.

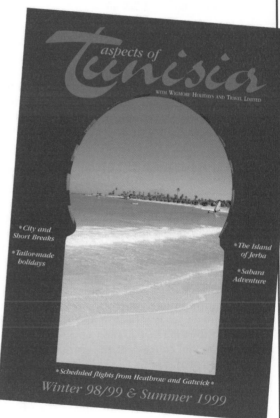

ADVENTURE CAMPING SAFARIS

Truck Africa operate overland tours for the adventurous traveller (18-40s) from 2 weeks to 7 months with regular departures throughout the year.

As a sampler:-
3 weeks Victoria Falls to Nairobi from £350.
5 weeks Cape to Harare via Namibia from £530.
11 weeks Harare - Harare including Victoria Falls from £960.
UK to Kenya & Zimbabwe with option on to
Cape Town - 5/7/9 months from £1780.
4 weeks Eastern Explorer visiting Mountain Gorillas and Game Parks from £530.

Our brochure has full details of these plus our Millennium Itineraries as well as our scheduled other tours in East and Southern Africa.

Tel: 0171 731 6142 for brochure and details.
Email: truckafrica@zambez1.demon.co.uk
Web site: www.truckafrica.com

Although disrupted by the fighting which in recent years has wrought widespread loss of life and dislocation along the borders of **Rwanda**, **Zaire** (now the **Democratic Republic of Congo**) and **Uganda**, the forested mountain regions of these countries have offered rare (and expensive) opportunities for visitors in small guided groups to watch gorillas, including those which inspired the naturalist Diane Fossey, whose book *Gorillas in the Mist* provided the basis and title for the subsequent film starring Sigourney Weaver. In late 1998, however, reports that tourists were offering bribes for closer access to the gorillas, possibly leading to unsustainable pressures on the animals, concerned conservationists.

West Africa, while lacking the wildlife of the great plains and bush states, has its own natural draws, as well as some more conventional tourist attractions. **The Gambia**, which in the late 1960s had a reputation for expensive exclusivity among a handful of Western visitors, moved to attract more mass tourism in the 1980s. After this policy produced its share of problems – including a form of sex tourism, in which some Western women tourists travelled to the country to enjoy the availability of young local men – the Gambian authorities governing the country since the coup of 1994 have sought to diversify tourism and introduced some new regulations, limiting the heights of tourist hotels to no more than four storeys, for example. The country is also seeking to draw visitor attention to its bird and insect life, as well as promoting a centre for the rehabilitation of formerly captive apes on Baboon Island. There is, however, local concern at the spread of 'all-inclusive holidays', where less tourist money is spent locally.

The wildlife of the Horn of Africa, and of those northern and sub-Saharan states, is less well known, and many travellers have in recent years been deterred by the conflict which has disfigured countries such as **Ethiopia**, **Somalia** and **Sudan**. Yet these countries are among the most scenic and culturally diverse Africa has to offer. In future they – as well as the North African states, such as **Libya**, **Tunisia** and **Morocco**, which also enjoy the advantages of Mediterranean beaches and historic cities – are likely to be more widely visited by travellers keen to explore mountains rich in birdlife as well as some of the rarer mammals.

Africa's islands have their own distinctive ecologies and attractions for the traveller. The **Seychelles** have mostly concentrated on traditional island tourism, taking advantage of excellent swimming, diving and sailing waters. **Zanzibar** is an extraordinary mix of

BOX 6.1

DEVELOPING TOURISM FROM THE
GRASSROOTS UP IN SENEGAL

One of the most radical experiments in grassroots tourism anywhere is to be found among the mangroves, silk-cotton trees and rice-fields of the delectably lush Lower Casamance region of Senegal. There, village-owned and operated campements (a cross between a guest-house and a youth hostel) have been running since 1976, the focus of a deliberate policy to enable local people to benefit from tourism.

The concept was conceived by a French ethnologist, Christian Saglio, who drew up a plan in the early 1970s with the Agency for Cultural and Technical Cooperation, under the banner of 'Tourism for Discovery', to counter what he saw as the negative impacts of mass tourism. Saglio's model gradually took shape: simple accommodation built by villagers (with a loan from central government), managed by a village council and run by local young people as a co-operative, with the profits reinvested and used to help build a health clinic, run a football team, or for agricultural projects. Saglio believed that a key prerequisite for the success of the campements was 'the ability to develop the interest of the people themselves so that the project benefits from their broad participation and becomes an integral part of the community'. In that way, tourism would bring economic opportunities but not destroy local cultural and social traditions and relations.

Only two village campements are on the coast (Kafountine and Abene); others are hidden among the creeks of the estuary of the River Casamance or in the centre of villages. Some are reached only by pirogue (wooden canoe); others by (occasional) public transport or by bicycle. Two of the campements (at Enampor and Affiniam) are built in the unique impluvium style of the Jola people of the region. These doughnut-shaped mud buildings have rooms opening on to a central courtyard and a drainage system which allows rain to be funnelled from the roof to a central reservoir.

Despite difficulties, the campements survive. Tourists are welcomed to the communities, enjoy a glimpse of village life and culture and contribute to a tourism evolved from a radical policy that is as about as grassroots and as 'fairly traded' as tourism can get.

Polly Pattullo, 1998
Contact: Campements Rurals Intégrés, Centre Artisanal, Zinguinchor, Casamance, Senegal.

cultures, expressed most strongly in the island's architecture and distinguishing it from mainland Tanzania. The **Cape Verde** islands are attempting to exploit both their quiet coves and green valleys as well as their European links through their Portuguese colonial past. **Madagascar** is emerging as a potential lure on account of its unique wildlife. Its hills, forests, savannah and mangrove swamps are home to a wealth of animals, most celebrated being the various and extraordinarily acrobatic lemurs. Although the island

LOVE OF AFRICA?

Tailormade Travel

Exclusive Safaris, using small personal camps and lodges in the remote wilderness of Eastern and Southern Africa, including hotels & lodges within the Indian Ocean Islands

ART·OF·TRAVEL

0171 738 2038

ATOL 2914

has experienced considerable deforestation (and mining continues to threaten the remaining forest) it remains a magnet for the adventurous traveller with environmental interests.

These days, travellers who go on most African safaris 'shoot' animals with nothing more harmful than a camera. Yet the tradition of trophy game hunting has continued in some countries, and may yet resume in others. Some argue that hunting gives wildlife additional value, encouraging local communities to manage it sustainably, and generating much revenue to plough back into conservation. Animal rights and many animal welfare groups, needless to say, disagree strongly.

Zimbabwe, where hunting is allowed for some abundant species, is an example among countries that are opting for small-scale, upmarket tourism. 'We don't want the problems that mass tourism brings,' warned Margaret Chinamora, Deputy Secretary (Tourism) at the country's Ministry of Environment and Tourism, speaking at the 1996 London World Travel Market. Zimbabwe's CAMPFIRE (Communal Area Management Programme For Indigenous Resources) scheme is an attempt to involve local people in managing, and profiting from, wildlife. 'If people think that there is a value in tourism, or hunting, they have a financial incentive to preserve the wildlife. Otherwise, it can be seen as a threat to their crops or even their lives,' she said. Like Kenya, Zimbabwe has increased entry fees to National Parks to boost revenue for conservation.

Positive developments to encourage sustainable tourism are taking place across Africa as evidenced by the numerous game reserves, wildlife projects and other conservation schemes which have received awards under the Tourism for Tomorrow scheme. The first Global Winner in 1992 was the Londolozi game reserve in South Africa's Eastern Transvaal which sought to combine in its management the care of land, of wildlife and of people. Other award winners have sought to achieve this balance (see listings at the end of this chapter)

Perhaps easily forgotten in the face of wildlife watching are the activity holidays offered by Africa's great physical features: desert ranging across the Sahara, climbing in the Atlas Mountains or on Kilimanjaro; white-water rafting in the southern rivers, including the waters of the Zambezi Gorges; or cruising down the Nile in Egypt. The coasts of many African countries offer opportunities for reef diving and sailing; dhow riding off the east and north east African coasts is gaining in popularity as cities such as Dar es Salaam and Mombasa become more popular with visitors. Several African holiday destinations offer horse-riding, camel riding, camping and cycling, and in some states in South Africa farm holidays are a new development.

For the green traveller, though, Africa's rich cultural heritage is as magnetic as its wildlife or landscape. Apart from the architectural remains of Egypt, other civilisations have made their mark upon the continent, from Carthage to Great Zimbabwe. The ancient yet still thriving cities offer impressive architecture and vigorous social and cultural life to be experienced from Tunis to Timbuktu, from the markets of Marrakesh to the mud-walled towns of Mali.

TOURISM FOR TOMORROW AWARDS

Hilltop Camp, Hluhluwe: Umfolozi Park, South Africa

Winner: Southern Region 1994

The park contains Africa's largest known population of white rhino and is vital to the conservation of wildlife resources in Kwa Zulu-Natal. Redevelopment of Hilltop Camp is important as South Africa is on the brink of a tourism boom. The development has been carried out with thought to the natural environment around the Camp and to the needs and wishes of the local community. A tarmac access road has been constructed and guided tours and educational materials introduced. Over 50,000 tourists visit the Camp each year. The BA citation highlights its 'non-elitist approach' to safari tourism and the value of consultation with local people, noting that the Camp 'could lead by example in the South African tourist trade'.

Natal Parks Board
PO Box 662
Pietermaritzburg 3200
KwaZulu-Natal
South Africa
T: +27 (331) 471961
F: +27 (331) 471037

Conserving a Vanishing Way of Life: Shamwari, South Africa

Highly Commended: Southern Region 1996

Situated in South Africa's Eastern Cape, the Shamwari Game Reserve protects a haven of plant and animal life. The area was coming under increasing development pressures until eight rangeland farms comprising 250,000 acres were set aside to create a stronghold for wildlife, including lion, elephant, leopard, buffalo and black rhino. Lodging for 58 visitors is provided in restored ranch houses. A conservation study centre has been built and jobs and welfare services created for local people, and a 'teaching village' salutes the area's cultural heritage.

Shamwari Game Reserve
PO Box 32017
Summerstrand
Port Elizabeth 6019
South Africa
T: +27 (41) 8511196
F: +27 (41) 8511224

Madikwe Game Reserve, South Africa

**Highly Commended: Southern Region and
BA Holidays 1998**

Madikwe Game Reserve
PO Box 4124
Rustemburg
South Africa 0300
T: +27 1466 55960
F: +27 1466 55964

Bordering on Botswana, the reserve was set up in 1991 on the site of an old cattle ranch and focuses on conservation of biodiversity and economic development. Over 8000 head of 21 species have been moved in; almost all large mammals that are historically indigenous to Madikwe have been or are in the process of being reintroduced. The local community was involved in planning and decision making, and a Trust channels income from the reserve into local development projects.

MTN Cape Whale Route, South Africa

Winner: Longhaul Special 1998

MTN Cape Whale Route
PO Box 797
Howard Place 7450
South Africa
T: +27 (21) 4017347
F: +27 (21) 4017303

Sponsored by a telecommunications organisation, the project promotes whale tourism along a 900km stretch of South African Coast, involving some 60 communities along the route. Visitors can tune into media reports or enquire through a whale hotline. The project sponsors three whale researchers and all sightings are recorded on a database. Interpretive and educational materials have also been produced. Local fishermen have been trained to become seasonal guides, while a start-of-season festival, beach clean-ups and road shows generate interest in the region as a whale watching destination.

Phinda Resource Reserve, South Africa

Winner: Southern Region 1997

Natal Parks Board
PO Box 662
Pietermaritzburg 3200
South Africa
T: +17 (70) 5212155
F: +17 (70) 5212079

The rehabilitation of 17,000 hectares of degraded farm land and the reintroduction of endemic species, combined with responsible tourism in partnership with the community, is the aim of this project. Carrying capacity for visitors has been determined and so far 36 double suites have been built out of a possible maximum of 48. Accommodation is built on stilts to avoid disturbance to ground habitat, solar power is the energy source and rubbish is separated and recycled. In 1995 the site was declared a Natural Heritage Site for its success in recovering fragile indigenous habitats.

Tortilis Camp and Wildlife Conservation Area, Kenya

Winner: Southern Region 1995

A development seen by the Tourism for Tomorrow selectors as especially important in 'an area that has gone full cycle in the tourism industry'. Safari tours have for many years affected not only the wildlife and habitats but also the indigenous peoples of Kenya. Tortilis Camp demonstrates that wildlife tourism, sensitively managed, can benefit local communities, landowners and other local stakeholders in the long run. Local staff are employed and the scale of the camp is kept small to ensure a high quality product and service.

Cheli and Peacock
PO Box 39806
Nairobi
Kenya
T: +254 (154) 22551
F: +254 (154) 22553

Il Ngwesi Lodge, Kenya

Highly Commended: Southern Region 1997

The Lodge and its 16,500 acre site is owned and run by the community as a small tourism enterprise to supplement meagre incomes from traditional land use. Accommodation is in four 'bandas'; thatched, open plan and built on stilts to maximise exposure to the wilderness, they are sited to minimise conflict with wildlife. Water is brought by camel from a nearby well and electricity is generated by solar power.

Lewa Wildlife
Conservancy
Private Bag ISIOLO
Kenya
T: +254 2 48314
F: +254 2 447310

Environmental Auditing for Small to Medium-Sized Hotels: Kenya

Winner: Longhaul Special 1996

Development planning scheme based on a handbook produced by a senior planner attached to the Inter-Continental Hotel, Nairobi, and distributed to more than 50 hotel businesses in Kenya and neighbouring countries. It suggests guidelines for low-cost and practical measures hotel managements can take to enable employees to adopt and implement best environmental practices. The aim is to help business prospects and back up national and global environmental protection efforts. Topics covered include energy conservation, protection of beaches, water conservation, landscaping, curbing CFC emissions and managing wastes.

Inter-Continental Hotels
and Resorts
PO Box 30353
Uhuru Highway
Nairobi
Kenya

Mnemba Club: Mnemba Island, Zanzibar, Tanzania

Highly Commended: Southern Region 1994

Mnemba Club
c/o Archer's Tours
PO Box 40097
Nairobi
Kenya
T: +254 (2) 224069
F: +254 (2) 212656

The Club was developed to provide an exclusive holiday resort that embraced environment-friendly principles and emphasised the use of natural materials and local skills in construction and decor, to ensure harmony with the surrounding landscape and help the local economy. Also mutually beneficial are arrangements with local fishermen to supply seafood and leisure trips. Solar energy is a primary power source. Interaction and consultation with the local community is a high policy priority.

Zanzibar Serena Inn, Tanzania

Highly Commended: BA Holidays
Special Hotel Supplier Award 1997

TIG Barrasford
PO Box 4151
Zanzibar
Tanzania
T: +33 3 44 484000
F: +33 3 44 572000

In a joint enterprise between the Aga Khan Trust for Culture, and Tourism Promotion Services (Zanzibar), historical build-ings were restored and converted to a 51 room hotel, and surrounding foreshore area rehabilitated. While traditional craft techniques ensure the authenticity of buildings, modern technology ensures environmentally safe waste disposal.

Friends of Conservation Tourist Awareness Programme: Kenya and Tanzania

Highly Commended: Southern Region 1995

Friends of Conservation
Sloane Square House
Holbein Place
London SW1W 8NS
T: +44 (171) 5598790
F: +44 (171) 5598792

In harness with a UK-based group, tourism authorities in both countries agreed on an integrated scheme combining training, monitoring, community development and publicity initiatives. Training for safari tour drivers, a community-led conservation pilot project and facilities for monitoring rhino populations were part of moves to discourage harassment of animals in National Parks and reserves. Guide books and leaflets defining standards of responsible behaviour towards local customs, and a Conservation Code, were produced and distributed to hotels and lodges.

Cameroon's Rainforests: Earthwatch Europe, Cameroon

Highly Commended: Southern Region 1995

This project was set up to marshal a critical mass of data about the rare and endemic plants of a little-known ecosystem with a view to building a case for conserving it as a genetic resource stronghold. Of over 2,000 specimens amassed in 1994, 20 are thought to be new to science. Immediate objectives of the project include negotiating protected status for the forest and launching an education programme among local people to promote agroforestry and other sustainable forms of land use. A full land-use plan is emerging over time.

Earthwatch Europe
Belsyre Court
57 Woodstock Road
Oxford OX2 6HJ
T: +44 (1865) 311600
F: +44 (1865) 311383

Central Region Project, Ghana – Conservation International

Winner: Global Award and Southern Region 1998

Funded by government and international conservation and aid agencies, the project aims to reverse environmental devastation in Ghana's forests due to logging and other human activities, and to restore historical sites while generating local income through ecotourism. At Kakum National Park, a visitor centre, canopy walk and forest trails operate in conjunction with scientific research, and training for local resource protection agencies. Tourism provides economic alternatives to logging and hunting endangered species such as Diana monkeys. Visitors to the Park in 1997 reached 40,000, from none in 1992.

Conservation
International
PO Box 1495
Cape Coast
Ghana
T: +233 42 33041
F: +233 42 33042

Rebuilding Bird Island Lodge: Seychelles

Highly Commended: Southern Region 1994

A privately owned estate, Bird Island is home to a large breeding colony of sooty terns and other sea birds. The introduction of coconut plantations encroached on the bird habitat and breeding populations were in decline until 1992, when a small-scale ecotourism project was launched. Many coconut trees have now been cleared and replaced by indigenous shrubs. As a result of this and other measures, bird numbers are now increasing. The Lodge accommodates 50 visitors, and the project has created jobs for 40 local people.

Bird Island Lodge
PO Box 404
Victoria, Mahe
Seychelles
T: +248 224925
F: +248 225074

CHAPTER 7
THE CARIBBEAN

For a collection of islands and mainland states, for the most part small and with relatively struggling micro-economies, the Caribbean has in recent decades exerted a growing influence on the international tourist market on both sides of the Atlantic. The attractions for many visitors are obvious: sun-soaked beaches, bright blue seas, and the prospect of an indolent week or two in a friendly culture. British links to much of the region add to the advantages for English speakers. The wildlife and other environmental aspects of the Caribbean (above and below sea-level) are now increasingly being advertised, particularly by such nations as Belize, Dominica and Guyana, as well as the more established, conventional tourist destinations.

Yet like island destinations everywhere, the Caribbean is a fragile paradise. The image of the brochures – palm-fronded white beaches and crystal blue seas – sometimes masks an acute vulnerability to the pressures exerted by large numbers of visiting tourists and their demands. Tourism does not just put pressure on the natural environment; it can also have repercussions for social and economic relationships, particularly when the perceptions held by tourists are at best superficial. As the writer Polly Pattullo has pointed out in *Last Resorts* (Latin America Bureau with Cassell, 1996), which any intending green traveller to the region would be well advised to pack:

'Those romantic "desert island" images of the brochures and the magazines triumph over the real and painful complexities and paradoxes of Caribbean life and culture. Those fantasies mock the history of the Caribbean: from the almost complete annihilation of the Amerindians, through slavery and the plantation system, to migration, the difficulties of nationhood and the forging of new identities and economic strategies. Most tourists know little of all this.'

Pattullo continues:

'Until recently, the fantasies projected by brochures and travel agents also failed to distinguish between one island and the next, building on the impression of nothing but sand, sea and sun from the Bahamas to Bonaire. Most tourists have a limited view of the Caribbean: the airport, the hotel, the beach and the sights. Their encounters with local people and their everyday life are limited. This is particularly true if the tourists stay in an all-inclusive [package holiday resort] where the resort becomes the centre of the holiday. In many instances, the only locals the tourists meet are the hotel staff and the tour operator rep (who is often an expatriate), the taxi-driver, the beach vendor and the hustler. Thus the tourist's impression of "local" is defined. This narrow definition tends to reinforce stereotypical images.'

In some parts of the Caribbean, this distance between tourists and local people is physically reinforced. Hotels and beaches are fenced off, patrolled by security guards and most locals discouraged, if not physically prevented, from entering. Although this may be due to fear of crime, or to prevent tourists from being hassled, it can of course heighten visitors' fears of the world beyond the resort perimeter and lead to prejudicial impressions of local folk.

An antidote to this divisiveness can be found in programmes run by some Caribbean tourist boards, such as the People-to-People scheme run in the Bahamas, where visitors get a chance to meet locals in their homes, workplaces or at other social functions, or in Jamaica's fledgling community tourism project in the town of Mandeville, where tourists can visit local gardens, factories, schools and even a crocodile farm.

An excellent listing of whale and dolphin watching tours is carried in the Trade and Travel Handbooks *series guide to the region. Specific cetacean watching holiday operators may be found through the* Whale and Dolphin Conservation Society, *or through the advertising sections of magazines such as* BBC Wildlife.

Similar tensions can be caused by the cruise ship business, which is highly developed in the Caribbean. Some argue that responsibly managed cruises minimise environmental impacts, and allow large numbers of holiday makers to enjoy a region without imposing themselves on one spot for any length of time. But they have many critics, who point out that many liners have routinely dumped rubbish overboard, while the damage caused by anchor dragging and oil pollution has been considerable.

The social impacts of cruise liners may also be divisive in those communities where only a few quayside boutiques or businesses may profit from the ships' arrival. An international agreement, the Marpol Convention, is supposed to prohibit dumping of human or food waste in coastal waters, and any dumping of plastics, but not all the Caribbean states have ratified it, lacking onshore disposal facilities. But some cruise lines have voluntarily cleaned up their act. The Carnival Corporation, which runs many cruise ships in the region, won a special long haul Tourism for Tomorrow commendation in 1995 (see listings at the end of Chapter 8, page 177). Reportedly, not all operators live up to the highest standards.

There is now growing recognition that the future of all tourism in the region is dependent on preserving the Caribbean's all too fragile environment. Since the late 1980s, a number of states have begun to develop ecotourism, and this has been paralleled by a new concern for conservation, with national parks opening on many islands. Ecotourism, Pattullo concludes, is likely to become ever more important to the region, though it is not without its difficulties – not least of which is the opening up of hitherto unexploited areas.

Space does not permit an island-by-island account of all the region's environmental attractions, nor the challenges they face. But there are many highlights. Ashore, walking, bird and animal watching and botanical expeditions are beginning to be seen as a way of taking holiday makers away from the coasts. Along most coastlines in the region the usual water sports remain popular but whale and dolphin watching is also growing in importance, with humpback and sperm whales to be seen at various times of the year in parts of the Caribbean, and dolphins widely distributed. A more recent tourism development – and one not without its critics – is underwater shark watching. Divers watch from protective cages; the sharks are often fed to bring them closer.

Belize, **Dominica** and **Guyana** are, perhaps, the Caribbean nations keenest to promote their ecological attractions. Belize, with its 150-mile chain of offshore islands and reefs – the cays (or cayes) – has many newly designated national parks or nature reserves, and wildlife protection legislation which is intended to prohibit the commercial trade in wildlife. It has attracted assistance from many US and UK conservation organisations (though also the interest of many commercial developers, who have bought up a lot of property). Coral Cay Conservation, a UK-based organisation, won a Tourism for Tomorrow global award in 1993 for its work. It offers diving holidays to the public who help survey the status of reefs, with the results helping to encourage better coastal zone management (see Chapter 2 for details). As a result, the Belize government has designated the South Water Caye a marine protected area. On the Belize mainland, Cockscomb Basin wildlife sanctuary is the world's only jaguar reserve, while the Community Baboon Sanctuary has been praised as a model of sustainable ecotourism, with local farmers adapting traditional methods to protect the black howler monkey, and prospering by the resulting tourist trade. From Caye Caulker, you can visit a manatee reserve.

Dominica, in the Windward Islands, has promoted nature tourism for many years. The mountainous and heavily forested island caters well for hill trekkers, forest walkers,

bird watchers (look out for the national bird, the rare imperial parrot) and botanists. One climb takes visitors to the 'boiling lake', a rare natural feature heated by underground thermal streams. Dominica has so far mostly managed to conduct ecotourism successfully: small-scale, locally owned and managed. But there are concerns that this could be threatened in the future by the government's need to develop tourism as the banana industry is threatened by changes in world trading patterns and law. Foreign investment is being wooed, including much from Taiwan, with consequent fears that larger hotel development is likely. Elsewhere in the Windwards, spectacular parrots and other birdlife can be seen on mountain forest excursions in **St Lucia** and **St Vincent**, two islands also intent on developing green tourism.

Guyana, on the South American mainland, has only recently begun to promote its tourist attractions: the former government of President Forbes Burnham was understandably concerned at dependence on foreign capital, and the country has largely lacked the scale of infrastructure for extensive tourism development. Up-market ecotourism has been mooted as the obvious alternative, though Pattullo's research indicates concern that, without regulation, it could threaten a largely unexploited hinterland, including the lands of native peoples.

Jamaica's tourist attractions are many, and tourism is now the island's second biggest source of foreign exchange; 1.2 million visitors stopped there in 1997, a fifth of them from the UK. But concerns over crime – somewhat misplaced, as it has mostly been confined to areas of the capital, Kingston – have led to many tourists opting to stay in secluded resorts, leaving only for brief coach excursions (or to catch their flights home). That is a pity: particularly in the hilly interior, Jamaica is a good place for wildlife watching, with large varieties of birds and mammals, and reptiles that include crocodiles and the rare Jamaican iguana.

East of Kingston, the Blue Mountain and John Crow Mountain National Park, established in 1989, marks an attempt not only at conservation, but also restoration: much of Jamaica's original forest cover has been logged, leading to erosion and topsoil loss. Planting programmes are now under way in an attempt to redress the loss. In the north west of the island, Jamaica's celebrated Montego Bay has given its name to a marine park, indicating the area's underwater riches, a draw for scuba divers, snorkellers and boat trippers. Ironically, the nearby airport was built on the site of an important wetland, home to many bird species.

Jamaica also has its share of golf courses, with attendant environmental problems, but one company is leading the field in new organic operating systems which ultimately will eliminate at least the need to use chemicals. In 1998 the Half Moon Club won both Tourism for Tomorrow and Green Globe awards for its innovations.

In 1994 **Barbados** hosted a UN conference for small island developing states. It was an appropriate venue: Barbados, by Caribbean standards a relatively prosperous (and populous) society, has an established tourist economy, still mostly concentrated on the south and west coasts, but it has also suffered from some of the problems of unsustainable tourism development. These have included inadequate sewage treatment (an issue now being addressed) and the development of water-consuming golf courses. At the same time, it is attempting to encourage visitors to see some of this small island's other sights, away from the established beaches. These include the more rugged Atlantic shoreline and aspects of the island's economic heritage, including sugar plantations and some of the many plantation houses established in this 'most English island of the Caribbean'.

For many people, the very name of **The Bahamas** suggests a playground for the wealthy, redolent with the lucrative adventures of 17th century pirates. Certainly, their proximity to the US has made some of the 700 islands popular for US visitors, and the range of tourist sporting facilities includes many yacht marinas, golf courses and tennis courts. (A further, unhappy legacy of the link with its northern neighbour is a drugs smuggling trade which still uses some of the remoter islands, and is currently being fought by both US and Bahamas authorities.) Some of the smaller islands are privately owned.

Seclusion is equally sought after in the **Cayman Islands**. For most people, the Caymans are synonymous with mysterious offshore banking and investment, modern financial secrecy to rival the legends of hidden pirate gold. But the British colony of Cayman Islands has also developed a growing tourist trade, much of it based on natural attractions. Chief among these is some of the best diving in the Caribbean, with a dramatic array of coral reefs and ledges dropping into some of the deepest waters in the region. Turtle watching is now being encouraged, while sport fishing is well established, with blue marlin and yellowfin tuna particularly sought after. High point of the anglers' year is the Million Dollar Month tournament.

Comparatively wealthy, the Cayman Islands authorities have designated conservation areas to protect mangrove swamps, opened a new botanic park, and sought to enforce legislation introduced in 1978 and 1986 to protect the marine environment. In 1993 new penalties were invoked, threatening vessels convicted of polluting the islands' territorial waters with fines of up to $625,000. Marine park officials and police officers equally seek to enforce legislation which forbids the collecting of hard corals in some areas. A new golf course has to be watered from a desalination plant, and this in part reflects concern that tourist damage has been mounting. In 1994, for example, one survey found that more than 300 acres of coral reef had been damaged through cruise ships anchoring off George Town, the capital.

Cuba has not traditionally promoted itself as a venue for green tourism, though attempts are now being made to exploit the country's relatively unspoiled marine life for scuba diving and snorkelling. But its history and culture – both in the colonial era and in more recent decades – warrant the attention of anyone interested in the region. When Sky Masterson whisked his girlfriend to Havana for a weekend of rum, sun, and rumba, in *Guys and Dolls*, he was reflecting a holiday trend which economically kept the regime of President Batista afloat in the 1950s; the prototype of the sex and gambling holidays which have become familiar today in the Far East.

Fidel Castro put paid to all that when his guerrilla forces overthrew Batista in 1959, introducing communist reforms in the next few years. In the 1980s Castro attempted to diversify Cuba's economy – perilously dependent on its sugar crop, together with extensive Soviet-bloc subsidies – and built his own version of a tourist industry based around cultural, musical features, as well as the beach theme. He reopened the fabulous Tropicana nightclub in Havana, where tree-top gantries supported lines of chorus girls and formed a backdrop for some of the country's most illustrious musicians and singers, and attempted to revive the fortunes of the city's hotels which had declined since the first years of the revolution. He also began to develop the nearby coastal resort of Varadero.

But the collapse of the Cuban economy following the fall of the Soviet Union, together with the intensifying of the draconian trade embargo imposed by Washington, has led to a sudden and drastic return of poverty and its attendant features: the sudden and very visible return of the sex trade; a more apparent two-tier society; frustration and at times resentment on the part of impoverished locals struggling daily to find food in the shops to augment meagre rations, and money to pay for it.

The blockade, and the partial state of siege which has characterised much of

Cuba's existence since Castro came to power, has, however, had the curious effect of preserving some ways of life that elsewhere have disappeared. On the streets of Havana you still see 1940s and '50s American cars, kept going by the ingenuity of their owners, and when petrol is available. The petrol shortage makes for transport difficulties throughout Cuba, although it has some environmental benefits, encouraging cycling and walking.

The old city of Havana, with some of the most remarkable 16th and 17th century buildings in the Caribbean, is a designated World Heritage Site (as is the Spanish colonial town of Trinidad, on the south coast), and is being (slowly) restored, with UNESCO funding. The Cuban countryside is worth exploring, particularly the area around the town of Vinales, but travel is harder the further you venture from Havana. Wherever you travel, however, Cuban music will stay with you, long after you return home. The Cuban government's rediscovery of and support for its cultural and particularly musical heritage has led to the establishment of a series of international music festivals throughout the year. Indeed, the green traveller can do worse than time a visit to the Caribbean to coincide with the carnivals and other musical events that punctuate the calendar.

Nor, too, is a visit to the Caribbean complete without an understanding of the complex historical currents that have fashioned today's island cultures. Each of the Caribbean nations reflects, in ways both predictable and less so, their relationship with their former colonial powers: France, Spain, Britain, the Netherlands and, of course, the US. These links still show in the social, cultural and economic environments of the Caribbean, as well as in the land and townscapes.

TOURISM FOR TOMORROW AWARDS

Programme for Belize (PFB) – Ecotourism Project, Belize

Highly Commended: Americas Region 1997

World Land Trust
Blyth House
Bridge Street
Halesworth
Suffolk IP19 8AB
T: +44 (1986) 874422
F: +44 (1986) 874425

The Programme for Belize, with financial support from government, aid agencies and corporate donors, bought 250,000 acres of rainforest land between 1988 and 1996. The programme involved the local community in education centres to promote the benefits of conserving the area and its many rare and endangered plant and animal species. Tourism developments use solar energy and other ecology sensitive methods.

Royal Naval Dockyard Restoration Project, Bermuda

Highly Commended: Americas 1995

West End Development
Corporation
PO Box MA 145
Somerset MA BX
Bermuda

The dockyard is a 17-acre fortified naval base dating from the early 1800s. Built by the British, it was purchased by the Bermuda government in 1954 together with a 200-acre chain of developed islets, but continued to fall into disrepair until restoration began in 1985. This vast Victorian fortress has now become the island's top tourist attraction, housing some 75 business enterprises and private tenants, and hosting, among other events, an International Food Fair and annual pop festival.

The St Lucia Marine Management Association, St Lucia

Winner: Americas Region and IUCN Award 1997

St Lucia Marine
Management Association
PO Box 727
Bay Street Soufriere
St Lucia
T: +758 4595500
F: +758 459550

The management programme for St Lucia Marine Park was set up in 1995 to protect the marine environment, and promote its sustainable multiple use for both traditional and modern uses, such as tourism. Zoning, and control of the numbers of divers, protects more fragile areas, while fisher-men who lost access to inshore fishing grounds due to the influx of tourism have been offered alternative employment and loans for small enterprise development.

Half Moon Golf, Tennis and Beach Club, Jamaica

Winner: BA Holidays Special Award 1996 & 1998

The Half Moon Club is a recognised leader in environmental practices, having won Green Hotelier Awards in 1995/96/97, a Green Globe achievement award in 1998, and a Jamaican Conservation Trust Environmental award also in 1998. Now the Club has implemented a six-month pilot project to reduce the use of chemicals on the golf course, nursery and gardens, and in the treatment of sewage by the use of Effective Micro-organisms (EM). EM is a naturally occurring microbial innoculant which helps break down organic matter. The ultimate aim is to eliminate the use of chemicals on the property, and maximise the use of recycled water for irrigation.

Half Moon Golf, Tennis
and Beach Club
PO Box 80
Montego Bay
Jamaica
T: +876 9532211
F: +876 9532731

Matura Turtle Conservation Project, West Indies

Winner: Americas Region 1998

As a result of the project, community attitudes towards the Leatherback Sea Turtle have shifted from a source of food for which up to 30 per cent were killed, to a scarce resource to be conserved and reap added tourism benefits. Nature Seekers Incorporated (NSI), established in 1990 to reduce the slaughter of endangered turtles, manages the project in cooperation with the Wildlife Section of the Forestry Division. Activities include cleaning beaches before nesting, patrolling beaches to protect nesting turtles and hatchlings, assisting damaged females to excavate nests, and excavating trapped baby turtles. Research is also carried out, and guided tours are offered to view nesting, but visitors are limited to 200 each night.

Matura Turtle
Conservation Project
Toca Main Road
Trinidad
West Indies
T: +1 868 6231932
F: +1 868 6233848

CHAPTER 8
NORTH AMERICA

North America – the US and Canada – is one of the most popular long-haul destinations for British holiday makers but a large number of these travellers are concerned only with one comparatively small corner of the continent – Florida. The attractions of winter sun, Disney World and similar ventures draw a disproportionate number of visitors, though cheap flights and inclusive holidays are equally beguiling. While understandable, it means that many parts of the US and Canada are comparatively unexplored. And although cities such as New York, Los Angeles, San Francisco, Boston, New Orleans and Vancouver have well-trodden tourist paths, some of the rural and wilderness areas of the two countries are still little known by Britons, with the exceptions of Yellowstone National Park and the Grand Canyon.

That is not to say that the national parks and other nature reserves and wildernesses of the US and Canada do not suffer from over-exposure to tourists. Parks managers in the US have been examining means of regulating numbers in sensitive areas of Yellowstone, as well as limiting the use of cars. And although awareness of some of the areas now defended as national parks was first encouraged by railroad companies wanting to encourage visitors, there is a strong feeling that wildernesses need protecting.

At the same time it is arguable that both countries, particularly the US, have suffered, environmentally, from the curse of space. Too many cities sprawl endlessly, and the cult of the car (and cheap petrol) has spawned roads to service the suburbs and satellite towns. This, together with the spread of consumerism, industry and farming on a scale that dwarfs European imagination, has caused environmental strain. But it would be wrong to suggest that North Americans are not aware of the environmental debate. On the contrary, Canada has played a leading role in many international conferences pushing for environmental programmes, and there is some evidence that environmental issues, particularly those connected with public health concerns, played a not insignificant role in the 1996 Congressional elections, with a backlash against Republicans seen to have an 'anti-environment' record. At the same time, questions of how to use as well as conserve natural resources continue to play an important part in US and Canadian politics. Green travellers in North America will find much to appreciate, whether it is in some of the oldest National Parks in the world or in the efforts that most Americans and Canadians are making to preserve their natural heritage.

THE UNITED STATES

For tourists and travellers, New York is still a major attraction. For sun seekers, however, Florida and California are increasingly popular destinations. Today, Florida's Disney World, Epcot, Sea World and the Miami Seaquarium, are major draws for thousands of Britons each year, but the environment has come under increasing strain from the development of the state since the 1890s. Much land has been given over to agriculture or to new development. In particular the demand for water has led to the draining of much of the Everglades, habitat for a variety of wildlife. In recent years, environmental awareness has given impetus to moves to protect the 'Glades, part of which was declared a national park in 1947 but, as with other parts of the state, the battle is far from being won. In Carl Hiaasen's darkly comic novel *Tourist Season*, a talented-but-crazed Miami newspaper columnist wages war on the tourist industry in an attempt to reverse the tide of development. Conservationists are currently trying other, more peaceful, strategies to preserve Florida's remaining wilderness. Perhaps ironically, the Everglades and the Florida Keys are also becoming increasingly popular visitor attractions which may yet provide further economic incentive for their preservation even if it brings the familiar problems of how to balance visitor numbers with preserving the environment and wildlife they have come to see.

That said, there are examples of 'win–win' tourism. As instanced in Melville's epic novel *Moby Dick*, New England was once home to one of the world's most vigorous whaling industries before the killing drove many species to near-extinction. These days, as elsewhere, whale watching is proving increasingly lucrative for the whalers' descendants. You can join whale watching trips from many New England ports, either as part of a pre-booked holiday or for a day trip. It is worth remembering that the US has wildlife protection laws which should be observed. These include not harassing whales, dolphins and other sea mammals.

What is popularly known as the American South is, more properly, the south east of the country. Such states as Alabama, Arkansas, the Carolinas, Georgia, Louisiana, Mississippi, Tennessee and Virginia have played their part in the economic revival of the region in the last 30 years but there is still a strong sense of history, particularly that evoked by the era of the Civil War and the southern Confederacy. There are a number of active Civil War Re-enactment Societies whose full-scale dramatisations of the battle lines bring history vividly to life. But American heritage is perhaps no better portrayed than in the restored and partially reconstructed Old Williamsburg in Virginia – a 'living museum' where colonial characters roam the streets or work their crafts, eager to talk to visitors about their life and times. More recently, the South was the original cockpit of the Civil Rights movement of the 1950s and '60s.

The city of Memphis sells itself to many tourist visitors through its links with Elvis Presley but, for all the cultural importance of the king of rock 'n' roll, a more moving experience than visiting Presley's home and grave at Graceland, or the legendary Sun Studio, can be had at the National Civil Rights Museum. Here, the story of African-American history since the 1940s is recounted in what was once the Lorraine Motel where Martin Luther King was assassinated in 1968.

If the natural environment can shape a culture, and vice versa, then the South is as much to be seen in lonely backwoods trails, on sharecroppers' farms and in the poor districts of towns and cities as much as it is in the showpiece sights of the region, or for that matter the clubs and bars of Memphis or Nashville, where the blues and country music have spawned a tourist industry. But beyond the towns and cities, the South has much to offer the green traveller: the Mississippi is a river calling out to ride, the Appalachian Mountains a range full of trekking routes, and the coast from Georgia to Virginia a magnet for bird watchers, swimmers and sailors alike.

Perhaps the US's most celebrated natural phenomenon, the Grand Canyon inspires awe for its sheer size, together with the eons of time needed for water to erode its way through such immensities of rock. In recent years US authorities have been aware that the impact of tourist numbers on the Grand Canyon has made some regulation necessary to prevent path erosion, litter and other damage. Even so, it continues to be an overwhelmingly impressive attraction for the visitor.

California's hold on the popular imagination has been due as much to the products of the modern film and entertainment industry as to what first attracted settlers but, for holiday makers and other travellers, the west coast is as much about a natural environment as an artificial one. Where the two meet, there are revealing environmental contrasts. The whaling industry used to prosper from the annual migrations of the gray whale from Alaska and the Canadian coast to the lagoons of Mexico's Baja California. Now whale watching is becoming an important part of the tourist industry. But equally, sprawling coastal settlements derived in part from the attraction of California's beaches have helped add to industrial pollution, while Los Angeles is as famous for its smog as its tourist attractions. Away from the more predictable tourist attractions, however, the state has a wealth of disparate attractions for the green traveller; whether it is the coastline of northern California; Yosemite National Park, the massive redwoods of the north, stretching into Oregon; the eminently hikeable Sierra Nevada mountains; or the harsh desert of Death Valley National Park.

To the north and east of California, the Rocky Mountains and the north west Pacific coast of the US are becoming increasingly desirable places for Americans to live or visit, in great part due to a clean and relatively unspoiled environment. In turn, the tourist interest in the region has increased. Winter sports enthusiasts know about the Rocky Mountains resorts and their reputation for skiing, but climbing, trekking and mountain biking, as well as kayaking and rafting, are enjoyed from Colorado up to Washington State.

National Parks

The National Parks of the US deserve special mention for their bewildering array of environments and habitats, their wildlife and sheer size. Including a handful in Alaska and Hawaii, they cover a vast range of ecosystems, from the Florida Everglades to Mount Rainier in the northwest, from Arizona's Petrified Forest to Yellowstone in Wyoming. Naturalists can indulge their passions, too, in the National Parks, with some of the US's most celebrated species, from buffalo to bear or bald eagles to be seen. The wealth of the US means that economic resources have been made available to the parks on a greater scale than in many nations. As a result, information, ranger services and communications are among the best in the world.

TAILPIECE

'CALL ME ISHMAEL.' I adopt my best weather-beaten look and murmur the first sentence from *Moby Dick* as I scan the waters from the crow's nest. Somewhere near here there are whales. The great white whale, maybe. 'Left your wooden leg behind, Cap'n?' Chris Peterson, marine biologist and enthusiastic whale watcher from California's San Diego Zoo, breaks my reverie as he climbs up alongside me. 'Oh, and if you're looking for Moby Dick, how about taking a peek over the port side?'

I wheel around. There, 50 yards away, a whale is blowing. Twenty yards beyond, another waterspout gleams in the Mexican sun. Then another, and another. The sea is alive with whales. Not the sperm whales of Melville's classic, though, let alone his white leviathan. These are Californian gray whales, up to 50 feet long and weighing almost as many tons, barrelling through the Sea of Cortez, the silvery waters separated from the Pacific by Mexico's Baja California peninsula.

Each year these grays travel from the Baja, 4000 miles north, to the summer feeding grounds of the Arctic Ocean and the Bering Sea. When the ice returns, they head back south, to the coast of California and the lagoons of Baja, where they mate and calve. To see them, the *Don Jose*, a 70ft vessel modelled on the local shrimping boats, is carrying a small group of whale watchers.

Ever since the West Coast was inhabited, North Americans have watched and followed the migration of the California gray whales. It has not always been a peaceful affair. In the north, coastal Eskimos have hunted the grays for meat, oil, blubber and skin. Near what is now the US–Canadian border, native people ventured out in hewn-cedar boats, armed with stone-tipped lances. Such aboriginal hunting was for sustenance: it was not until the 1840s that commercial whalers started to harry the grays.

Chief among the hunters was Captain Charles Scammon. In 1857 he discovered the whales' breeding and calving lagoons along the Baja peninsula: Magdalena, San Ignacio and the lagoon that grateful whalers were to name after Scammon himself. Over the next decade, thousands were slaughtered; within 50 years the species dwindled to the point where commercial whaling was barely profitable. In 1937 the International Whaling Commission declared the California gray a protected species.

Slowly, the gray whale has rallied. Though the annual migration is still a faint echo of its former size, each year it grows. And so does the number of watchers. From Vancouver to San Diego, from land and on sea, people gather to watch them go by. And at the end of the journey south, the lagoons of Baja are again home to calving whales, safe from the hunter's harpoon. The entry channels are narrow and tortuous. The water here is thick and salty; though to us it is still chilly, for a new-born gray whale – 12 feet at birth and gaining 35 pounds a day – it is a warm and gentle nursery.

To follow the whales now, we must abandon the *Don José* and take to 15-foot motorised skiffs. Away off, in calmer waters, the tell-tale, heart-shaped spout of a gray, a heaving back, barnacled and scarred by parasites, and then the wondrous kick of the fluked tail as the whale dives deep. We draw near, idling the outboard engine, counting the seconds till the whale surfaces again.

Whoosh! We spin about in the boat, fumbling for cameras, squinting into the southern sun. As we do so we are showered with a pungent spray – the whale has surfaced 10 feet from us, its vast lungs emptying in seconds. Make that whales, plural – there's a sleek black shape beside the gray: it is a young calf, perhaps a week old and some 15 feet long.

Then the mother reappears. Not the porpoising, broad-shouldered back breaching the surface: instead, like a totem, suddenly the head is erect, six or seven feet clear of the water, a dark eye beadily regarding us, before just as suddenly sliding back, away into the water. 'She's spy-hopping,' Peterson excitedly explains, 'virtually standing on her tail!'

Too soon, the audience is over. The sun sets low among the sand dunes on the Pacific side of the lagoon. The lights of the *Don José* welcome us back, to the chatter of the other whale watchers, eager to recount their own sightings, and just as keen for a hot tortilla supper, a bottle of Mexican beer and a shower.

And talk. 'People who come whale watching here like to get close to the whales. It is a peculiar experience … they get quite emotional,' observes Henk Nienhuis, a rangy, laconic Dutch marine biologist, who worked for UNESCO before settling in the Baja to work with the whale watching tours. 'So I think, I hope, that they will also come to understand a little better how the whales live as part of an ecosystem. And when they get back home, that we cannot go on polluting the world, destroying the seas. I hope they make those whales that part of their lives.'

Based on an account by Greg Neale (originally featured in *The Daily Telegraph*) of a whale watching expedition organised by Baja Expeditions, San Diego, US, and Twicker's World, Twickenham, UK, in 1989.

Though it is not within the remit of this book to offer an assessment of the plethora of guide books, any account of the US would be incomplete without a mention of the Smithsonian series of guides to natural and historic sites. A useful adjunct to a general guide, this series concentrates on the natural or historic sites within reasonably limited and well-defined regions (Northern New England, for example), so their scope is relatively concentrated.

CANADA

Canada is slowly emerging from a long and undeserved reputation among many travellers as the staid northern neighbour of the US. Now it is seen for what it is: a society with a distinctive cultural mix, and a wide range of environmental attractions for the visitor. Of course, it also has its own share of environmental problems, but the response of many Canadians suggests that green thinking is closer to the surface than in many comparable industrial nations. It is perhaps not surprising that some of the most active early Greenpeace campaigners came from Canada's British Columbia coast, where such issues as US nuclear testing in the Pacific, the campaign against whaling and the arguments over intensive forestry came to prominence.

Across Canada – a journey that can memorably be made by train – a series of national parks provides opportunities for the naturalist to see a host of native species, from the black-tailed prairie dog to the polar bear. Cross-country trekking, mountain climbing, fishing, canoeing, long-distance cycling – it is a country that can only truly be experienced out-of-doors, though its varying urban cultures range from the smaller, maritime provinces, through French-influenced Quebec and the plains provinces of Ontario, Manitoba and Saskatchewan, Alberta and the Rocky Mountains, to Pacific Vancouver.

Vancouver and its island offer perhaps the most concentrated array of attractions for green travellers. The oft-quoted remark about Vancouver being a spot from which one can travel from beach to mountain top in a day sums up its geographical wealth. And on Vancouver Island, the visitor can enjoy a variety of holiday activities. But it is also a point at which environmental conflicts can be appreciated. Debates continue over logging coastal rainforests, over the rights of native Canadians, over old jobs and new; and how tourism can best serve both the wild and the needs of people.

NATIVE AMERICANS

The squalid and shabby treatment meted out to Native Americans since Europeans began arriving in numbers should not entirely obscure the wars between the indigenous tribes that predated it. But the expansion westward from the early settlements of New England, the so-called Middle Colonies and the South, which gained new impetus in the 19th century, left many Native American peoples dispossessed, and others driven to effective social extinction. The inglorious record continued well into the 20th century. These days, poverty, joblessness and social problems such as alcoholism persist. Examples of tribes that benefit from the legal operating of casinos scarcely offset this continuing oppression.

For most travellers, contact with Native American peoples is likely to be brief – a tourist visit to a 'genuine Indian village' or the like. This should not obscure the wide range of Native American history that can be discovered in the US and Canada; whether in the Anasazi cities and cliff palaces in Arizona, Colorado, New Mexico and

Utah, or the meticulous assembly of artefacts and reconstructions at the Royal British Columbia Museum in Victoria, to give just two examples. Nor should it obscure the traveller's responsibility; the cultural awareness hints in Chapter 1 apply as much to North America as to anywhere else in the world.

TOURISM FOR TOMORROW AWARDS

Sustainable Living Centers: American Youth Hostels, US

Highly Commended: Americas Region 1995

There are over 150 youth hostels in the US, all comply with the qualifying standards of the International Youth Hostel Federation. Under the Sustainable Living Center scheme, they have now been upgraded to exacting building and service standards in water and energy conservation. Purchasing policies support cleaning and maintenance firms with green credentials. The Tourism for Tomorrow citation notes that: 'This initiative reaches people from all walks of life, from all over the world. It has the potential to spread environmental awareness and practices far and wide.'

American Youth Hostels
733 15th Street NW
Suite 840
Washington DC 20005
USA
T: +1 (202) 783 6161
F: +1 (202) 783 6171

Creating Ecowaves: Carnival Cruise Lines Corporation, Florida, US

Highly Commended: Longhaul Special 1995

The Carnival Corporation carried over a million passengers on its 20 cruise ships in 1994 and employs over 18,000 people worldwide. The company invests heavily in systems to control ship-borne pollution and otherwise curb adverse environmental impacts. All solid wastes are crushed into fine particles on board the ship before disposal. All refrigeration has been converted to CFC-free versions and all decking is made from certified sustainably-harvested timber. Each Superliner's freshwater requirements are largely met by a seawater desalination unit, easing reliance on supplies at ports-of-call.

Carnival Cruise Lines
Corporation
Carnival Palace
3655 NW 87 Avenue
Miami
Florida 33178-2428
USA
T: +1 (305) 599 2600
F: +1 (305) 599 8626

Maho Bay Camps, US Virgin Islands

Highly Commended: Americas Region 1994

Maho Bay Camps
17a East Street
New York
NY 10021
USA
T: +1 (212) 472 9453
F: +1 (212) 861 6210

Based in the US Virgin Islands National Park, Maho Bay Camps consists of 114 units and a campground linked by elevated walkways. A range of environmental management initiatives has been introduced here to minimise the adverse impacts of recreational tourism on the surrounding ocean and coastal zone. These initiatives include building design innovations, including wind scoops for natural cooling and wind and solar energy collectors, as well as aspects of the running of the resort, such as wastewater recycling.

Cascadia Marine Trail System: Washington State, US

Winner: Americas Region 1996

Washington Water Trails
Good Shepherd Center
4649 Sunnyside Avenue N
Room 305
Seattle WA 98103–6900
USA
T/F: +1 (206) 545 9161

Human-powered vessels ranging from kayaks and canoes to small sailing and rowing boats ply this 160-mile-long watercourse across and around Puget Sound, the first national recreational trail officially designated offshore by the US Department of Interior. Users can put in to some 33 onshore sites where they have the option of an overnight stay in campsites, urban hostels or waterside inns. Around 200 such sites will be developed over time, located at least every five to eight miles along the trail. The project's chief aim is to make people aware of the Sound's marine ecology, ocean-going commerce and historic uses of waterways. Another trail is now being set up in Willapa Bay in South West Washington State.

Irving Eco-Center, New Brunswick, Canada

Highly Commended: Americas Region 1997

Irving Eco-Center
PO Box 577
Saint John NB E2L 4M3
Canada
T: +1 (506) 444 5649
F: +1 (506) 453 7127
E: ladune@nbnet.nb.ca

The Center is located in the Bouctouche area of New Brunswick where in the past industry has been the mainstay of the economy but is now adjusting to environmental planning and tourism. Through close collaboration with the community, the private company project has restored and preserved one of the few remaining great sand dunes on the north-eastern American coastline, and provides research and environmental education opportunities.

Redberry Pelican Project: Saskatchewan, Canada

Highly Commended: Americas Region 1995 and 1998

Redberry Lake is a 6000-hectare freshwater lake near Hafford, a Provincial Wildlife refuge and federal Migratory Bird Sanctuary. The Redberry Pelican Project Foundation (RPPF) was established in 1989 to conserve a colony of White Pelicans. Local residents also successfully opposed a plan to develop a 400-cabin lakeside resort. A guide to the natural history of the area was produced and in 1992 an Interpretive Centre was opened. Wildlife monitoring and ecotourism research are combined with practical clean-up measures, including steps to make safe a nearby refuse dump. The RPPF emphasises the importance of ecotourism for both the environment and the economy, and is preparing a regional tourism strategy.

Redberry Pelican Project
Box 221 Hafford
Saskatchewan
Canada S0J 1AO
T: +1 (306) 549 2400
F: +1 (306) 549 2199

The Little Town That Did: Chemainus, British Columbia, Canada

Winner: Americas Region 1994

This community regeneration project has restored vitality to a small rural community whose main industry (long in decline) had been the lumber trade. Celebrating the many skills that spin off from forest-based industry, it centres on creative interpretations of the past lifestyle of people of Chemainus and has conjured up a tourism industry in an area where none previously existed. Many formerly unemployed sawmill workers have found livelihoods that include installing mural art and other landmark exhibits in the neighbourhood.

[no contact details]

The Biodome: Montreal, Canada

Highly Commended: Americas Region 1994

The Biodome
c/o Quebec Tourism
59 Pall Mall
London SW1V 5JH
T: +44 (171) 930 8314
F: +44 (171) 930 7938

The Biodome was created from the relics of a former velodrome or cycle track. The arena was disused and the people of Montreal, who have for some time grown increasingly aware of issues relating to heritage and environment, backed the development of the drome into a multi-purpose exhibition and teaching space offering natural history living displays and nature trails, lecture areas and heritage exhibits. The project scores by applying principles of ecotourism to the mass market using high quality environmental awareness and mass communications techniques to establish the connection.

Oak Hammock Marsh Interpretive Centre: Manitoba, Canada

Highly Commended: Americas Region 1996

Oak Hammock Marsh
Box 1160 Stonewall
Manitoba ROC 2Z0
Canada
T: +1 (204) 467 3279
F: +1 (204) 467 9028

A joint project of Ducks Unlimited Canada and the Government of Manitoba, the Centre aims to boost conservation of wetland ecosystems throughout North America by fostering public approval, awareness and knowledge of their inherent value. Oak Hammock Marsh is a reclaimed relic of a wetland which once covered 450 square kilometres. A massive rehabilitation programme has saved 36 square kilometres. The Centre offers interactive displays, remote marsh cameras, a theatre, a cafeteria and 32 kilometres of hiking trails. It attracts over 200,000 visitors a year.

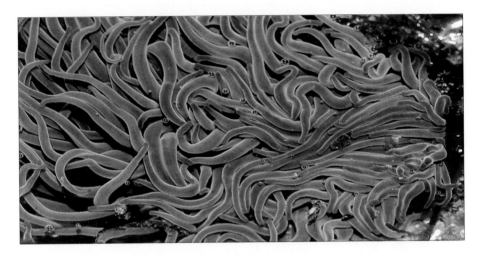

CHAPTER 9
CENTRAL AMERICA

When Hurricane Mitch swept across a swathe of Central America in autumn 1998, it devastated many parts of a region that has slowly begun to impinge on the British traveller's conscience for other reasons. Central America – which in this Guide includes Mexico – has recently begun to attract British travellers in greater numbers. The northern and coastal regions of Mexico, so accessible from the US, have long been popular with North Americans, but by and large the other central American states have suffered from a not always accurate reputation for poverty, lawlessness or dictatorial regimes, often supported or tolerated quite benignly by Washington. Central America has also suffered from being defined for what it is not: not the US, with its American sense of space and culture, not the Caribbean with its image of 'holiday' islands, and not quite South America either.

Thankfully, that is now changing, and the attractions of the region are becoming more widely known. For the green traveller there are numerous areas of interest, with a variety of holidays now being offered for the specialist, such as bird watching or diving, and a wide range of alternatives for those who like to make their own way. Recent years have seen exciting advances in archaeological excavation of Aztec, Olmec and Mayan civilisations, including the use of satellite imagery. This has increased awareness of cultural history in Central America and increased interest in the music and traditions which have survived.

Mexico's history since the Spanish occupation of 1519 and the subsequent overthrow of the Aztecs has left a tangled legacy. Economically and politically, Mexico has always been buffeted by political winds blowing from the US. In the mid-1990s, together with the US and Canada, it formed a North American Free Trade Area. Environmentalists have warned – and subsequently have claimed justification – that this could lead to US companies relocating some of their more polluting industries south of the border, where environmental restrictions were thought to be less rigorous. That said, many Americans, together with an increasing number of Europeans, head for Mexico's Baja California peninsula for holidays with a distinctly green tinge: whale watching in the Sea of Cortez and Pacific Ocean. And while the wealthy continue to flock to the resort developments of Acapulco and Cancun, the country's natural attractions are becoming better known. The Ecology Park in Xochimilco (famous for its lapidary craftsmen at the time of the Aztecs) won a Tourism for Tomorrow Award in 1996.

The countries of **Guatemala, El Salvador, Honduras, Nicaragua** and **Panama** have all undergone differing degrees of social and political upheaval this century and such events tend to dominate their image overseas. In Nicaragua, for example, less well known is the increasing interest in environmental issues inspired and spearheaded by official and non-governmental organisations alike. The country is also fortunate in encompassing Lake Nicaragua, the tenth largest freshwater lake in the world, with freshwater sharks among its wildlife, though there have been recent reports of pollution.

Of all the states of Central America to make a pitch for the green traveller, however, two have in recent years sought to emphasise the environment: **Belize** and

Costa Rica both publicise themselves as ecotourism destinations, advertising their coasts, forests and wildlife. (The coast, reefs and islands of Belize are referred to in this Guide's section on the Caribbean.) Costa Rica, which fifty years ago famously decided to abolish its army and whose former president Oscar Arias received the Nobel Peace Prize for his efforts to secure political settlement in the region, is rich in biodiversity, and has vigorously promoted wildlife tourism in the country: visitor figures almost doubled between the late 1980s and early 1990s. Perhaps symbolically, it was also chosen for the location of the Earth Council, set up by Maurice Strong, organiser of the 1992 Rio Earth Summit, to further work on sustainable development. Strong also owns a resort centre which he set up to serve as a model of sustainable tourism development.

Costa Rica abounds in birdlife, with more than 800 species including humming birds, parrots, toucans, and many others. Mammals include monkeys, jaguars and tapirs as well as smaller animals. Many are found in some of the country's 30-plus national parks and other protected areas which cover about 11 per cent of the country. Outside of this there is little major forest left and Costa Rica's dilemma is how to accommodate increased tourism without the numbers leading to strains on its natural and social environments. The last surviving populations of spider monkeys in Costa Rica are found only in Manuel Antonio National Park, and they are threatened by excessive visitor numbers and tourism infrastructure. Half of the park area has now been closed to tourism to protect the ecosystem but there is opposition from the tourist industry to further restrictions. At the moment, however, Costa Rica is still among the leaders in countries consciously promoting ecotourism. Uniquely among tropical nations, it has also commissioned a full-scale inventory of its wild genetic resources as a first step towards a systematic national policy for safeguarding biodiversity.

TOURISM FOR TOMORROW AWARDS

Lapa Rios: Osa Peninsula, Costa Rica

Winner: Americas 1995

Lapa Rios is a shoreline resort accommodation designed and built to blend with the surrounding rainforest and taking on board many aspects of sustainable building practice, including energy conservation, waste management and use of wood from sustainable sources such as windfall trees. Only local people are employed as guides and the selectors esteem the project 'a good example of tourism giving direct benefit to the community in which it is located'. Funds are injected into conservation measures and into the improvement of local schooling.

Lapa Rios
c/o PO Box 025216
SJ0706 Miami
Florida FL 33102
USA
T: +1 (506) 735 5130
F: +1 (506) 735 5179

Parque Ecologico de Xochimilco: Mexico City, Mexico

Winner: Longhaul Special 1996

Patronato del Parque
Ecologico de Xochimilco
AC
Periferico Oriente #1
Cinega Grande CP 16070
Mexico DF
T: +52 (5) 673 8061
F: +52 (5) 673 7653

This ecological park was set up in the peri-urban fringe of the world's biggest and most polluted 'mega-city', to help preserve a marshland wilderness threatened by destructive development and to contribute to the recovery of its diverse ecological zones. It comprises 60 lakes and swamps in a 189-hectare protected area. Natural vegetation has almost doubled in extent since the scheme began. Channels have been cut to renew water flow to areas drained by irrigation activities and less damaging farming methods have been piloted. More than 250,000 flowering plants have been re-introduced by school groups and horticulturists. Sheltered areas with disabled access have been built on key sites. More than a million people visit each year.

CHAPTER 10
SOUTH AMERICA

Given global concern for the fate of the rainforests, it was appropriate that the 1992 Earth Summit – the biggest ever gathering of world leaders to discuss environmental issues – should have been held in the Brazilian city of Rio de Janeiro. Although new evidence suggests that some of South America's forest cover has undergone various cycles of existence, including clearance and subsequent regrowth, in this century far greater tracts have been under threat from logging both for the timber trade and for land clearance. The forests' fate is our concern: not only do they play a part in regulating the climate cycle, but they are also home to a large proportion of the Earth's wildlife, its biodiversity. That is not just important for naturalists, nor for the indigenous forest peoples: plants and animals as yet unrecorded could hold vast potential wealth.

Sadly, just as European colonisation of Latin America from the early 16th century onwards was accompanied by the destruction of indigenous cultures and the exploitation of its precious metals, so in this century the process has continued, albeit under South American governments and the more influential international corporations. Mining, oil and gas exploration and the conversion of land for crop production, sometimes with uncontrolled use of pesticides or fertilisers, has given rise to widespread river pollution, while the clearance of forest for slash-and-burn farming, or for cattle grazing, has caused considerable problems of erosion, depleted soil fertility and habitat loss. South America's indigenous tribal peoples – some of the last to be 'discovered' by Western explorers – have suffered grievously: from introduced disease, loss of their traditional lands and resources, and the destruction of much of their original culture.

Yet the lure of South America for the green traveller is as strong as it was for the early *conquistadores*. Governments and conservation groups are working on schemes to help preserve the continent's flora and fauna, and sensitive tourism development can help this process. On the other hand, tourism can also exacerbate the social divisions in a continent where extremes of wealth are among the greatest in the world. And the relative lack of developed infrastructure can make tourism a threat to the natural environment, bringing problems of litter and waste disposal, the destruction of local habitats and new burdens on natural resources. As elsewhere, the issues of whether tourism should be encouraged in areas of wilderness and ecological fragility are central to the environmental debate in the continent. The trade in wildlife products (from parrots to animal pelts and skins) has done great harm in South America and travellers should steer well clear of it.

For British travellers, of course, the distances involved in getting to South America in the first place pose the question of the energy consumed, and the resultant pollution. If nothing else, this suggests that the conscientious traveller should think of making a visit to South America a lengthy one, rather than indulge in shorter, more frequent trips. Once made, the journey will not be wasted. From the high mountains of the Andes to the forests of Amazonia, on the islands of Galapagos or the Falklands, or in the deserts of Chile or Peru, the green traveller will find much to do and see in South America.

In the north of the continent, **Venezuela** has in recent years been keen to advertise its environmental attractions. Visitors can explore a diverse range of landscapes: from the beaches and offshore coral islands of the Morrocoy National Park to the Cordillera de la Costa range, and taking in Lake Maracaibo. But the country also possesses its own portions of Amazonian forest and Andean mountains as well as extensive savannahs, punctuated by raised rocky tepus, the vast plateaus said to have inspired Conan Doyle's *The Lost World*. The variety of Venezuela's wildlife is impressive: capybaras and red howler monkeys, ocelots and the spectacled caiman, while the range of birds is equally wide, notably in the Henri Pittier National Park, with cloud forest species spread over 1,000 hectares.

Though **Colombia**'s recent reputation for its international cocaine trade has dominated its coverage by western news media, the drugs industry's effect on the country's environment has been little reported. It has been destructive not just for the populace but for those areas where drug production is intensive – and where US-financed anti-drugs operations have been carried out, and much vegetation sprayed with herbicides. Similar environmental damage has been caused by the flower industry, which supplies millions of blooms to Europe. Sickness among the low paid flower nursery workers is widespread, often as a result of indiscriminate pesticide use.

The architectural heritage of Cartagena, on Colombia's Caribbean coast, and the nearby Islas del Rosario archipelago (a national park), may draw the visitor away from the country's capital, Bogotá, but nature tourism is also beginning to develop in other areas. The Los Katios National Park, on the Panamanian border, is an attraction for campers, while the Farallones de Cali National Park has facilities for horse riding, and in the Purace National Park, climbers can ascend the eponymous volcano. More adventurous travellers visit the Colombian Amazon, if possible by river boat, a form of transport green travellers to the continent should endeavour to use.

Ecuador's geographical diversity – ranging from the peaks of the Andes through dense forest to the celebrated islands of the Galapagos – is paralleled by a rich mix of flora and fauna. Accordingly, it has long been an attraction for visitors interested in wildlife. There are other draws: the capital, Quito, is itself an architectural gem of the Spanish colonial era. Adventure tourism, including trekking, rafting, mountaineering and volcano climbing, is on the increase. For the nature lover or ecotourist, however, an additional interest is the number of conservation projects designed to harness tourist revenues to practical environmental use.

One example of an international conservation programme is the Choco-Andean Rainforest Corridor project which is attempting to link the cloud forests of the Ecuadorian Andes to the mangrove swamps on the country's Pacific coast. The intention is thus to create 'biological corridors', to safeguard animal and plant migration, and maintain species diversity. Peter Bennett, of the London-based charity Rainforest Concern, explains: 'Monkeys, for example, will travel through the forest following ripening fruits on which they feed and the ocelots follow the monkeys on which they, in turn, depend. The corridor is necessary to protect the rainforests from slash-and-burn agriculture, cattle ranching, charcoal burning and logging which are relentlessly destroying them.' The area covered by the project is home to much endemic wildlife including more than 325 species of birds and 45 types of mammal. Among them are the black and chestnut eagle, the plate-billed mountain toucan, the spectacled bear and the jaguar.

A beginning has also been made in Ecuador to involve indigenous peoples in a tourism project, claimed to be an example of sustained community development. At the Kapawi Ecological Reserve, in addition to canoeing and forest trekking, visitors are offered the opportunity of spending time with local Achuar tribespeople. The Achuar have been involved with the building of a 20-cabin lodge and research station, constructed from local materials and using solar energy. Time will tell if the project

can be truly sustainable and help the Achuar, but the project's efforts were recognised in a Tourism for Tomorrow Award in 1998, detailed at the end of this chapter.

An interesting educational aspect of some of Ecuador's developing ecotourism is that offered by one company, Emerald Forest Expeditions. Its trips into the equatorial rainforest of eastern Ecuador (the Oriente) are not only advertised as opportunities to 'gain insight into the incredible diversity of the rainforest' but also to 'experience the deforested areas caused by the pursuit of petroleum in this fragile ecosystem, and the consequences of slash-and-burn agriculture. See first hand what is being done by the oil industry and how this experience can be used to educate others about the importance of conservation and preservation.' It is a commendable alternative to the brochures that are glossy both in appearance and in what they omit.

Most green travellers to Ecuador are likely to want to visit the Galapagos Islands. To biologists, the islands where Darwin made some of the initial collections and observations that were later to help him develop his ideas on evolution are places of veneration. To the less specialist visitor they are still islands of astonishment, not least because many of the wildlife species found there (giant tortoises, marine iguanas, boobies and frigate birds) show little fear of human interlopers. Yet the impact of tourism on the islands is controversial. Attempts by conservationists to limit the numbers of visitors have been balanced by Ecuador's need to earn foreign currency and by local people's desire to improve their standard of living. The more responsible tourist operators seek to limit numbers, employ trained guides, and reduce waste, either in terms of fuel, water or food. Not all do.

Photo © Trish Nicholson

Inca remains at Machu Picchu, Peru

The government of **Peru**, Ecuador's southern neighbour, appears to be winning its battles with the revolutionary guerrilla and bandit groups that have made travel in parts of the country hazardous during the past decade. It is likely, therefore, that the country will see an increase in visitors including those attracted by its mixture of natural and archaeological riches. The latter include the Inca remains at Cuzco and Machu Picchu, and the mysterious vast sand engravings, the Nazca lines (whose fragility deserves the respect of conservation-minded visitors). Trekking and hill walking are well established, with the Inca Trail being perhaps the most celebrated. The country has established a network of national parks and conservation areas, including the Manu Biosphere Reserve, which is officially claimed to have the world's richest biological diversity – up to 5,000 species of flowering plants, 1,000 bird species, and 13 types of monkey. Better known, perhaps, is the vast mountain lake Titicaca, or the Amazonian city of Iquitos, which is used by many travellers as the starting point for journeys down the river. Peru's coastline is also beginning to be promoted for nature tourism as well as sailing, surfing, diving and beach tourism.

Brazil's sheer size endows it with considerable geographical variety. Its environmental, social and economic problems are equally sizeable. Perhaps because of Brazil's size as much as its history of social and economic problems, conventional tourism has been in the past largely limited to the beaches and bars of Rio de Janeiro (especially at carnival time), and, more recently, to the old colonial coast of Bahia. This is beginning to change, and ecotourism is now developing; ironically enough, in pace with the economic development, road-building, logging and agricultural clearance that is putting extra strain on many of Brazil's natural resources.

The Pantanal wetlands, for example, a wilderness to the west of the country that is home to numerous bird, mammal and reptile species, are threatened by canal and drainage programmes designed to bring economic benefits. Yet moves are being made to develop adventure holidays or ecotourism, at the same time bringing sustainable revenues to communities marked by extremes of wealth and poverty. Along the Amazon many companies now specialise in small expeditions into the forest, as well as cruises along the river itself. It is not only the wildlife – from pink river dolphins to the parrots of the forest canopy – that can excite the traveller: there is the sheer size of the river, not to mention the phenomenon of the *encontro das aguas* where the black waters of the Rio Negro and the muddy pink waters of the Solimoes come together just a few miles east of Manaus to form the Amazon, but flow side by side without the colours mingling.

Landlocked Bolivia and Paraguay, together with the southern trio of Chile, Argentina and Uruguay, have until recently not attracted the same degree of tourism as their northern neighbours in Latin America. Partly this has been a function of distance, but it is also, perhaps, because tourism advertising has boosted the glamour of the other nations. Political attitudes may also have played a part; a reputation of dour dictatorships for at least four of the southern nations is now lifting. As a result, visitor numbers are likely to rise over the next few years.

Bolivia, South America's fifth-largest country, is one of its most sparsely populated. Many of its diverse geographical zones (they include the Amazon basin region to the north east, the dense Gran Chaco scrubland of the south east and the mountainous high plains region in the west) are relatively inaccessible. For those interested in wildlife or geology, however, there is much to reward a journey.

Neighbouring **Paraguay**'s population density is greater, with consequent pressure on the land and its wildlife, but the remoter northwestern areas of the Chaco region are home to many bird and reptile species, including several rare macaws, as well as big cats including the ubiquitous jaguar. Economic development has been slow, but even so, indigenous tribes people in the Chaco region have protested recently at the pace of agricultural expansion depriving them of traditional lands.

Cycling is increasingly popular for travellers to **Argentina** and **Chile**, in those regions where well-made roads allow for greater speeds and comfort. But the two countries are also trying to develop other activity holidays: whitewater rafting, skiing, trekking and mountaineering, as well as sailing and diving off their extensive coastlines.

To the south, cruises are one means of exploring the rugged coastline, especially in the heavily glaciated areas of southern Patagonia. Wildlife includes penguins and albatrosses, sea lions and elephant seals. The Argentinian authorities, meanwhile, are now promoting a tourist railway, the Ferrocarril Austral Fueguino, as a low environmental impact means of visiting the Tierra del Fuego National Park.

In the **Falkland Islands** too, nature tourism is being encouraged as a means of diversifying the islands' economy. Colonies of many bird and seal species will attract nature watchers. But while you can rarely miss out on a view of Falkland sheep, you are unlikely to see – alive, at least – the most prolific and potentially controversial of the Falklands' wildlife species. The future of the marine squid stocks, already a contentious one between fishing nations, is a reminder that here, as elsewhere in South America, environmental issues still play a dominant part in shaping the politics of the continent.

TOURISM FOR TOMORROW AWARDS

Kapawi Ecological Reserve, Ecuador

Highly Commended: Americas 1998

Kapawi Ecological Reserve, located in the Amazon Basin, is accessible only by small aircraft and is owned by the Achuar indigenous people who joined with a private tour operator, Canodros SA, to develop an ecotourism lodge. Traditional materials are used and solar power is the main energy source. The company will operate the lodge for 15 years while training Achuar to manage the enterprise independently in the future.

Luis Urdaneta
1418 y Ave Del Ejercito
Guayaquil
Ecuador
T: +593 (4) 285711
F: +593 (4) 287651

CHAPTER 11
INDIA, THE SUBCONTINENT, HIMALAYAS AND CENTRAL ASIA

Whether it is because of the enduring images of the Raj, or the decades-old view of India and Nepal as favourite destinations on the hippy trail, or even the more recent popularity of Goa for laid-back lifestyles, the Indian subcontinent remains a staple must-see experience for many British travellers who prefer to wander off the beaten track. Spiritual, cultural and historical associations also make the region attractive for many visitors, as do the environmental assets: awesome mountain ranges, lush forests, an array of wildlife; so much so, the green traveller might well feel that this is a part of the world that evokes all manner of eco-sympathies.

All this is true. But it is equally important to realise that the environment of this region can be as fragile as any others. Decades of hill trekking by Western visitors have had their impact on the Himalayan foothills, just as years of Western mountaineering expeditions to the peaks have left mini-mountains of rubbish. To satisfy the need for fuel, forests have been felled, resulting in soil erosion and flooding. Traditional cultures in Nepal and parts of India have been assailed by the impact of many young Western travellers, enjoying relatively cheap prices and soft drugs. Some notable attempts to reverse this trend have received recognition in Tourism for

Tomorrow awards detailed at the end of this chapter. Even so, more intensive tourism has begun to threaten the very architectural fabric of some of India's ancient cities. In Goa, the spread of sex tourism, and the loss to local people of water and access to the sea caused by hotel and resort-building, have become controversial issues, as in the island state of Sri Lanka.

India offers bewildering variety to the visitor but most Western travellers are likely to gravitate to a number of traditional tourist 'draws' at some stage: the capital, New Delhi; Agra, with the Taj Mahal; the ancient cities of Rajasthan; Goa with its beaches and remnants of Portuguese colonialism; Kashmir's lakelands and the high plateau of Ladakh. Each has experienced environmental problems: the effects of industrial air pollution on the Taj Mahal, for example, have recently led to a government attempt to close down many small factories, in a move designed to preserve the Taj and the tourism revenue it generates.

India's wildlife reserves and national parks are beginning to be better known, in part because they are sometimes threatened 'island' sanctuaries for wildlife species and habitats disappearing elsewhere in the face of agriculture and other development. They include the Bharatpur Bird Sanctuary, near Agra; the Kaziranga National Park in Assam, and the Corbett National Park in Uttar Pradesh. Among the species to be seen are tigers (sadly declining in numbers although efforts are being made to reverse this), lions, leopards, one-horned rhinos, bears and elephants, as well as a range of other animals, including deer, wild buffalo and crocodile. It goes without saying that, as in other parts of the world, green travellers should support conservation efforts, especially those of locally based organisations, and refrain from buying wildlife products as souvenirs.

Public transport, cheaper and less resource-consuming than hiring a car, is often the only means of travel in much of the subcontinent. Though slow, it is a good way of seeing the countryside and meeting people. India, in particular, is a delight for train buffs; while the experience of many bus rides is something impressed on the memory – though given the state of roads and standards of driving in some regions, not always for the most relaxed of reasons!

Given India's diverse cultural and religious traditions, it is, as elsewhere, important to attempt to understand and respect local mores, as far as dress and conduct are concerned. So, too, does it help to understand that India is a developing nation: some of the problems that tourism expansion in Goa has caused – including the growth of sex tourism as well as the annexation of beach access and water supplies – have in part come about because of the increase in the numbers and demands of Indian holiday makers.

An interesting attempt to keep some of the cultural influences of Western tourism at arm's length can be seen in the Indian Ocean republic of the **Maldive Islands**. Here the government has sought to preserve a relatively relaxed Islamic culture by limiting tourist development to a specific number of islands, usually those without existing

Photo © Trish Nicholson

A ready-made camp site typical along the trekking route skirting
Mount Chomolhari in Bhutan

settlements. But as visitors to the island are aware, including those who come to swim, snorkel and scuba dive in some of the most exciting of the coral reef areas, the Maldives have their own environmental problems. Some of the coral has been taken for building work including, it was reported, the expanded airport runway at the capital, Malé, where most tourists arrive. Given the low-lying nature of the islands (none is more than a few metres above sea level), the Maldives are likely to be among the most seriously affected by the rise in sea level and increased incidence of tropical storm surges that are a predicted consequence of global warming.

Cultural erosion is as much a threat as is the physical erosion of land in the Himalayan states. **Bhutan**, unique as a Buddhist Kingdom, heeded lessons from neighbouring **Nepal**'s excessive tourism impact. Bhutan limits tourism numbers to around 2000 per year through visa control and relatively high fixed daily charges, and, perhaps as a result, the state tourism agency, Bhutan Tourism Corporation, has an excellent reputation for efficiency, friendliness and environmental sensitivity. The popular trekking route skirting Mount Chomolhari in the west, uses restored old stone shelters as camp sites, water and fuel use are kept to a minimum, and local foods – including ubiquitous butter tea – are the staple trekkers' diet. But Bhutan's current non-citizenship policy for long standing Nepalese immigrants in the south has environmental implications. Without future security, long-term care of the environment is unlikely to be a high priority for immigrants.

Different travel companies have tried in different ways to ensure that their holidays are environmentally sustainable: the British company Steppes East encouraged a high degree of local involvement in its trekking expeditions in the Pamir mountains in **Uzbekistan** and **Tajikistan**, while its founders were determined to ensure that the arrival in remote regions of Western visitors did not lead to disruption of local cultures.

The London-based organisation Tourism Concern has produced a code for hill walking and trekking in the Himalayan region. It can also be considered widely applicable elsewhere – and not just in mountain regions!

TOURISM FOR TOMORROW AWARDS

Resurrection of Khajuraho: Orient Express Company, India

Winner: Longhaul Special 1995

Orient Express Travel
70 Janpeth
New Delhi
110 001 India
T: +91 (11) 3322142
F: +91 (11) 3325198

In 1965 Orient Express Company representatives visiting India's central forest hinterland found a group of ruined temples dating from roughly 1000 years ago, in the village of Khajuraho. Backed by Indian Airlines and the Civil Aviation Authority, the company pressed for restoration of the temples and the development of the site as a tourist destination. State and federal government agencies subsequently lent the scheme support and a luxury hotel was developed in the village. The temples (which have since been declared a World Heritage Site) stand amid forest lands rich in wildlife which enjoy protected area status as part of the Panna National Park, a Project Tiger Reserve.

ECOTAJ, South and South-East Asia

Winner: BA Holidays Special Hotel Supplier Award 1997, and Highly Commended for Longhaul Special and Southern Region.

Indian Hotels Company Ltd
Taj Mahal Hotel
Apollo Bunder
Mumbia 400 001
India
T: +91 (22) 2023366
F: +91 (22) 2029298

An initiative to standardise good environmental practices across the entire chain of 60 hotels located in 9 different countries of SE Asia. The programme follows the International Hotel Environment Initiatives (IHEI) environmental guidelines relating to water and energy conservation, recycling of paper, reduction in use of plastic, and chlorine-free water treatment for swimming pools is being introduced. New hotels use environmentally friendly construction materials and, where possible, local labour and products.

Turtle Conservation Project, Sri Lanka

Highly Commended: Southern Region 1998

Local fishing families in Rekawa were deprived of fishing income by illegal mining on a coral reef and a causeway which blocked the natural lagoon. Subsequently they turned to raiding the nests of green sea turtles for food and income, threatening the turtles' survival. An international wildlife conservation agency initiated the project which pays local people to protect turtle nests, while tourists pay for a Turtle Watch experience that contributes to local incomes.

Turtle Conservation Project
73 Hambantota Road
Tangalle
Sri Lanka
T: +94 (047) 40581

CHAPTER 12

CHINA AND NORTH-EAST ASIA

The return of Hong Kong to Chinese rule in July 1997 attracted world attention to a region of the world seeking to develop its tourist industry in the next century. **China** and **Japan** dominate the region, and their economic and political influence extend beyond it, as they will continue to do in the next century. Indeed, if we are entering the era of the 'Pacific Rim' as many commentators predict, the two countries will be highly influential, especially China. Again, as powerful and historic nations, both attract their fair share of criticism as much as praise. China, once largely inaccessible to Western visitors, is now embracing tourism with almost as much enthusiasm as it is undertaking economic reforms that bring the world's last nominally communist power its own brand of state-centred capitalism. From the point of view of this book, both have their attractions and potential disadvantages. China's human rights policies have been criticised – notably since the killings of pro-democracy student demonstrators in Tiananmen Square – and in recent years there have also been questions raised about some of its environment policies, particularly the deforestation of Tibet (reoccupied by Chinese forces in 1959, since when supporters of the exiled Dalai Lama have pointed to continuing human rights abuses) and the construction of the vast Three Gorges dam. That having been said, China's critics include those whose past history of industrial pollution (or, for that matter, human rights) is not particularly outstanding. Japan also has long been the object of criticism from some green groups whether for the activities of its whaling fleets, its domestic market for ivory, or its consumption of timber, much from the forests of South-East Asia. Yet, both countries exercise a fascination for the visitor, and offer much to see and do, both in terms of their natural attractions as well as their historic cultures.

Hong Kong is likely to remain a stepping-off point for many visitors to China, as well as a destination in itself. The energy of the city areas contrasts sharply with the relative tranquillity of its less well known islands and the more remote parts of the New Territories, as a visit to the placid Po Lin monastery on Lantau island will prove. But it is for the city that Hong Kong deserves to be known: perpetually busy, offering a bewildering range of sights, smells and experiences, including almost every kind of cuisine, and the once-legendary opportunities for cut-price shopping. If you're doing the latter, remember that while the intricately carved ivory on sale in some stores may look impressive, it is against the law to export it to Britain. 'Hong Kong' means 'fragrant harbour' in Cantonese and not so long ago it was anything but. But in recent decades, Hong Kong began to clean up its act as far as environmental policies are concerned. More recently, however, the building of a new international airport has brought some criticism from green groups, concerned that, among other things, it could jeopardise local colonies of porpoise and other species.

By contrast to the bustle of Hong Kong, the nearby enclave of **Macau** seems extraordinarily sluggish (save for the frenetic activity in its casinos and around the trotting track). Its mixture of Portuguese colonial and traditional Chinese architecture is engaging, but the green traveller might want to avoid the various wildlife species caged outside Macau's many restaurants.

Exploring China could well take many lifetimes. The modern traveller, with rather less time, is likely to look for some of the traditional tourist sights: Beijing's old Forbidden City, the Great Wall a few hours away (incidentally, you no longer have to shuffle along in a crowded mass of visitors to see it; get your guide to take you to less frequented sections which are now open); Shanghai and perhaps the army of terra-cotta statues in the tomb of Qin Shihuang at Shaanxi. But there are almost inexhaustible (if sometimes exhausting) experiences around the country, though travel can be difficult. In many towns cycling is the best way around while over longer distances bus, train and boat services are the best way to see the country. A voyage down the Yangzi, for example, is increasingly popular. China is only just beginning to experiment with the idea of ecotourism but it is becoming easier for the traveller to move around without having to be a member of an official tour party.

To the north, **Mongolia** is beginning to appear on travel itineraries. Although mass tourism is unlikely to present problems, the challenge for the country will be to ensure that it can generate sufficient revenue while not conflicting with lifestyles in the more remote areas of the country. One movement towards this is the availability of visitor accommodation in a traditional dome-shaped 'gur' on the outskirts of Ulaanbaator, involving low environmental impact from the point of view of reducing the amount of travel, as well as being operated on a low resource-use basis.

Famed for magnificent mountain scenery, hot springs, rocky islands, gardens and cherry blossom, Japan also abounds in exotic wildlife – snow monkeys, black bears, dancing cranes, bul-bul birds.

But many of Japan's rare species are threatened by ignorance or by tourism itself, Snow monkeys, which delight holidaymakers by their antics of bathing in hot springs, have been encouraged to beg for food. Now the increase in numbers, particularly in the last Winter Olympics region, has led angry farmers to shoot them. Captured live Japanese monkeys often end up in labs or zoos. In the overcrowded, badly-run zoos, creatures like monkeys, bears and wild birds are cramped into small cages with no real care or relief from boredom.

Pet animals suffer, too. It is not unusual in cities and villages to see dogs tied up without proper shelter outside private homes and workshops, or running homeless in the streets. Unwanted cats breed freely on rubbish dumps, lucky to avoid traps and sale to labs. Small pets are sold in poor conditions in pet shops and stores, or given away as free prizes in raffles.

JAWS raises funds to run rescue centres which care for ill-treated and stray animals, finding them new, loving homes. The charity encourages neutering as a means of reducing unwanted kittens and puppies. JAWS is now campaigning vigourously with other animal organisations in Japan for stronger laws to protect all animals in Japan.

Please help by sending donations to:

Japan Animal Welfare Society
Lyell House,
51 Greencoat Place
London
SW1P 1DS
Tel/fax 0171 630 5563

Reg. Charity No. 244534

Membership, £5 a year;
pensioners and
under-18 years, £2;
life membership, £25

Japan not only exports planeloads of tourists each year, their cameras poised; it also attracts an increasing number of Western visitors. The range of activity holidays is increasing: Japan can offer skiing, climbing and canoe holidays as well as the opportunities for trekking and cycling in scenic areas of the country. Japanese culture invests particular qualities in the landscape and some of the country's formal gardens, temples and shrines offer an insight into that relationship. Modern cities offer another insight as Japan's embrace of new technologies and urbanisation is also startling. By contrast, the city of Kyoto (venue for the crucial talks in December 1997 on climate change) is perhaps the 'greenest' city in the country, with a wealth of historic buildings and parks. The environmentally minded traveller may also want to visit Hiroshima's Peace Memorial Park; more than 50 years after the atomic bombing of the area at the end of the Second World War, it is a vivid but sensitively portrayed reflection on one of this century's more apocalyptic episodes.

CHAPTER 13
SOUTH-EAST ASIA

Before the financial crisis of 1998 unfolded, South-East Asia had seen an explosion of tourism development in the two decades since the end of the Vietnam war. Modern jets have put the region in relatively easy reach for travellers from Europe or North America. Such visitors are now joining, in ever increasing numbers, the Australians and New Zealanders for whom the region has long been the nearest destination for a foreign holiday or a stopover on the way to Britain. The attractions include a rich mix of cultures and cuisines (a mix compounded by a history and legacy of European and American colonialism) and a wealth of environmental interest, from mostly unspoiled shorelines to forest and mountain regions, with a diverse and surprising variety of wildlife (a new species of wild ox was recently discovered in a forest area of Vietnam).

If some parts of South-East Asia have been synonymous with low-cost, backpacking holidays in the past, that image is changing. In 1991, as the Indonesian authorities proclaimed 'Visit Indonesia Year', they and the governments of **Singapore**, **Malaysia** and the **Philippines** were planning concerted campaigns to promote part of the region as 'the Caribbean of the East'. Such slogans should be a warning. Certainly, tourism has already had an adverse impact in many parts of South-East Asia, which has also experienced – and continues to experience – environmental abuses and human rights violations amid the process of reconstruction and development. Wars have racked **Vietnam, Laos** and **Cambodia** in recent decades: millions of landmines and other munitions remain uncleared and a significant threat, and hundreds of thousands of refugees are still displaced.

Myanmar (Burma) is currently under the control of a military regime, and some human rights groups have urged a tourist boycott, noting that the government's attempt to boost tourism has involved forced labour and village relocations. Similarly, human rights activists have condemned Indonesia's occupation of East Timor since 1975, and there is some indigenous peoples' resistance to Indonesian rule in Irian Jaya. Indonesia, one of the world's most populous countries, is pursuing a vigorous policy of resettlement. Its forestry techniques have also been criticized by environmentalists, particularly since 1997's disastrous fires. As in neighbouring Malaysia and in the Philippines, there has been environmental criticism of some development projects, including dam building and forestry. Illegal logging continues to be a serious threat to the forests of Cambodia and Myanmar. The trade in wildlife products continues to endanger some species, particularly in the poorly policed areas of northern Thailand, Laos and Myanmar as well as the remoter regions of Indonesia.

Tourism, of course, brings its own problems as well as development opportunities. Perhaps the most serious problem in South-East Asia is the spread of prostitution, particularly child prostitution in areas being developed for tourism. The proliferation of golf courses, catering both to visitors and local players, is in some

Photo © Trish Nicholson

'The Caribbean of the East' or a disaster waiting to happen? The authorities of Indonesia, Malaysia, Philippines and Singapore must act fast to prevent environmental and social exploitation from tourism

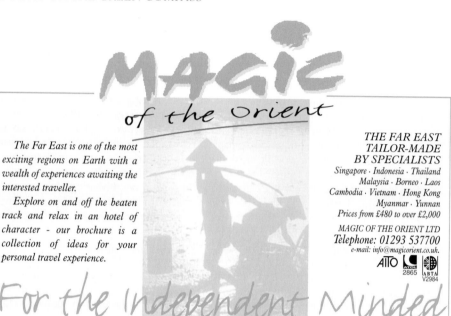
cases causing a strain on local water supplies. You also need to be very aware of your own behaviour – tourists or travellers should avoid buying wildlife products unless certain that they can be brought home legally, and that the trade is sustainable. If you are caught trafficking or in possession of drugs, you are liable to extremely stiff punishment across most of the region.

Thailand perhaps sums up a diverse region with its mixture of attractions and environmental problems. To some Western tourist brochures, it is a brew of Buddhist temples, beaches and bars – and many travellers leave out visiting the former altogether. But though there are parts of Thailand where environmental problems are evident (including the capital, Bangkok, with its choking roads and polluted water-ways) there are signs that the risks are being understood. Some of the first coordinated actions against sex tourism, for example, have come from coalitions of Thai religious groups, and recent Tourism for Tomorrow awards in the region indicate benchmarks for future improvements.

Away from the more heavily touristed areas, more independent travellers can visit the more remote regions of northern and central Thailand. The focus of such expeditions may be to see some of the wildlife in the Khao Yai National Park, or to trek into the hills where traditionally independent tribespeople are to be found (some trekking companies offer tours specifically designed for those wanting to learn more about tribal cultures). More traditional holiday sports, such as diving, canoeing and rafting, are also being developed in Thailand.

BOX 13.1

ETHNIC MINORITIES IN VIETNAM'S TOURISM INDUSTRY

Vietnam's national tourism Master Plan, drawn up in 1991 with assistance from the United Nations Development Programme, anticipated 1.5 million foreign visitors by the year 2000. But actual growth far exceeded forecasts and had already reached 1.6 million by 1996, when foreign visitors accounted for approximately 40 per cent of all tourists. Ethnic minorities in scenic mountain areas are a growing tourist attraction. While this brings cash incomes to remote communities, their poverty and poor bargaining power can result in exploitation.

Lao Cai province, in the north western mountains bordering China, is home to about one million of Vietnam's eight million ethnic minority population. The four major ethnic groups in Lao Cai are Hmong (more than half), Dao, Tay and Zay. Almost half of the population live below the official poverty line; local rice production feeds families for less than 6 months of the year. Most villages lack adequate electricity and water supplies and have no roads, which limits the potential for production and marketing of local produce. Not surprisingly, ethnic minorities are turning to tourists as a potential source of cash income.

The town of Sa Pa, with its cool climate and forested mountain environment, was a popular retreat for French colonists during the 1920s. Little of the old French resort now remains, but in the last five years both state and private guest houses and hotels have mushroomed, and now provide over 2,000 beds. Sa Pa's economy is dependent upon tourism. It is one of the most keenly marketed and accessible mountain resorts – two hours by bus from Lao Cai town where there are road and daily rail links with Hanoi (a 10–12 hour journey). Tour operators all over the country offer trips to ethnic groups around Sa Pa.

Part of the 'exotic' appeal of ethnic minorities is their colourful traditional costumes decorated with panels of fine and intricately-worked hand embroidery. The Hmong Den weave linen from hemp fibres. Women and girls constantly shred and wind hemp around their hands while looking after small children, or carrying produce on their backs to the market in Sa Pa. They soften the fibres with a tedious process of repeated washing and rolling between stone slabs, using their feet to rock one slab over the other. The fibre is then twisted into yarn, woven – usually on a back-strap loom – and immersed for up to two months in vats of indigo dye, made from indigo plants grown in the villagers' gardens. For special garments the cloth is crushed between wooden rollers, giving a very smooth finish and deep sheen to the fabric. Finally the garment is made up and collars and sleeves delicately embroidered.

The Dao Do of Ta'phin do not weave their own cloth. They buy linen from neighbouring Hmong weavers, or lengths of unbleached machine made cotton from traders in Sa Pa, and dye it themselves. But they use more embroidery than the Hmong, decorating jackets, skirts, loose fitting trousers, and dresses with large panels of very fine yellow, white and blue stitching. Embroidery is carried out during the day between other agricultural, domestic and marketing activities. A complete Dao Do woman's dress takes about a year to complete in this way. A young woman will make at least one complete new outfit for her marriage, and more if she can afford it and has the time. Designs are handed down from mother to daughter (although some men can and do embroider), and girls learn the skill from the age of eight or ten. Although there are individual preferences for combinations of colour and motif, characteristic designs identity different ethnic sub-groups. Embroidered garments have cultural significance in other ways too, in the exchange of gifts for example, especially during courting. The extensive time and skill involved in embroidery is conserved within the culture – when the base fabric wears out, embroidered panels are removed and reapplied to new cotton or linen garments.

Now, however, all this is changing because ethnic embroidery has become important souvenir material. Both old and new embroidered panels and garments, made for personal and family use, are diverted to the market because of the need for cash income. There is a constant stream of ambulant vendors, mostly women and girls, selling embroidered collars and panels to local souvenir shops and tailors for whatever they can get. A finely embroidered collar in good condition may fetch less than a dollar. These are made up into new items and sold on to gift shops in Hanoi, where middle men and retailers reap the benefits.

Many craft vendors walk into Sa Pa on a Thursday, carrying their goods in back-baskets, and stay until Monday, sleeping under the awnings of buildings or in quiet corners of the market. But the trade is exploitative. The skill, time and cultural values involved in making traditional garments are not comparable with market values. To cut out the middle men, vendors also sell direct to tourists, but they often lack the skills to make and market souvenir products. They take short cuts to produce items more quickly, for example attaching cheap Chinese trims bought in the market. They also have less time for traditional embroidery work unless they extend their long working day even further.

Major expansion is planned for tourism in Sa Pa, including a new cultural centre in the town. Ethnic minorities cannot avoid their absorption into the tourist industry nor the commodification of their cultural products, but these new trading practices represent an economic 'survival strategy' which will further erode their position in the longer term. While at the centre of attraction, they are at the periphery of economic benefits. There is an urgent need for their conditions of participation in tourism to be improved, and for broader based development alternatives to reduce dependence on tourism. In 1997, The World Conservation Union (IUCN) in partnership with Vietnam's National Tourism Authority, started on a new project, 'Capacity Building for Sustainable Tourism Initiatives.' Sa Pa is one of their pilot areas where they are initiating research into the impacts of tourism, especially the views and needs of ethnic minorities. The project is at an early stage but anticipates the creation of a Sa Pa Tourism Association and assistance to ethnic minorities, enabling them to have a greater say in tourism planning for the area.

IUCN, 13 Tran Hung Dao
Ha Noi, Vietnam
T: +844 8265172
F: +844 8258794
E: tourism.iucnvn@
netnam.org.vn

Source: Trish Nicholson (1997) *Culture, Tourism and Local Strategies for Development*. Research report for Department For International Development, London.

By comparison, **Vietnam** still has the cachet for some travellers of its being a relatively new addition to the list of the region's holiday destinations. Although joint commercial enterprises between a range of state departments and large foreign owned corporations dominate Vietnam's tourism development, new economic freedoms – 'doi-moi' – during the last ten years have enabled small local enterprises to flourish in many areas, notably in the proliferation of mini-hotels. Outside the attractions of Ho Chi Minh City (formerly Saigon) and Hanoi, visitors wanting to see more of rural Vietnam are likely to head for the outlying parts of the Mekong valley or to the hill country of the north, where Vietnam's ethnic minorities are already experiencing some of the less desirable aspects as well as some of the benefits of tourism. Coastal regions are also undergoing rapid development, not only in previous rest and relaxation centres for US troops, such as the famous China Beach, but in the north also, around the massive and extraordinary rock formations of Halong Bay, designated by UNESCO in 1995 as a World Heritage Site.

For a country where public transport is in places dilapidated, green travellers might well consider cycling, particularly in Hanoi where traffic is still dominated by the ubiquitous scooter, and where many of the numerous 'tour cafés' offer cycle hire at a reasonable cost.

Following the recent demise of Pol Pot, **Cambodia** is slowly recovering from political instability and civil conflict in parts of the country, which included the kidnapping or killing of Western travellers in recent years. Even so, the lure of the country's countryside and architectural heritage remains strong, particularly the temples of Angkor, of which Angkor Wat is the most celebrated. It is a monument as enduring in its beauty as the country's many mass graves dating from the Khmer Rouge rule of the late 1970s are testimony to the horrors of the period.

Wildlife enthusiasts are perhaps most likely to focus on **Indonesia** with its archipelago of more than 13,600 islands, some barely mapped. The two species of wildlife associated with the archipelago are, probably, the orang utan and the Komodo dragon, but the list is almost endless; biodiversity in this part of the world is among the richest. Forest trekking is one way of seeing such wildlife in situ, possibly as part of an expedition that also includes rafting or hill climbing. Diving and snorkelling are being developed in some unspoiled islands in coastal areas where the coral reefs are home to a vast array of marine life.

Equally diverse are Indonesia's human cultures; the country's challenge is how to reconcile economic development with preserving the rights of indigenous peoples. As parts of Bali demonstrate, unthinking tourism can ravage local culture, reducing it to a walk-on role in a 'tourist experience'. Perhaps more equitable, assuming their size and frequency do not overly increase, are small expeditions where travellers may meet such tribes as the Dani of Irian Jaya or the Tadjas of Sulawesi.

BOX 13.2

COMMUNITY-BASED SUSTAINABLE TOURISM
IN THE PHILIPPINES

Although renowned for its white powder beaches, sun, sea, smiles and... sex, the Philippines offers much more to the discerning traveller. Ecologically it has one of the highest biodiversity and endemic species ratings in South-East Asia, and international and national groups are working to develop tourism experiences which combine ecological sustainability with economic benefits for local host communities.

In the village of Poctoy on the south east coast of Marinduque island, fishing is the main livelihood activity. But here, as in many coastal areas of the Philippines, overfishing has reduced fish stocks, creating both environmental and economic problems for the future. The community devised a plan to zone part of the near shore fishing ground as a 'no fishing' sanctuary to enable fish stocks to recover. The difficulty, however, was that a reduction in fishing would reduce the already meagre incomes of local fishing families. To overcome this, the community looked into the feasibility of controlled use of the fish sanctuary for snorkelling and diving by tourists as a possible alternative source of income.

Tourism in Marinduque has, since the 1960s, been largely confined to a short season at Easter, when visitors come to see the processions, parades and dramatic re-enactments which make up the island's very distinctive celebration of Holy Week. Only recently have the island's authorities drawn up a tourism plan in an attempt to spread tourism further throughout the island, and extend the season throughout the year.

Poctoy had the advantage of having the only white sand beach in the island, and although there was no existing tourist accommodation or facilities, the village association sought assistance with planning their project from the local branch of an environment and rural development group, Philippines Rural Reconstruction Movement (PRRM). The result was a four day 'rural life' tour package in which Poctoy would participate along with other villages on the island. Visitors would stay overnight in Poctoy, sampling village home-stay accommodation and food. The programme would include information on the local environment, swimming and snorkelling among the coral in the fish sanctuary, and participating in various local craft and agricultural activities. PRRM set up a link between the village association and a Dutch ecotourism tour operator, Multatuli Travel, for their first pilot tours at the end of 1998.

Multatuli has offered 'sustainable tours to developing countries' since 1994, and emphasises in its publicity material that it works closely with local non-government organisations to coordinate community based tours which protect local people and their environments. As well the Philippines, it offers tours to Indonesia, Ecuador, South Africa, Tanzania and Nepal.

To what extent such community based sustainable tourism projects can be part of mainstream tourism is uncertain, although there may be scope for successful examples to increase the awareness of sustainability issues among tourists and the industry in general.

One of the problems is that, in order to protect local environments and cultures, the numbers of visitors need to be kept relatively low. Whether such projects can generate sufficient income to be economically viable is one of the many challenges to be faced.

Trish Nicholson

Multatuli Travel

Max Euweplein 24

1017 Amsterdam

T: + 31 (0) 20 627 7707

F: + 31 (0) 20 627 4886

E: travel@multatuli.nl

TOURISM FOR TOMORROW AWARDS

Banyan Tree Hotels & Resorts, Singapore

Highly Commended: Pacific Region 1998, and

BA Holidays Special Hotel Supplier Award 1998

The company operates three luxury resorts in Phuket in Thailand, the Maldives, and in Bintan in Indonesia. All are designed and sited to minimise environmental impact and modelled on local architecture. The Phuket hotel is built on regenerated land from an abandoned tin mine. Water and energy conservation is observed and a sewage treatment system in Bintan protects fragile corals.

Wah Chang House

211 Upper Bukit Timah Road

Singapore 588182

T: +65 (460) 5814

F: +65 (462) 3800

Ulu Ai: Towards Responsible Tourism, Malaysia

Highly Commended: Pacific Region 1994

A niche tourism project in Sabah, the Malaysian part of the island of Borneo. Local Iban people host tourists as guests to their village. The Iban culture is integral to the tourist experience. Visitors are accommodated in a traditional longhouse and are briefed about local customs before they arrive. Locals work for the project. Orang utan live in the area and local guides can earn extra commission for spotting them, so gain a vested interest in conservation measures.

Borneo Adventure

PO Box 2112

93741 Kuching

Sarawak

Malaysia

T: +60 (82) 245175

F: +60 (82) 422626

Sukau Rainforest Lodge, Malaysia

Winner: Pacific Region 1997

Sukau Rainforest Lodge
Sukau
Sabah
Malaysia

T: +60 (88) 234009
F: +60 (88) 233688

The Sukau Rainforest Lodge is a privately owned enterprise in a remote 40-bed property, adjacent to extensive rainforest which is soon to be gazetted as Kinabatangan Wildlife Sanctuary. Most staff are local and benefit from a comprehensive education and training programme. Solar power, electrically powered boats, waste water treatment, organic waste composting and recycling of cans and bottles are among the environmentally friendly management practices in operation.

Environmental Education and Information Campaign: Palawan, Philippines

Highly Commended: Pacific Region 1995

Ten Knots Development Corp
2/F Builder's Center Building
170 Salcedo Street
Legaspi Village
Makati City, Metro Manila
Philippines

T: +63 (2) 894 5644
F: +63 (2) 894 1134

This campaign hinges on making resort guests and members of the El Nido island community more conscious of the natural assets within the El Nido Marine Reserve. It seeks to generate awareness of the need to manage resources along sustainable lines. It also aims to encourage local people to curb destructive development activities such as wildlife poaching. The campaign uses radio, teaching packs, posters and many other tools.

El Nido Marine Conservation Programme: Palawan, Philippines

Winner: Pacific Region 1996

Ten Knots Development Corp
2/F Builder's Center Building
170 Salcedo Street
Legaspi Village
Makati City
Metro Manila
Philippines

T: +63 (2) 894 5644
F: +63 (2) 894 1134

Ten Knots Development Corporation owns and operates two El Nido Resorts on Pangulasian and Miniloc Islands. In 1995 it launched the El Nido Marine Conservation Program, with a view to maintaining the marine ecosystems of the El Nido region and to boosting the area's attractions and appeal to international and domestic tourists. The scheme has succeeded in boosting local economic growth and the well-being of local communities. Waste management and clean-up programmes, a system of mooring buoys, regular sea surveys and continuous monitoring of marine resources are combined with training and awareness drives.

Sea Canoe: Phuket, Thailand

Winner: Pacific Region 1995

A range of tours through a maze of inland waterways known in Thailand as klongs, entered by a system of caves, this scheme offers access to an area of natural beauty in a way that is low in destructive impact compared with other tourism in Thailand. It represents a conservation benchmark as well as an ingenious use of local resources. Selectors regarded it as 'truly sensitive to the need for taking pressure off other areas of a very busy tourist resort whilst protecting an important site of natural heritage'. Sea Canoe also won a Green Globe commendation in 1996 for environmental achievements.

Sea Canoe
PO Box 276
Phuket 83000
Thailand
T: +66 (76) 212252
F: +66 (76) 212172

Siam Safari Nature Tours – Ecotourism and Elephant Conservation

Highly Commended: Pacific Region 1997

The project protects the welfare of elephants in captivity no longer used for traditional purposes, by employing them for elephant treks. This encourages elephant owners to care for their animals and educates tourists on the management and future survival of elephants, of which there are some 3000 in captivity in Thailand. Treks provide funds to assist an endangered species experience while providing quality ecotourism.

Siam Safari Nature Tours
17/2 Soi Yod Sane
MOO 10
Chalong
Phuket
Thailand
T: +66 (76) 280116
F: +66 (76) 280107

Togean Ecotourism Network, Indonesia

Highly Commended: Pacific Region 1998

The network is a community-based group working with assistance from Conservation International, to provide a forum for all those involved in tourism to learn about environmental management and promote responsible practices. The introduction of boardwalks, guided tours and education materials on how tourists can help, aims to promote the Indonesian islands as an ecotourism destination while reducing environmental impacts.

JL. H. Samali No 54
Pejaten Barat
Jakarta 12510
Indonesia
T: +62 (21) 7993955
F: +62 (21) 7947931

CHAPTER 14

THE PACIFIC

The description 'paradise' is so frequently and glibly used in travel brochure-speak when it comes to describing the islands of the Pacific Ocean that it is often forgotten how environmentally fragile many of them are. In many ways, the image presented in the West is still a curious amalgam of the images evoked by Gauguin's paintings, Rodgers' and Hammerstein's musical and the advertisements for a coconut-filled chocolate bar: a languid playground for the occasional Western visitor. But the Pacific islands are emerging as distinctive and vigorous political entities, with different cultures and colonial pasts, and disparate views on their futures – as evidenced by their reaction to the French nuclear tests at Mururoa Atoll in 1995 and 1996. Equally, the islands present differing attractions to the traveller.

Environmentally, the Pacific islands are far from unchanging, or unchanged. Human impact on the Pacific environment did not begin with the American, British and French nuclear tests in the early 1950s. As happens so often, some of the indigenous wildlife species of the Pacific have been driven close to extinction by introduced domestic, agricultural or feral species. Economic activity has also played its part. Perhaps the strange giant carved heads that stare out to sea on **Easter Island** are symbolic: archaeologists believe that the indigenous Rapanui people, descended from original Polynesian settlers, waged bitter civil wars as a result of deforestation disrupting local economies. Now, the defoliation worsened by sheep introduced by a British company around the turn of this century, the island's environmental tragedy is a reminder of the fragility of the local ecosystem, and the social systems that relied on it.

Deforestation is not peculiar to Easter Island. Commercial logging has removed much of the original forest cover in New Caledonia and the Solomon Islands, as well as in Fiji, Western Samoa and Vanuatu. Loss of tree cover can not only threaten wildlife, but also lead to greater water run-off (a serious problem for islands with water shortages), silting, flooding and eventual drought, while also affecting coral reefs. A more bizarre example of unsustainable use of an island's resources has been the history of Nauru, to the north of the Solomons, where the island's rich deposits of phosphate in the form of seabird excreta have been strip-mined, leaving the islanders rich in cash, but poor in land. Mining has also caused serious environmental and social damage in Papua New Guinea, heightening political tensions and leading to resistance movements among various indigenous peoples.

Nuclear testing has left its legacy. The US programme of testing atom bombs and hydrogen bombs caused many islanders to be evacuated from their homes, some already suffering from the effects of exposure to radioactive contamination. In March 1954 the US exploded the first hydrogen bomb at Bikini Atoll, showering the islanders at Rongelap, 150 km away, and Utirik Atoll, as well as a Japanese fishing boat, with nuclear fall-out. In 1966, three years after France transferred its nuclear test programme from north Africa to the Pacific, General de Gaulle, on a visit to Polynesia, insisted that a test at Mururoa went ahead, even though the wind direction meant that fall-out would land on many inhabited islands. Many islanders now ascribe incidences of cancer or still-births to this nuclear legacy.

Today, visitors to the **Tuamotu Islands** are warned against eating toxic fish; the seafood poisoning known as ciguatera caused by a microscopic algae is more prevalent in parts of French Polynesia than anywhere else in the region, and has been linked by some researchers to the nuclear test programme. Another potentially disastrous environmental threat to the Pacific islands is the prospect of global warming, with the resultant increase in sea levels and more violent fluctuations in weather patterns. To low-lying islands, these changes may spell catastrophe. Paradise may well be imperilled.

Tourism, needless to say, is also creating as many problems as possibilities in the Pacific. **Tahiti**, the main island in French Polynesia, shows the effects of an economy distorted by the military and concomitant expenditure by Paris since the early 1960s (which in part explains why many Tahitians, particularly those of French extraction, supported the nuclear tests). While new luxury hotels provide work for local people, they also make demands on water and other local resources; money can flow out of local economies to enrich foreign tourism developers, as well as paying for expensive imports of foreign foods for the tourists.

In **Hawaii**, American statehood has quickened the development of tourist resorts, all with their demands on the environment, including the water-thirsty, fertiliser- and weedkiller-intensive golf courses. At sea, yachts and cruise liners alike contribute their share of litter and other pollution, or add to the damage done to coral reefs. But local communities are beginning to assert their rights for better environmental management. The efforts of Friends of Hanauma Bay to control environmental degradation in the Bay was recognised in 1997 by the Tourism for Tomorrow award scheme (see listings at the end of this chapter). Although Hawaii is popularly seen as a destination for American-style high-consumption holidays, with mall-shopping as important as topping up the tan, the national parks that have been established, such as the Volcanoes Park on Hawaii itself, Haleakala Park on the island of Mauai and Waimea Canyon Park on Kauai, offer greener alternatives.

Tahiti, too, is beginning to look beyond the mix of beach and bar holidays, not to mention the exhaust fumes of the capital, Papeete, where ancient colonial buildings and an ancient market are now challenged by new office blocks and malls. Hill walkers and climbers focus on mountains such as Aorai or Orohena, but less arduous walks are beginning to be used more widely. Whale watching is an enjoyable experience in the Pacific, where some of the world's most spectacular species can be seen, including the humpback, the most acrobatic of them all.

Western Samoa and **Vanuatu** are among countries to declare new national parks, with legislation designed to preserve wildlife habitats from the downside of tourism and other economic activity. Vanuatu has rich birdlife to attract the ornithologist, while local magical lore has a special place for the tiger sharks which are abundant in its waters.

Fiji has suffered its fair share of deforestation (interestingly, a fact now acknowledged in official tourist literature) but there are new ventures that emphasise conservation: a resort hotel on the island of Namena (sometimes known as Namenala), for example, is limited to ten guests at any one time. The island is home to the flightless banded rail, a bird wiped out by cats and other introduced predators on other islands.

Away from the attractions of scuba diving and snorkelling among the Pacific coral reefs, many islands are developing forest hiking trips, in part as their coastal resorts are becoming more established. **Raratonga**, in the Cook Islands, illustrates one example of how resort growth has alarmed many visitors.

Papua New Guinea, where over 900 ethnic languages within a population of a little over three million give it the distinction of having the greatest cultural diversity of any nation on Earth, has the bird of paradise species among its glories, and still has some of the best coral found anywhere. The adventurous will find challenging opportunities for whitewater rafting and jungle trekking, but it is inadvisable to attempt these activities without a competent guide or expedition group. All travellers should also take advice as to the prevailing political situation in parts of Papua New Guinea when they visit.

If the Pacific Rim nations are the economies that will help shape the future, the states of the Pacific islands are likely to see more attention paid by travellers. It is to be hoped that they tread lightly.

TOURISM FOR TOMORROW AWARDS

Environmental Targets (Asia-Pacific): Inter-Continental Hotels & Resorts

Highly Commended: Pacific Region 1995

Part of a seven-year environmental programme by a major international hotel group, this Asia-Pacific regional initiative far exceeded expectations in 1994 in terms of general improvements in such areas as saving fresh water through re-use and recycling of wastewater, installation of CFC-free fridges, recycling of useful materials such as cork and a collaboration with the Royal National Park in Sydney, Australia, to propagate and supply plant seedlings to restock the Park after a disastrous bush fire.

Inter-Continental Hotels and Resorts
Devonshire House
Mayfair Place
London W1X 5FH
T: +44 (171) 3556586
F: +44 (171) 3556592

Vanua Rapita Lodge, Solomon Islands

Highly Commended: Pacific Region 1998

Vanua Rapita Lodge, on a one-hectare island, accommodates up to 12 visitors at a time in three leaf houses overlooking Marovo Lagoon. Local food is used and cooked without electricity. The enterprise is owned by the Tobakokorapa Association, a consortium of three tribes encompassing about 300 villages. A percentage of revenue is used for village projects such as water supply, health and education.

Vanua Rapita Lodge
c/o Seghe Postal Agency
Marovo Lagoon
Solomon Islands
T: +66 (7) 60191
F: +66 (7) 60294

Hanauma Bay Nature Reserve Management Plan, Hawaii

Winner: Americas Region, Special Longhaul, and Global Award 1997

Friends of Hanauma Bay was formed in 1990 to lobby for better environmental management of the 50-acre Bay Reserve, which was suffering severe degradation of its aquatic and terrestrial ecology. The community group worked closely with government agencies and a number of management options have been implemented, including better interpretive information, regulations regarding safety and limitation of the number of visitors, more staff, charges for parking, and better sewage facilities and rubbish collection. The near shore reef and the landward environment are now showing signs of recovery.

Hanauma Bay Nature Reserve
680 A la Moana Avenue - 411
Honolulu
Hawaii 96813
T: +808 5211742
F: +808 5211743

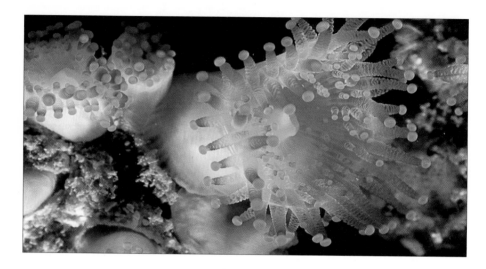

CHAPTER 15
AUSTRALASIA

Australia and New Zealand hold almost infinite attractions for the green traveller. The Australian city of Sydney is already billing the Olympic Games to be held there in the year 2000 as the 'Green Olympics', and New Zealand's commitment to environmental issues was demonstrated in 1995 when, together with her larger neighbour and many of the South Pacific island states, she led the opposition to French nuclear tests at Mururoa Atoll. For lovers of unique wildlife and outdoor activities, the two countries offer almost endless opportunities. Australia, for example, has some 2000 national parks and reserves, including 11 World Heritage areas. Notably, Australia also proudly boasts that it was the first country to proclaim a national park – in Sydney in 1879.

Having said that, both countries have experienced environmental controversy. Early British settlers and colonial governments dispossessed the Native Australian and Maori people (in some cases driving tribes to extinction) and issues of land rights and political recognition remain sensitive. The history of settlement also meant interference with the two countries' island species, as hunting and the introduction of new forms of agriculture spelled disaster for such creatures as the Tasmanian tiger, which is believed to have died out in the 1930s, and the Moa, the giant flightless bird of New Zealand. More recently, there have been political controversies over such issues as logging, the construction of roads and hydroelectric dams in rainforests (the environmentalist David Bellamy was arrested at one protest in Tasmania some years ago) and mining in areas important to Aboriginal culture.

Tourism is increasingly important to both countries – annual tourist visitors to Australia doubled from one to two million in the late 1980s – and there is a widespread concern that its development should be controlled, especially among the relatively fragile ecosystems of the Great Barrier Reef and Aboriginal cultural sites, such as Uluru (Ayers Rock). The involvement of indigenous people in the tourism industry, on terms of equality, is seen as increasingly important.

AUSTRALIA

To the chagrin of Canberra, the capital, or Melbourne, which sees itself as the country's cultural focus, the city most people associate with Australia is Sydney, the bustling port on the New South Wales coast best known for its two distinctive landmarks – the shell-shaped Opera House and the Sydney Harbour Bridge.

Many travellers use Sydney as their jumping-off point for the rest of the country but a growing number of tourists are flying direct from Britain to the northeastern coast of Australia. The vast distances involved mean that green travellers wanting to explore more than a fraction of the land must be prepared for long hauls. If time permits, rail and bus services are an excellent way to see the country rather than by car or plane, with both services offering economy passes which keep travel costs down, as well as going some way towards reducing vehicle pollution.

Each of Australia's states has its own environmental attractions, as you would expect from a country that boasts some 300 bird species found nowhere else in the world – and about 500 varieties of eucalyptus. But in this land which bills itself as the world's 'largest island and smallest continent', Queensland, the north easterly state, has one of the biggest natural attractions on the planet: the Great Barrier Reef. Some 1200 miles (2000 km) long, the reef is, biologically, the world's largest living organism. As a result it is a magnet for anyone interested in marine life, with the multicoloured corals a haven for a bewildering array of fish. Swimming in these waters, especially if snorkelling or scuba diving, can be like taking part in a technicolour extravaganza.

Needless to say, the Queensland tourist industry has been ready to exploit the marvels of the reef with a plethora of cruises, boat trips and day tours – some even by helicopter – to take swimmers out to the coral. But the coral can be fragile, and

damage has been done by some careless tourism, such as boats dragging their anchors or tourists being allowed to 'reef walk'. In the 1980s some sections of the Great Barrier Reef were found to be suffering from coral dying off at a high rate, as well as being attacked by a plague of the crown of thorns starfish. A number of theories were advanced to account for this, including an increase in sea temperatures caused by global warming. Whatever the cause, the starfish plague abated during the early 1990s, but the reef is still closely monitored as a barometer of the coast's environmental health.

Away from the beaches, rainforest trekking and river cruises, whitewater rafting, back-packing and bungee jumping are part of the state's outdoor thrills. As elsewhere in Australia, green travellers who are enjoying outback life should remember that during the dry season, bush fires are literally a burning issue: take care to avoid starting them.

By contrast to Queensland's popularity, or the larger numbers that flock to Sydney and the surrounding areas of New South Wales, the vast state of Western Australia has only recently begun to develop its tourist attractions. But two are of interest to almost any green traveller. Some 830 kilometres north of Perth, the inlet of Monkey Mia in Shark Bay is remarkable for the large numbers of dolphins that swim close in to shore, apparently enjoying the contact with holiday makers who wade out among them. Wildlife rangers are now employed to make sure that the contacts remain enjoyable to both parties.

Hundreds of miles further north are the remarkable rock formations that make up the Purnululu range; the area is also known as the Bungle Bungle and is protected as a national park, with access to visitors limited by the passability of the tracks as much as a desire to protect the environment. That desire was recognised when the Purnululu National Park was the first global winner of the inaugural Tourism for Tomorrow Award. Employing Aboriginal custodians of the area (representatives of the four local language groups, Kija, Jaru, Malngin and Miriwung, sit on the management board) together with concentration on low-impact camping holidays, helped the park restrict undesirable commercial tourist development.

Still further west is the Pilbara region. Here the landscape seems in places hammered hard by a combination of climate and geology. Appropriately, this is an area rich in minerals, whose extraction has had its impact on both natural and social environments. Iron ore mining has left its trace in spoil. Ore trains, hundreds of wagons long, trundle over the horizon. Mining and port towns, such as Tom Price, Newman and Dampier, reflect the struggle to win the metals from the soil. Other settlements fared less well: abandoned towns such as the former pearl-fishing port of Cossack hint at the harsh lives of the early settlers.

At the heart of the Australian continent, in the southern reaches of the Northern Territory, looms the vast Ayers Rock, Uluru. The rock, surrounded by the Uluru-Kata Tjuta National Park, has been designated a World Heritage Site, both for its natural beauty and its Aboriginal cultural significance. The exploitation for tourism of Aboriginal culture continues to divide anthropologists, as well as environmentalists and

BOX 15.1

WHAT THE LAND IS ABOUT

The Millstream-Chichester National Park, in Western Australia's Pilbara region, is a green oasis in this rugged, iron-hard country, where temperatures can rise over 100 degrees in the high summer months of December and January. The park headquarters are in a converted sheep station, close to groves of palm, cadjebut and eucalyptus fed by a freshwater aquifer.

The Chinderwarriner Pools, deep and deliciously cool, sparkle in the tree-filtered light, giving a jewel-like quality to the darting fish and the blue-green dragonflies that hover, sapphire-bright, above them. The trees are hung with the dark, leathery umbrellas that are fruit bats, and resound to the call of birds.

The Chinderwarriner Pools have been a traditional sacred site for the Injibarndi people who came there for rituals as well as for food and water. Now plans to involve present-day Aborigines in the park's development are progressing well. 'Anything we do in the park, we first talk to the Aboriginal elders,' says Hugh Chevas, one of the local officers of CALM, Western Australia's Conservation and Land Management Department. 'They have their people's responsibility for looking after the sacred sites, identifying them and telling us where they are.'

Chevas wants to build on the scheme with more Aborigine park rangers. A local tour company, Snappy Gum Safaris, is also employing Aborigine guides who explain the significance of sacred sites and rock carvings, as well as how to survive off the land. On the northwest coast, Emma Withnell, one of the first Victorian settlers there, is recalled through a heritage trail which links the old pearl-fishing port of Cossack – abandoned early this century and now being carefully restored – with nearby Point Sampson and Roebourne. She lived in Roebourne and befriended Aboriginal women.

Not all European settlers or their descendants were so minded: the death in police custody of John Pat, a young Aborigine, in 1983, was one of a series of such incidents that sparked a Royal Commission of Inquiry, and highlighted the injustices faced by the Aborigines. The town's old jail, now a tourist attraction, still casts a shadow.

David Daniels, a member of the Ngarluma people, lives on the outskirts of Roebourne with his family. He is the author of a guide to the Thalu Aboriginal ritual sites of Western Australia and helped set up a dance group to preserve some of his people's cultural traditions. He also works as a tour guide, demonstrating how to gather, catch and cook 'bush tucker' – the food of the Outback – and explaining rock paintings and Aboriginal lore.

'Black fellahs, white fellahs, we all live in this country. We have to live together now,' he said as we sat with his uncle and tribal elder, James Solomon, in the shade of his verandah. Daniel sees Aboriginal involvement in tourism as acknowledgement of his people's intimate association with the continent. 'We can tell people what the land is about, its history, its life,' he said. 'To you people, a lot is just legends. To us – we know, we know.'

Source: Greg Neale writing in the *Daily Telegraph*, 1991

conservationists. But tourist income from Aboriginal culture is considerable – of the four million visitors to Australia in 1995, 11 per cent visited Aboriginal sites or cultural centres, and sales of Aboriginal art and crafts alone amounted to A$100 million.

In recent years a serious effort has been made not only to use Aboriginal knowledge and to encourage the employment of Aboriginal peoples as guides and cultural advisers, but to recognise their right to self-management and an equal share of economic benefits from tourism. The 1991 Commission of Enquiry into Aboriginal Deaths in Custody identified tourism as one of three industries which offered indigenous Australians significant opportunities for self-determination and self-sufficiency. As a result of the Commission's findings, a National Aboriginal and Torres Strait Islander Tourism Industry Strategy has been established. One of its programmes is the setting up of Aboriginal Tourism Australia to represent the interests of indigenous tourism operators. For the green traveller, the guidelines have to be based on avoiding exploitation.

The island of Tasmania may not have the arid deserts of central Australia or the sweltering heat of the tropical north, but its environmental diversity is almost as rich. Sailing is an almost obsessional sport for many Tasmanians, but so too is fishing, walking in the hills and forests, or whale and dolphin watching at the appropriate time of year. Equally obsessive are those Tasmanians and their visitors who keep an eye open hoping to see a surviving Tasmanian tiger. Though the last recorded specimen of this carnivorous marsupial died at Hobart zoo in 1936, there are occasional reports of unexplained sightings on lonely roads and in remote forest clearings.

NEW ZEALAND

New Zealand's environmental enthusiasms strike the visitor from the outset. Auckland, point of arrival for most visitors, is busily developing a kerbside recycling scheme. Not all visitors reciprocate: in July 1985, French secret agents planted two bombs under the hull of the Greenpeace ship *Rainbow Warrior*, which was due to sail on a voyage around the South Pacific, protesting against French (and American) nuclear testing. A Greenpeace photographer, 34-year-old Fernando Pereira from Portugal, was killed.

After the bombing, the vessel was eventually towed north, to Matauri Bay, where it was scuttled as a memorial to Pereira and to the environment group's mission to the South Pacific. The episode has, however, left a legacy of even deeper environmental concerns among most New Zealanders. When in 1995 France began a new series of tests, the sense of national outrage was palpable. In many ways, it coincided with the country's pride in its own environment as well as a sense of unity with the other island nations of the region, an identification deepened by several generations of migration to New Zealand by people from other South Pacific countries.

Maori identification with the land is a similarly strong factor in moulding New Zealand's green image. The outdoor life is a popular one. Auckland is often dubbed the 'City of Sails', and the enthusiasm for boating is evident here, as it is in Wellington, the capital. Hill walks are plentiful around the Auckland area, but serious trekkers may want to spend time in the South Island, where skiing and other Alpine sports are also being developed, so far without the intensive mass-tourism approach that has marred much of the European Alps. Extensive rural bus routes, uncluttered roads for cycling, plenty of bed and breakfast places, and a well developed network of youth hostels in really prime sites, makes getting around South Island an easy task for the green traveller. Most youth hostels have detailed information about walks and wildlife in their locality, but perhaps the ultimate trek is the Milford Track running through Fiord National Park from Lake Te Anau to Milford Sound for 55km (33.5 miles). The route, which takes up to four days, was pioneered by explorer Quintin MacKinnon in 1888. As well as the drama of MacKinnon Pass and the thousand feet high Sutherland Falls, the track passes through primeval forest considered by some naturalists to be the closest ecology to the ancient forests of Gondwanaland. The track is carefully managed and the number of walkers is limited.

Whitewater rafting is also popular, and New Zealand can claim the dubious credit of being home to the 'sport' of bungee jumping. For geologists, or the simply curious, however, the thermal mud springs of Rotorua, in the North Island, are internationally famous and have long drawn the visitor, as well as those wanting to take the spa waters for health purposes.

Whale watching is increasingly enjoyed in New Zealand. In 1994, the Whale Watch group at Kaikoura, in the South Island, won the global prize in the Tourism for Tomorrow awards sponsored by British Airways. The Maori-run venture is helping to revive an area which had suffered from high unemployment, in some part due to the end of the former whaling trade. Two other projects in South Island, involving colonies of black petrel, and the rare crested penguins, were highly commended by the award scheme in 1993.

TOURISM FOR TOMORROW AWARDS

Savannah Guides: Queensland, Australia

Highly Commended: Pacific Region 1996

A professional body unique within the tropical savannah regions of Northern Australia, Savannah Guides is a network of local tour guides who conduct tours along environmentally and culturally sensitive lines. The skills they acquire ensure that they win general recognition as 'specialists in, and protectors of, their own region'. Regular Savannah Guide training schools maintain skill levels and registered Guides have exclusive permission to take visitors through areas that would otherwise be off-limits. In addition, the organisation has developed eight Savannah Guide Stations from traditional fishing, mining and stock rearing structures, which now provide full visitor facilities.

Savannah Guides Ltd.
PO Box 6268
Cairns
Queensland 4870
Australia
T: +61 (70) 317933
F: +61 (70) 317939

Crystal Creek Rainforest Retreat: Australia

Highly Commended: Pacific 1994

Crystal Creek Rainforest
Retreat
PO Box 69
Murwillumbah
NSW 2484
Australia
T: +61 (66) 791 591
F: +61 (66) 791 596

Formerly a run-down banana plantation, this small lodge resort is located in a rainforest setting adjoining Numinbah Nature Reserve in New South Wales. No trees have been removed but many indigenous species have been replanted, and feral animals are being eradicated to allow native wildlife to reclaim the area. A maximum 20 guests can be accommodated at any one time. Wastewater and effluent are treated and the liquid residue used to irrigate trees. Solid wastes are segregated for recycling, composting and use as mulch. Guided walks and educational visits are among the recreations on offer. Crystal Creek also won a Green Globe commendation for environmental achievement in 1996.

Quicksilver Outer Barrier Reef, Australia

Highly Commended: Pacific Region 1998

Marina Mirage
PO Box 171
Port Douglas
Queensland 4871
Australia
T: +61 (7) 4099 5455
F: +61 (7) 4099 5525

The project reduces the impact of tourists on fragile coral of the Great Barrier Reef. Quicksilver is the largest cruise operator on the Reef and the first to use floating platforms for viewing to reduce the impact of anchor lines, and avoid the need for visitors to 'reef walk' to appreciate the coral. Through qualified marine biologists in its Reef Biosearch department, the company also conducts monitoring and research in the reef environment, and provides interpretation to visitors.

Seal Rock Sea Life Centre, Australia

Highly Commended: Longhaul Special 1998

Seal Rock Sea Life Centre
7 Bennet Street
Dandenong
Victoria 3175
Australia
T: +61 (3) 9793 6767
F: + 61 (3) 9793 6868

A run-down kiosk and car-park on Phillip Island, Victoria, has been transformed into a viewing centre to educate visitors about Bass Strait marine life including Australian Fur Seal, Silver Gulls and Little Penguins. A solar and wind powered camera system nearly 2km from the Centre sends back images of Fur Seals for viewing and monitoring without disturbing the seals. The Centre's design is energy efficient, and has drainage and filtering systems to prevent soil erosion and ocean pollution.

Eco Beach Resort, Australia

Winner: Pacific Region 1998

This purpose built eco-lodge, south of Broome on the north west coast of Western Australia, was designed and built to be environmentally friendly as well as economic. Over 70 per cent of construction materials were recycled including floors, walls and walkways. Trolleys rather than motor vehicles were used for transport. In operation the Resort uses minimal energy drawn from a hybrid solar and diesel system. The local Aboriginal population was involved in initial approval for the project, and some work as guides ensuring that local sacred sites are respected. Other awards gained by the resort include 1998 Western Australia Environmental Tourism Award; 1998 Jaguar Award for Excellence/Innovation in Travel; the 1997 Western Australia Best Hotels Award; and *Tatler* magazine's list of Top 101 Hotels in the World 1998

Eco Beach Resort
PO Box 2965
Broome
WA 6725
Australia
T: +61 (8) 9192 4844
F: +61 (8) 9192 4845

Binna Burra Mountain Lodge, Queensland, Australia

Highly Commended: Pacific Region 1997

Originally built in 1933, lodging and camping accommodation at Binna Burra is adjacent to the World Heritage listed rainforest of south east Queensland. The original buildings are listed by the National Trust and new buildings emulate the old style. Where possible, the lodge employs local people and purchases local supplies. Water supply is by gravity, glass and metals are recycled, and organic waste is processed by a worm farm.

Binna Burra Mountain Lodge
Binna Burra Road
Beechmont
Queensland 4211
Australia
T: +61 (7) 5533 3622
F: +61 (7) 5533 3658

Oamaru Blue Penguin Colony: New Zealand

Highly Commended: Pacific Region 1996

Set up to protect the breeding ground of the rare blue penguin of Oamaru Harbour and to protect the natural environment of the Oamaru Quarry area, the project provides opportunities for researchers and the visiting public to observe and appreciate the bird colony's behaviour and surroundings. A visitor centre has been established and volunteers participate in beach clean-ups, access projects and production of nesting-boxes. An educational project involving local schools has also begun.

Tourism Waitaki
Private Bag 50058
Oamaru
New Zealand
T: +64 (3) 434 1655
F: +64 (3) 434 1657

Whale Watch: Kaikoura, New Zealand

Global Winner 1994

Whale Watch Kaikoura Ltd
PO Box 89
Kaikoura
South Island
New Zealand
T: +64 (3) 319 5045
F: +64 (3) 319 6545

This small former whaling community had a high level of unemployment until Maori people of the Ngai Tahu group set up an owner-operated fleet of whale watching vessels, run from offices in a refurbished railway station in Kaikoura. Today, part of the profit from tours is invested in cultural education and training courses that take place in a customary Maori meeting-place. World-wide, whale watching is a growth area (over four million visits yearly) and this project can be regarded as a model. It helps prove the long-term value of live whales as a tourist attraction. Out of every 100,000 visitors to Kaikoura, 37,000 come to see whales. Whale Watch Kaikoura also won a Green Globe Distinction award in 1997.

SECTION THREE
THE GREEN
TRAVELLER'S
DIRECTORY

CHAPTER 16

THE TOURISM INDUSTRY: GLOBAL INITIATIVES

Although its strongest critics view the tourism industry as a rapacious predator – moving on to fresh conquests after one environment has been spoiled, and forever fuelling the desires of holidaymakers with the prospect of a new paradise that must be enjoyed 'before it's gone' – there are many within the industry who reject the claim. They are at least partly right. There are examples where the travel trade is doing better.

Of course, reforming initiatives often come after the damage has been done and in some cases for public relations purposes rather than from a commitment to sustainability. In addition, the growth of the travel industry puts increasing strain on natural and social environments by its sheer size and volume. Yet it would not do to overlook examples of improvements. Pressure for reform has come from many sources: market demands, consumer pressure, organised lobbying and by local, national and international agreements involving governments and non-governmental organisations. This chapter examines some of the initiatives that have been taken by the industry, by government bodies, non-governmental organisations and others to address the various issues thrown up by the expansion of tourism.

WHAT IS SUSTAINABLE TOURISM?

Definitions of sustainable development vary. Definitions of sustainable tourism vary still more. For some purists, any encroachment by tourism or non-indigenous travellers in some of the world's wilderness areas is unsustainable. A single footfall is sufficient to disrupt the (albeit probably temporary) ecological balance; a lone traveller enough to impact on the cultures he or she encounters. But while arguments around the need for various forms of wilderness to be preserved are likely to rumble on, the controversy over tourism presents more immediate problems, even if the possible solutions become more varied. Until recently, most international travellers and tourists have come from the European and North American countries (as well as Australasia and Japan). Changing economic and political circumstances are now seeing more tourists from Eastern European countries, and the so-called 'tiger economies' of South-East Asia. Trade liberalisation is likely to swell these numbers in the decades to come.

A basic definition of sustainable development might be necessary, therefore, to see whether it can be applied to those individuals, groups, corporations, governments and other public authorities who are attempting to reform travel and tourism to meet environmental needs. Possibly the most enduring definition of sustainability was that coined by the Brundtland Commission, chaired by the former Norwegian prime minister, Gro Harlem Brundtland, in 1987 in its milestone report, *Our Common Future*. The Commission declared that sustainable development was development which 'meets the needs of the present without compromising the ability of future generations to meet their own needs'. Of course, such a definition may be criticised as excessively vague, or even as concentrating implicitly on human needs, without reference to the more fundamental workings of natural ecosystems. Yet in the end, attempts at ever-more-precise definitions are probably doomed to irrelevance. What is appropriate in one situation may be inadequate elsewhere.

This chapter therefore looks at some of the initiatives undertaken by various institutions holding a stake in travel and tourism. They are not always compatible: industry bodies and conservation groups frequently seek different objectives and often pursue seemingly colliding agendas. Yet each of them merits consideration in its way. The green traveller needs to be aware of them, if only as potential sources of further information, and for when it comes to making choices about holiday and travel plans.

GLOBAL RESPONSES TO THE CHALLENGE: OFFICIALDOM, TRADE AND INDUSTRY

The World Tourism Organization (WTO)

World Tourism
Organization
Capitán Haya 42
28020 Madrid
Spain
T: +34 (91) 567 8100
F: +34 (91) 571 3733
E: omtweb@world-tourism.org
URL: www.world-tourism.org

The WTO, which has its offices in Spain, was set up in 1975 as a United Nations intergovernmental organisation, amid increasing awareness of the growing impacts of tourism. Some 134 nations are members of the WTO, as well as more than 300 affiliates, including private companies, regional and local government bodies. Though its critics argue that, possibly because of its linkages with the private sector, it is overly concerned with the promotion of tourism, and the lowering of trade barriers, it has increasingly become concerned with environmental issues, especially as they affect poorer countries, and has helped promote projects and programmes aimed at making the industry more environmentally sustainable. This in part reflects its mission statement of intent to 'develop tourism as a significant means of fostering international peace and understanding, economic development and international trade'.

The WTO is currently working on Agenda 21 initiatives, and publishes, among other documents, a sustainable tourism guide for local planners. WTO staff and consultants are also working to develop a series of environmental indicators for tourism destinations. It has arguably the most comprehensive intake of regular data on the tourism industry – it publishes an annual *Yearbook of Tourism Statistics* – and contributes to wider campaigns, such as that against child sex tourism. In harness with the World Travel and Tourism Council and the Earth Council, WTO has prepared a report, *Agenda 21 for the Travel and Tourism Industry: Towards Environmentally Sustainable Development*. It attempts to translate the Rio Agenda 21 document into an action plan for the industry (Box 16.1)

Other international organisations taking an active interest in tourism and environment issues include the Paris-based Industry and Environment programme activity centre of the UN Environment Programme (UNEP), and the International Labour Organization (ILO), which looks into questions of employment law and conditions. Both promote 'best practice' guidelines and codes of conduct.

Certain regional treaty organisations also pursue technical co-operation and training programmes for safe and prosperous tourism, involving several neighbouring destination states. An example is the work of the Department of Regional Development and Environment of the Organization of American States, which co-funds sustainable tourism master plans and development programmes in Brazil, Guyana, Panama, El Salvador and six other Caribbean and Latin American countries.

> *'We need to recognise that there are limits . . . to the patience and welcome of our hosts, and limits to the numbers who can visit natural resources.'*
> WTTC

> *'Tourism is the world's largest employer, employing 112 million people worldwide: that is, one in every 15 employees.'*
> WTTC

The World Travel and Tourism Council (WTTC)

The World Travel and Tourism Council is a 'global coalition' of chief executives from travel and tourism companies – mostly major firms, including international airlines, hotel and holiday groups – which was set up in 1990 to promote the tourism industry. Its goals are 'to convince governments of the strategic and economic importance of travel and tourism, to promote environmentally compatible development and to eliminate barriers to growth of the industry'.

While sustainable development may seem to sit at times uneasily with an elimination of all trade barriers, the WTTC,

World Travel and Tourism Council
20 Grosvenor Place
London SW1X 7TT
T: +44 (171) 838 9400
F: +44 (171) 838 9050
E: via CompuServe
100421.702

with a membership of more than 70 corporate heads, has nevertheless been responsible for a series of environmental initiatives, such as the Green Globe programme and more recently the ECoNETT system (see below).

Green Globe and Green Flag

Green Globe (at WTTC)
20 Grosvenor Place
London SW1X 7TT
T: +44 (171) 930 8333
F: +44 (171) 930 7779
E: 100104.2605 (via
Compuserve)

Another initiative WTTC has developed, together with the Earth Council, is the Green Globe programme. Its objective is to provide a low cost practical means for travel and tourism companies to improve their environmental practice. 'Good environmental practice is not only morally right; it makes sound business sense and can lead to significant cost savings', is the message it seeks to put across to would-be corporate members. The Green Globe scheme is designed to give participating companies advice in changing their environmental practice, as well as the means of evaluating them and information about cost-saving techniques and technologies. Green Globe membership can also be useful for its public relations value.

Green Flag International
PO Box 396
Linton
Cambridge CB1 6UL
T: +44 (1223) 890250
F: +44 (1223) 890258

Linked with the Green Globe programme is the Cambridge-based Green Flag International, an independent organisation, but still closely allied to WTTC. Its programmes are now running around the world. Among the support services the scheme offers to those who join it are telephone and fax helplines as well as electronic databases with information on environmental best practice and regular surveys, training materials, and access to advisers who may visit Green Globe member organisations to help with environmental improvements.

ECoNETT

As its acronym suggests, ECoNETT, the European Community Network for Environmental Travel and Tourism, is a European Union funded initiative to use the Internet to disseminate information on these related areas. The initiative was set up in December 1995, with initial three-year funding from the DG XXIII tourism unit of the European Commission to the World Travel and Tourism Council.

The ECoNETT web site is designed to provide information for the travel industry, tourism destinations, governments, academics and media, as well as the general public.

ECoNETT Project Office
(at WTTC)
20 Grosvenor Place
London SW1X 7TT
T: +44 (171) 235 2135
F: +44 (171) 235 2445
E: 106316.2226@
compuserve.com
URL: http://www.wttc.org

BOX 16.1

BLUEPRINT FOR BETTER PRACTICE

The *Agenda 21 for the Travel and Tourism Industry* report asserts that travel and tourism, peace, development and environmental protection are interdependent. It calls on national authorities to cooperate with trade interests to promote an open economic system in which global trade in travel and tourism services can take place on a sustainable basis. Governments should hence take steps to remove trade barriers affecting travel and tourism services. They should also adopt a policy of warning one another of natural disasters that could affect tourists or tourist areas. In general, travel and tourism should (says the report):

- Assist people in leading healthy and productive lives in harmony with nature
- Contribute to the conservation, protection and restoration of the earth's ecosystems
- Be based upon sustainable patterns of production and consumption

For their part, travel and tourism developers on the industry side are urged to:

- Integrate environmental protection into the development process
- Handle development issues with the participation of concerned citizens
- Ensure that planning decisions are adopted at local level
- Use their capacity to create employment for women and indigenous peoples to the fullest extent
- Recognise and support the identity, culture, and interests of indigenous people
- Respect international laws protecting the environment

The Agenda posits ten priority areas for action:

- Waste minimisation, reuse and recycling
- Energy efficiency, conservation and management
- Management of freshwater resources
- Waste water management
- Hazardous substances
- Transport
- Land-use planning and management
- Involving staff, customers and communities in environmental issues
- Design for sustainability
- Partnerships for sustainable development

To these ends WTTC commends the following environmental guidelines:

- Travel and tourism companies should show commitment to environmentally compatible development
- Targets for improvements should be established and monitored
- Environmental commitment should be company-wide
- Education and research into improved environmental programmes should be encouraged

More generally, travel and tourism companies should seek to implement sound environmental principles through self-regulation, recognising that national and international regulation may be inevitable and that preparation is vital. WTTC suggests the following 'systematic and comprehensive' programmes:

'For years I have tried to defend it [tourism] as a valuable asset to a poor region. I stood up for the vast caravan parks which disfigure so much of our coast on the grounds that the caravan was the poor man's holiday cottage. No longer; something has cracked in me. I have come to detest all aspects of mass tourism. It has gone too far, has got out of control.'

Jan Morris (1987)
'Sick of the Tourist Roller-coaster'
The Independent
December 9

- Identify and continue to reduce environmental impact, paying particular attention to new projects
- Pay due regard to environmental concern in design, planning, construction and implementation
- Be sensitive to conservation of environmentally protected or threatened areas and species
- Attach value to scenic aesthetics, achieving landscape enhancement wherever possible
- Practise energy conservation
- Reduce and recycle waste
- Practise freshwater management and control sewage disposal
- Control and diminish air emissions and pollutants
- Monitor, control and reduce noise levels
- Control and reduce environmentally unfriendly products, such as asbestos, CFCs, pesticides and toxics, corrosive, infectious, explosive or flammable materials
- Respect and support historic or religious objects and sites
- Exercise regard for local people, including their history, traditions, culture and future development
- Factor environmental issues into overall development of travel and tourism destinations

HUMAN RIGHTS WATCHDOGS

Tourism Concern

In a relatively short time, the London-based educational charity Tourism Concern has become a leading and serious focus for academic and general debate on the nature and effects of tourism. The charity's stated aims include resolutions to:

- promote greater understanding of tourism's impact on host communities and environments;
- raise awareness of the forms of tourism that respect the rights and interests of people living in tourist receiving areas, promoting tourism that is just, sustainable and participatory;
- work for change in current tourism practice;
- enable tourists and travellers to travel with critical insight and understanding.

A particular focus to which the charity lays claim is in drawing attention to the development issues raised by tourism in developing countries. This does not preclude, however, attention being paid to domestic tourism. Though it keeps a watching brief on environmental issues where these impinge on community concerns, human and civil rights, poverty and inequality, the agenda of Tourism Concern has a decidedly 'People First' emphasis.

Tourism Concern
Stapleton House
277–281 Holloway Road
London N7 8HN
T: +44 (171) 753 3330
F: +44 (171) 753 3331

Survival International

Survival International concentrates on one of the issues that has increasingly come to the fore in recent discussion of the effects of tourism: its impact on indigenous peoples. Of course, tourism development also affects mainstream or large-scale societies, their lives and cultures, in ways that may be far-reaching, but some groups have argued that the impact on indigenous, tribal peoples is potentially more devastating.

Survival International
11–15 Emerald Street
London WC1N 3QL
T: +44 (171) 242 1441
F: +44 (171) 242 1771

It is not just the more recent development of 'ecotourism' or 'nature' tourism, where travellers and holidaymakers travel into more remote regions and come into contact with indigenous tribal peoples, where these impacts are observed. More traditional tourism development has already impinged upon local tribal cultures. 'To all the tourists, visitors, travellers or whatever other name you are called: I beg you, please don't come to Hawai'i,' Puhipau, native Hawaiian film maker and

*'Tourism is killing us . . .
Our lands have been
sucked dry.'*
Native Hawaiian
activist Puhipau
(1994) *In Focus*

BOX 16.2

RESPECTING OTHER CULTURES

Survival International issues a *Danger, Tourists* leaflet giving basic hints for travellers. They include:

- **DON'T** bring in disease. Care must be taken in areas where tribal peoples' immunity to outside diseases may be poor. Some contagious diseases (colds, influenza etc) which affect tourists only mildly can kill tribespeople.
- **DON'T** demean, degrade, insult or patronise tribal peoples. This includes travel advertising and also should govern the behaviour of tour company staff, as well as their customers.
- **DO** recognise land rights, ask permission (or make sure your travel company has done so) before entering tribal peoples' territories, and pay properly for their services or handicrafts.

'In the late twentieth century, international business tourism has become a sophisticated industry... The per capita spending power of the business tourist is considerably higher than that of the leisure traveller, by a ratio of three to one, and the sheer volume of international business tourism has reached an impressive level, the World Tourism Organization estimating that [it] now accounts for 30 per cent of all international tourism.'

Gareth Shaw and Alan M Williams (1994) *Critical Issues in Tourism* Blackwell, Oxford

political activist, wrote in Tourism Concern's magazine, *In Focus*, in 1994. 'Tourism is killing us... We are running out of sweet water. Our lands have been sucked dry. Where once there were taro fields and fishponds, today there are golf courses, hotels and urban sprawl.'

Countries such as Hawaii, which move quickly to intensive tourism development, highlight the impact on local indigenous people: loss of land, access to beaches, water and traditional fishing grounds, as well as the bulldozing of local culture (in Hawaii's case, quite literally: foreign-funded tourist development has often been on sacred sites).

The rise of ecotourism has added to this assault, taking it to more remote regions. The London-based organisation Survival International, which seeks to support tribal peoples in protecting their lives, lands and human rights, is particularly concerned at this new development. 'Even small groups of people, or for that matter, the lone traveller, no matter how sensitive, may have a disruptive effect on local culture. This is true especially if the host community has had little contact with "mainstream" society, as is still the case with some tribal peoples,' a Survival International document argues.

Equally, says the pressure group, tourist development, including that which has nature conservation as an objective, is frequently achieved by moving tribal peoples off their lands, or denying them access to traditional resources. 'For example, in west Nepal, the Chhetri people were moved from their lands to make way for Lake Rara National Park, disrupting their community and leading to new deforestation at the relocation site,' Survival International says. On the other hand, Survival International concedes that many tribal peoples have had long-term relations with the outside world, and may themselves encourage tourism, which can help preserve local cultures and generate employment. It cites as examples North American and Siberian tribal peoples who have set up and run local tourism projects.

PRO-ENVIRONMENT INITIATIVES

World Wide Fund For Nature (WWF)

In 1995 WWF's International Board resolved to 'engage constructively' with travel and tourism industry leaders 'to explore ways to share responsibility for environmental protection' around the world. The Fund's President, HRH The Duke of Edinburgh, proposed a levy of $1 or the equivalent sum on every international tourist visit.

A scheme along these lines was launched the same year, focused initially on the most visited region of the globe, the Mediterranean. The idea was to develop a simple mechanism, in co-operation with IATA and other leading tourism and travel industry stakeholders, to offer tourists the option of making a voluntary one-dollar contribution to a fund which would then be committed to environmental care projects around the Med. WWF National Organisations (NOs) in four Nordic countries (Denmark, Finland, Norway and Sweden) followed up by launching, in late 1996, a pilot partnership with a leading Scandinavian package tour group that involves channelling $1 from each customer buying into a Mediterranean package holiday to WWF to finance conservation projects. The exclusive deal was set up to run for two trial years, with an option to renew each year thereafter. The travel group also committed itself to 'as far as possible' provide and regularly audit environmentally responsible services, products and transport facilities.

More recently, WWF has enlarged the scope of the scheme to embrace other National Organisations and other destination regions, and to tie all activities in with a new global conservation agenda, the WWF 2000 Living Planet campaign. This campaign hinges on conserving 200 natural areas that WWF has identified as top priorities for conservation action, linked to modern sustainable development planning and practice. Participating National Organisations

WWF-UK
Panda House
Weyside Park
Godalming
Surrey GU7 1XR
T: +44 (1483) 426444
F: +44 (1483) 426409
URL: www.wwf.org

'At one extreme is the small number of drifters and explorers who are prepared to try new, exotic and challenging situations in which there is a degree of risk. Such people are absorbed into different cultures with minimum impact. In contrast, organized mass tourists prefer the security of a family environment from which risk has been largely eliminated.'

France, L (ed) (1997)
The Earthscan Reader in Sustainable Tourism

'*Over 500 Mediterranean plant species are threatened with extinction, and three quarters of European sand dunes on the coast between Gibraltar and Sicily have disappeared.'*

UN Environment Programme (1992) *Industry and Environment*, Vol 15, No 3

1 Eber, S (ed) (1992) *Beyond the Green Horizon: Principles for Sustainable Tourism*

2 Forsyth, T (1996) *Sustainable Tourism: Moving from Theory to Practice*

in the WWF family also share in 25 per cent of the scheme's benefits. For its part, WWF commits itself to promote and publicise the involvement of trade partners, apply the proceeds to constructive conservation use and report regularly back to partners on progress at the project delivery end. The $1 levy idea is now being considered or developed by WWF NOs in Austria, Australia, France, Germany, Japan, the Netherlands, the UK and the US. Details of the scheme and Global 200 maps and factsheets are available from WWF-UK.

WWF-UK has also been engaged for some time in background and action research into the environmental impacts of travel and tourism. Among the fruits of these activities are a major 1992 report *Beyond The Green Horizon*[1] developed jointly with Tourism Concern, which includes a wealth of case studies and guidelines for better practice; and a controversial report on the impact of aircraft engine emissions on the ozone layer, published in 1994. A more recent collaboration with Tourism Concern, *Sustainable Tourism: Moving from Theory to Practice* (1996)[2] surveys UK tourism 'greening' trends and questions the worth of industry self-regulation as a sufficient safeguard in itself, calling for official checks and incentives as an essential complement to self-regulation.

Centre for Environmentally Responsible Tourism (CERT)

Centre for Environmentally Responsible Tourism
Indaba House
1 Hyde Way
Thundersley
Essex SS7 3BE
T: +44 (1268) 795 772
F: +44 (1268) 759 834
E: certdesk@aol.com

The Centre for Environmentally Responsible Tourism marks an attempt to evaluate, through customer reports, how well individual holiday companies perform from an environmental perspective. The organisation's methods thus reflect the experience of Liz Gillings, the organisation's founder (together with Will Travers, the environment and animal welfare campaigner).

'Some years ago, I was on holiday in East Africa when I went on a safari trip,' she explains. 'Several minibuses of tourists were parked in scrubland near a tree in which a leopard was resting. Incredibly stupidly, one of the tourists threw a cigarette butt out of one of the vans – and it ignited the dry grass. Within minutes the area was ablaze, and with it the tree where the leopard had been, causing it serious injuries.'

The experience convinced Gillings of the need for a personal initiative to combat poor tourist behaviour, and mitigate tourism impacts on similarly sensitive wildlife areas. As a result, CERT launched a scheme to bring limited consumer pressure on holiday companies. Under the CERT Environmental Kitemark scheme, companies must have a published environmental policy, ensure that their staff are aware of it, and distribute CERT literature and a questionnaire to customers. In addition, the company includes a £1 donation to conservation projects in its holiday prices, and undertakes to match every donation itself. The questionnaire asks holidaymakers simple questions about their holiday, and how they assess the company's environmental performance. After the questionnaires are reviewed, the company may be awarded a gold, silver or bronze star which it may then use in its promotions. The idea is to give the companies an incentive to improve their performance.

'I don't believe in boycotting companies, or proclaiming that tourism is irredeemably bad,' Gillings says. 'Instead, as tourism is clearly going to continue, and can bring pleasure to many people, we are trying to encourage good practice within the industry, and help it contribute to the ideals of conservation and sustainability.'

CERT distributes leaflets, including its guidelines on which the customer questionnaire is based. Though both are relatively simple and non-quantitative, Gillings argues that this is most likely to encourage responses, particularly from holidaymakers who have not previously considered tourism's environmental implications.

> '... one of the tourists threw a cigarette butt out of one of the vans – and it ignited the dry grass. Within minutes the area was ablaze.'

> 'Please do not think that I criticize or cavil
> At a genuine urge to roam
> But why oh why do the wrong people travel
> When the right people stay at home?'
>
> Noël Coward, *Sail Away* (1962)

TRAFFIC – Watching Out for Wildlife

Bringing home a coral necklace, a pair of sunglasses framed in sea turtle shell from the Caribbean or a wild orchid from Thailand's tropical forest lands could become a very costly wrong turn for the unwary (or unscrupulous) European tourist. A new law on international trade in wildlife products came into force on 1 June, 1997, which means illegal importers of products listed under the international CITES (Convention on International Trade in Endangered Species (of Wild Fauna and Flora)) could face imprisonment and fines.

Organisers of the campaign which led to this legal crackdown include the European Commission, WWF and

TRAFFIC International
219c Huntingdon Road
Cambridge CB3 0DL
T: +44 (1223) 277 427
F: +44 (1223) 277 2375
http://www.traffic.org

TRAFFIC (Trade Records Analysis of Fauna and Flora in Commerce). They are currently working in harness with customs and police authorities in all EU States, as well as 11 airlines, 32 airports and at least 25,000 tour operators and travel agencies to distribute leaflets, videos and other materials to alert travellers and traders to the law.

Friends of Conservation

Friends of Conservation
Sloane Square House
Holbein Place
London SW1W 8NS
T: +44 (171) 559 8790
F: +44 (171) 559 8792

Friends of Conservation is an example of a sectoral tourism initiative. It was founded in 1982, its leading figures being Jorie Butler Kent and her husband Geoffrey, of the safari holiday company Abercrombie and Kent. Together with other figures in the safari business, the Kents were concerned at the threat to wildlife from poaching, loss of habitat and at uncontrolled tourist development, particularly in East Africa, where in the early 1980s pressure on national parks and their wildlife was increasing.

The organisation, a registered charity, has initiated several conservation programmes aimed at increasing environmental awareness among tourists and the tourism industry, notably in Kenya, where it has funded the production and wide distribution of leaflets and other educational material. It has helped train local tourist staff, stressing such issues as the need to avoid tourist bus harassment of wildlife, and also funded scientific programmes, such as rhino monitoring. It has also established the Friends of Conservation community conservation and education centre in the Maasai Mara national reserve. It draws for its funding from its member companies as well as a regular round of charitable functions, and regularly sponsors lectures around conservation themes at the Royal Geographical Society in London.

The strength of bodies such as Friends of Conservation lies in its relatively narrow focus and in its ability to bring together commercial operators within the same tourist sector. This, in turn, has the effect of exerting informal peer pressure within an industry that is still known for its individual operators, and their knowledge of one another. As a result, it is arguable that, though it does not seek to lay down industry-wide standards, it has had a wider effect than simply the sum of its individual projects. For a small body, it boasts an impressive list of board members and supporting companies (from British Airways and Inter-Continental Hotels and Resorts through to Thomson Tour Operations, as well as smaller, specialist firms), as well as distinguished African conservationists on a panel of scientific advisers. It also has an individual membership scheme.

The Conservation Foundation and Ford Conservation Awards

The Conservation Foundation was set up in London in 1981 by David Bellamy, the botany professor and TV celebrity famed for his nature documentaries, and an academic colleague, David Shreeve. After collaborating success-fully on a high-profile national campaign to save trees and hedgerows threatened by Dutch Elm Disease, Bellamy and Shreeve wanted to put other conservation projects in need of funding in touch with companies that showed willing to put up cash for environmental initiatives.

The Conservation
Foundation
1 Kensington Gore
London SW7 2AR
T: +44 (171) 591 3111
F: +44 (171) 591 3110
E: conservef@gn.apc.org

The Foundation has since played a significant part in getting a vast range of conservation projects off the ground, from schemes within Britain and Europe to set up nature reserves, restore built heritage and nurture conservation skills and traditions, to scientific research in tropical rainfor-est areas, tree planting and education programmes in Africa and, more recently, primary environmental care and conser-vation programmes in Eastern and Central Europe and the former Soviet Union.

From an early stage in its development, one of the Foundation's most energetic sponsors on the industry side was Ford of Europe, initially in the person of its former Vice President of Public Affairs, John Waddell, a dedicated naturalist and the origina-tor of a highly successful 'Save the Village Pond' campaign mounted in the early '70s by Ford of Britain. The Ford connection was later cemented by the creation of a Europe-wide award scheme, the Henry Ford European Conservation Awards, adminis-tered by the Conservation Foundation since 1984. Though not specifically directed towards supporting projects linked to tourism issues, the scheme has become increas-ingly engaged in such projects over recent years, in keeping with the Foundation's view that responsibly managed tourism can be a resounding conservation plus in many situations that might otherwise seem strictly limited by economic and social pressures.

Federation of Tour Operators (FTO)

Set up in 1967, the Federation of Tour Operators (originally known as the Tour Operators' Study Group) is an alliance of 17 UK-based package tour operators, responsible for 90 per cent of the British market in overseas holidays. It keeps a watching brief over conditions and standards of travel, accommodation, safety, health and hygiene overseas and in transit from UK points of departure. Delegates from each member operator confer every month in open forum to debate issues and developments in the travel industry, as they affect holidaymakers. Through a trust fund, it also administers a bonding system for underwriting compensa-tion claims against its members. In 1970, the FTO set up an international chapter, the International Federation of Tour

Federation of Tour
Operators
170 High Street
Lewes
East Sussex
BN7 1YE
T: +44 (1273) 477 722
F: +44 (1273) 483 746

'Only some 30 per cent of sewage from coastal towns receives any treatment before being discharged into the Mediterranean.'

UN Environment Programme (1992) Industry and Environment, Vol 15, No 3

Operators (IFTO), which links tour companies from 19 countries and represents the interests of over 40 million package tour holidaymakers a year.

Environmental issues are recognised by FTO and IFTO alike as a key concern of any modern tour company though, as FTO Secretary-General Alan Flook notes, national responses differ. 'In Britain, the dominant pressure from the customer side is for improving health and safety standards in resorts and hotels. In mainland Europe, especially Germany and Scandinavia, clients appear far more concerned with broader environmental quality issues. They are much fussier about making sure the destinations they visit offer unspoilt surroundings and opportunity to sample wide open spaces and off-the-beaten-track experiences,' he reflects, though he adds that 'there are signs that this split is growing narrower year on year as British tourists wise up to the rewards of insisting that quality holiday environments mean more than taps that work or swimming-pools that don't get dirty.'

In 1990 IFTO conceived the ECOMOST project, a systematic effort to gain a better understanding on the industry side of how tourism could be made more sustainable and how ills arising from mass tourism in resort areas could be countered and designed out of packages. The ECOMOST report, authored by Peter Hughes and published in 1994, sums up the outcomes of a health-check run on the package tour phenomenon in two classic Mediterranean island resort destinations, Mallorca and Rhodes. Among its decidedly outspoken conclusions appear the following observations:

- Tourism is a stimulant for good and bad. It can lead to degradation and disorder but it can also work ... as a powerful preservative for landscape, species and historic monuments. It can do the same for people.
- More effort has to be devoted to making local people aware of the value of the scenery and wildife that surround them... It is unrealistic to expect any earnest efforts towards conservation [to succeed] if the ecology of an area is underrated by the people who should be its custodians.
- Tourism is the last domain where individuality should be sacrificed. Why should resorts slavishly emulate the culture of their visitors? ... Tourist destinations neglect their singularity at their peril.
- Nor should resorts shy from excellence... The most successful tourist destinations know exactly the kind of tourism that they want. They define it, plan for it, stick to it and profit by it.

If such prescriptions represent the considered view of the modern tour industry, then we have indeed come a long way from the lager-lubricated sun, sea and sex packages of the '70s. The problem, of course, is moving from such words to deeds.

CONSULTANCIES

Centre for the Advancement of Responsive Travel (CART)

A number of organisations now offer consultancy advice on travel and tourism from the point of view of its ethics and sustainability. Roger Millman, a geographer at the University of North London who now also works as a development consultant, established the Centre for the Advancement of Responsive Travel in 1988 after, in his own words, seeing a need for such a service. 'CART offers hints and tips to people travelling for a variety of reasons to places near and far, but especially to those planning

---

BOX 16.3

CREDO FOR THE CARING TRAVELLER

- Journey with an open mind and gentle heart. Travel in a spirit of humility and with a genuine desire to meet and talk with local people.
- Appreciate all the cultures you discover. Be aware of the feelings of the local people; prevent what might be offensive behaviour. Photography particularly must respect persons.
- Cultivate the habit of listening and observing, rather than merely hearing or seeing or knowing all the answers. Offer your friendship to everyone you meet, heeding local custom.
- Accept with grace and gratitude the diversity you encounter. Realise that other people may have concepts of time and have thought patterns which are very different, not inferior – only different, from your own.
- Respect and protect the natural environment which sustains all life. Instead of seeing only the beach paradise or the game reserve, discover the richness of another culture and way of life.
- Respect and thank your hosts for your welcome. Get acquainted with local customs and respect them.
- Remember that you are only one of many visitors; do not expect special privileges.
- When shopping through bargaining, remember that the poorest merchant will give up a profit rather than give up his/her personal dignity.
- Make no promises to local people or to new friends that you cannot implement.
- Spend time each day reflecting on your experiences in order to deepen your understanding. What enriches you may be robbing others. Encourage others to travel the world in peace, by your spirit, words and actions.
- If you really want a home away from home – why travel?

Source: Centre for the Advancement of Responsive Travel

---

individual and group visits and exchanges between North and South countries who are concerned for better cross-cultural understanding.'

CART is a personal consultancy – it does not actually train tour guides or travel agency staff – but it concentrates on what Dr Millman, a founder-member of Tourism Concern, believes are the six main aspects of planning any visit: preliminary planning and management; group processes and dynamics; social and cultural considerations; gathering information about the places to be visited; organisational details; and the means for reflection, before, during and after the travel experience. 'CART aims to raise issues and questions which many tour planners, tour group leaders and members of tour groups feel (if only, maybe especially, from heeding their past travel mistakes) need to be heeded by others as they get ready to travel,' he says.

Centre for the
Advancement of
Responsive Travel
70 Dry Hill Park Road
Tonbridge
Kent TN10 3BX
(include sae with enquiries)

CART also issues a Credo for the Caring Traveller which (while incorporating many of the points already discussed, and shared by many other commentators) makes its own distinctive points.

AN ISSUE APART: CURBING CHILD SEX TOURISM

According to United Nations estimates, there are at least a million children involved in prostitution in Asia alone. 'Tourism is not the cause of child sexual exploitation, but it often provides easy access to vulnerable children,' the ECPAT coalition against child sex tourism argues. Research by ECPAT and other bodies suggests child prostitution is increasingly associated with tourism in a number of countries. These include, in South America: Costa Rica, Cuba, the Dominican Republic and Venezuela. In Africa, 'the Gambia has become a popular holiday destination for middle-aged European women seeking sex with Gambian males, some as young as sixteen,' the coalition says. In Kenya, it reports increasing sex tourism, including the exploitation of children, both in Nairobi and the coastal resorts of Mombasa, Malindi and Lamu. Sex tourism is also believed to be developing in Senegal, while prostitution of young boys is said to be on the increase in Mauritania, and links with the tourist trade and child exploitation are reported in north African cities such as Alexandria, Marakesh and Tunis.

ECPAT UK (formerly The
Coalition on Child
Prostitution and Tourism)
Unit 4
The Stable Yard
Broomgrove Road
London SW9 9TL
T: +44 (171) 924 9555
F: +44 (171) 738 4110
E: antislavery@gn.apc.org

In Asia, sex tourism has spread beyond Thailand and the Philippines, and is also found in Goa, Sri Lanka and in parts of Indonesia, the coalition says. The trafficking of young women for the sex trade also involves Burma, Cambodia, Bangladesh and Vietnam. The richer Asian nations, including Japan and Taiwan, are reported to have a sex industry that recruits women from other countries in the region – while the phenomenon of Japanese men travelling to Taiwan, Thailand and the Philippines on 'sex tours' has sparked opposition within those countries.

Nor is Europe immune from the effects of sex tourism and trafficking. Police and non-governmental bodies have reported increasing sex industry activity in tourist areas. This includes the trafficking of young women, and some boys, from the eastern European nations to the west, as well as a flourishing sex industry in Romania, Russia and Poland.

An international trade in pornography, including child pornography, is also well established. Recently the travel industry has begun to take action to discourage sex tourism, while several nations are initiating laws against some of its aspects, particularly those involving children. In 1994 the United Federation of Travel Agents drew up a charter which pledges 'to combat the prostitution of children connected to so-called "sex tourism" and to protect the child victims of such tourists'.

In October 1996 the World Tourism Organization, meeting in Cairo, passed a motion calling on the industry to 'educate staff about the negative consequences of sex tourism, to develop and strengthen professional codes of conduct and industry self-regulatory mechanisms against the practice of sex tourism, and to warn tourists particularly against engaging in child sex tourism, denouncing its criminal nature and the manner in which children are forced into prostitution.'

In Britain, groups such as the Association of British Travel Agents (ABTA), the Association of Independent Tour Operators (AITO), the Council for Travel and Tourism, the Federation of Tour Operators (FTO), and the UK Chapter of the Pacific-Asia Travel Association (PATA) have expressed support for curbs on sex tourism. The Co-op TravelCare company gave out leaflets to its customers in 1996, calling on them to lobby their MPs for laws against the child sex trade. Overseas, some German and Australian tour companies have begun to press the hotels they use in Asia to prohibit child prostitution on their premises, while in France and Switzerland some travel agents are also beginning to do more to inform their customers about the issue.

Most recently, many governments as well as tourism bodies, law enforcement agencies, child welfare organisations and other groups sent delegates to the World Congress Against the Sexual Exploitation of Children which was held in Stockholm in August 1996. This declared that the sexual exploitation of children 'amounts to forced labour and a contemporary form of slavery', and adopted a declaration and agenda for action, committing 119 governments to introduce measures to end the trade in child sex tourism.

Many nations have begun to clamp down on sex tourism. Some western countries have legislation which allows their citizens to be tried at home for sexual offences committed abroad. They include Denmark, Finland, Iceland, Norway, Sweden and

BOX 16.4

SEX TOURISM

As we have already seen, many early travellers and tourists found the possibility of amorous encounters an added inducement to journey away from home. Romance – or sometimes simply sex – is a lure that is still employed in its advertising by the modern tourist industry. Sometimes the suggestion of romance is implicit, with holiday brochures showing carefree, swimsuited couples. Other approaches are more explicit, with advertising for some tour companies seeking to woo younger holidaymakers with the thinly disguised promise of a week or two's unbridled hedonism, of the 'sun, sea, sand and sex' variety.

Recent decades, however, have seen a rise in a more disturbing form of 'sex tourism' – the phenomenon in which travellers deliberately seek out those parts of the world in which sex with local people is readily available. The effect of this development is to create an economy where sex, whether heterosexual or homosexual, becomes a commodity, and where local people are exploited. Along the way, local social patterns and cultures are degraded.

While adult prostitution occurs in many if not most cultures, and is subject to varying degrees of legality, the advent of mass travel has led to a more direct link with the tourist trade in parts of the world. At one extreme, Amsterdam's central red light district, for example, has effectively attained the status of an accepted feature on the conventional tourist map, visited by tourists who are seeking sights, not sex. Parts of New Orleans' French Quarter, suitably sanitised, have achieved the same reputation. Elsewhere, however, sex is the draw, and the visitors, whether from elsewhere in the country or from abroad, are the willing consumers.

Tourism per se may not initially generate a sex industry. Prostitution may be a result of many factors, economic, social, political, legal and cultural. The red light quarters that grew up in some South East Asian cities in the 1960s and 1970s, for example, were in large part a result of the social and economic dislocation caused by warfare across much of Indo-China. In particular, the presence of large numbers of foreign troops with money and desire to spend – notably those of the United States – fuelled the development of the sex trade, with its proliferation of girlie-bars and brothels. Subsequently, the growth of peace-time tourism has simply brought new customers to places like Thailand or the Philippines.

For many people living in relative poverty, the attraction of tourists is the money they can bring, and again sex can become a tradeable commodity. But for both tourist and local, this can bring with it dangers. Early European travellers around the globe brought back syphilis; today, the spread of sexually transmitted diseases, notably Aids, can also be increased through tourism. Green travellers should also be aware that not only are they likely to be at risk of disease through unprotected sex, but that the sex-tourism trade is in many cities connected with organised crime, including the trafficking of drugs and thousands of young people.

Perhaps the most notorious example of sex tourism is the child sex trade which has developed in many parts of the world, particularly but by no means exclusively in Asia. In some cases, this has arisen because tourists looking for sex believe that younger women or men are less likely to be infected by transmittable diseases (in some countries, a girl's virginity may be repeatedly 'restored' to persuade a client of her safety as well as her desirability). In other cases, however, the greater ease of travel has led to a growth in paedophile sex tourism.

A number of groups are campaigning against the child prostitution trade, and some sections of the tourist industry are beginning to give them their support. In Britain, the group ECPAT UK is working to curb the sexual exploitation of children by tourists. The group is the British branch of ECPAT, the international campaign against the commercial sexual exploitation of children, which was originally set up in Asia. In Britain, the campaign is supported by the charities Anti-Slavery International, CAFOD, Christian Aid, the Jubilee Campaign, the NSPCC, the Save the Children Fund, NCH Action for Children and World Vision UK. Recently, the travel industry has begun to take action to discourage sex tourism, while several nations are initiating laws against some of its aspects, particularly those involving children.

Switzerland. According to the Coalition on Child Prostitution and Tourism, similar laws are also being introduced or debated in Germany, France, Australia, the USA, Belgium, New Zealand, Ireland, Italy and Canada. In November 1996 the British Government announced that it would introduce legislation to provide for the extra-territorial prosecution of child sex offenders. Several Britons have in recent years been jailed abroad (in Thailand, Cambodia and the Philippines) for child sex offences. In late 1997, this new legislation entered into force as part of the Sex Offenders Act. It is now an offence for UK citizens and residents to engage in underage sexual activity with a child in another country where it is also illegal. It is also an offence for individuals, groups or organisations to conspire or incite others to travel overseas to engage in sexual activities with children. By late 1998, however, there had been no reported charges or prosecutions under the new law.

CHAPTER 17

CONNECTIONS: ABC LISTING OF ORGANISATIONS, OPERATORS AND RESOURCES

This list of postal and electronic mail addresses, websites, telephone and fax lines offers initial access to a selection of organisations professing a stake in promoting environmentally and socially responsible travel and tourism. It provides leads for readers interested in personally researching and planning holidays that don't cost the Earth, or in networking with others who share such concerns. Wherever possible, readers seeking information should contact the source closest to their intended destination or the most specialised body in their area of interest, then follow up any further leads they suggest.

Every effort has been made to update the information at the time of publication but details are liable to change. Please write to the publisher if you have corrections or additions to offer for possible sequel editions of this Guide, or a cautionary tale to share!

INTERNATIONAL INDUSTRY, CROSS-SECTORAL AND INTERGOVERNMENTAL BODIES

Earth Council/Consejo de la Tierra/Conseil de la Terre
PO Box 2323-1002
San José, Costa Rica
T: +506 256 1611
F: +506 255 2197
E: ecouncil@igc.apc.org
URL: www.ecouncil.ac.cr

ECoNETT Project Office (at WTTC)
20 Grosvenor Place
London SW1X 7TT
T: +44 (171) 235 2135
F: +44 (171) 235 2445
E: 106316.2226@compuserve.com
URL: http://www.wttc.org

European Blue Flag
Seymour House
Muspole Street
Norwich NR3 1DJ
T: +44 (1603) 766 076
F: +44 (1603) 760 580

Federation of Nature and National Parks in Europe
Kröllstrasse 5
D-8352 Grafenau
Germany
T: +49 (8552) 96 10 00
F: +49 (8552) 961019
E: europarc@t-online.de

Green Flag International
PO Box 396, Linton
Cambridge CB1 6UL
T: +44 (1223) 890 250
F: +44 (1223) 890 258

Green Globe
PO Box 396, Linton
Cambridge CB1 6UL
T: +44 (1223) 890 255
F: +44 (1223) 890 258
E: GreenGlobe@compuserve.com

UN Environment Programme
Industry & Environment Programme Office
Tour Mirabeau 39–43
Quai André Citroen
75739 Paris
Cedex 15
France
T: +33 (1) 44 37 14 50
F: +33 (1) 40 58 88 74
E: unepie@unep.fr
URL: www.unepie.org/contact.html

World Conservation Union (IUCN)
Rue Mauverney 28
CH-1196 Gland
Switzerland
T: +41 (22) 999 0001
F: +41 (22) 999 0002
E: mail@hq.iucn.ch
URL: http://www.iucn.org

World Tourism Organization
Capitán Haya 42
28020 Madrid
Spain
T: +34 (91) 567 8100
F: +34 (91) 571 3732
E: omt@dial.eunet.es

World Travel and Tourism Council
20 Grosvenor Place
London SW1X 7TT
T: +44 (171) 838 9400
F: +44 (171) 838 9050
E: 100421,702@compuserve.com
URL: www.wttc.org

WWF International
World Conservation Centre
CH-1196 Gland
Switzerland
T: +41 (22) 64 91 11
F: +41 (22) 64 42 38

INDEPENDENT ETHICAL AND PRO-ENVIRONMENT PRESSURE AND INTEREST GROUPS

British Trust for Ornithology
The Nunnery, Thetford
Norfolk IP24 2PU
T: +44 (1842) 750 050
F: +44 (1842) 750 030

Blue Flag Federation for Environmental Education in Europe
Friluftsradet Olaf Palmes Gade 10
DK 2100 Copenhagen
Denmark

Centre for Environmentally Responsible Tourism (CERT)
Indaba House
1 Hyde Way
Thundersley
Essex SS7 3BG
T: +44 (1268) 795 772
F: +44 (1268) 759 834

Centre for the Advancement of Responsive Travel
70 Dry Hill Park Road
Tonbridge
Kent TN10 3BX, UK
(include sae with enquiries)

ECPAT UK, formerly The Coalition on Child Prostitution and Tourism
Unit 4
The Stable Yard
Broomgrove Road
London SW9 9TL
T: +44 (171) 924 9555
F: +44 (171) 738 4110
E: antislavery@gn.apc.org

Common Ground
PO Box 25309
London NW5 1ZA
T: +44 (171) 267 2144

Council for National Parks
246 Lavender Hill
London SW11 1LJ
T: +44 (171) 924 4077
F: +44 (171) 924 5761

The Conservation Foundation
1 Kensington Gore
London SW7 2AR
T: +44 (171) 591 3111
F: +44 (171) 591 3110
E: conservef@gn.apc.org

Council for the Protection of Rural England
Warwick House
25 Buckingham Palace Road
London SW1W 0PP
T: +44 (171) 976 6433
F: +44 (171) 976 6373

EGA Ecology Unit (UK)
Environmental Golf Services
51 South Street
Dorking
Surrey RH4 2JX
T: +44 (1306) 743 288
F: +44 (1306) 742 496

European Golf Association Ecology Unit (Europe)
Chaussée de la Hulpe 110
B-1050 Brussels
Belgium
T: +32 (2) 675 8743
F: +32 (2) 675 4062

Friends of Conservation
Sloane Square House
Holbein Place
London SW1W 8NS
T: +44 (171) 559 8790
F: +44 (171) 559 8792

London Cycling Campaign
Unit 228
30 Great Guildford Street
London SE1 0HS
T: +44 (171) 928 7220
F: +44 (171) 928 2318

Marine Conservation Society
9 Gloucester Road
Ross-on-Wye
Herefordshire HR9 5BU
T: +44 (1989) 566 017
F: +44 (1989) 567 815

The National Trust
36 Queen Anne's Gate
London SW1M 9AS
T: +44 (171) 222 9251
F: +44 (171) 222 5097
URL: www.nationaltrust.org.uk

The Soil Association
Bristol House
40–56 Victoria Street
Bristol BS1 6BY
T: +44 (117) 929 0661
F: +44 (117) 925 2504
E: soilassoc@gn.apc.org

Surfers Against Sewage
Unit 2 Workshops
Wheal Kitty, St Agnes
Cornwall TR5 0RD
T: +44 (1872) 553 001
F: +44 (1872) 552 615
E: info@sas.org.uk
URL: http://www.sas.org.uk

Survival International
11–15 Emerald Street
London WC1N 3QL
T: +44 (171) 242 1441
F: +44 (171) 242 1771

Tourism Concern
Stapleton House
277–281 Holloway Road
London N7 8HN
T: +44 (171) 753 3330
F: +44 (171) 753 3331
E: tourconcern@gn.apc.org
URL: www.oneworld.org/tourconcern

TRAFFIC International
219c Huntingdon Road
Cambridge CB3 0DL
T: +44 (1223) 277 427
F: +44 (1223) 277 237

Transport 2000
Walkden House
10 Melton Street
London NW1 2EJ
T: +44 (171) 388 8386
F: +44 (171) 388 2481

The Vegetarian Society
Parkdale
Dunham Road
Altrincham
Cheshire WA14 4QG
T: +44 (161) 928 0793
F: +44 (161) 926 9182

The Whale and Dolphin Conservation Society
Alexander House
James Street West
Bath
Avon BA1 2BT
T: +44 (1225) 334 511
F: +44 (1225) 480 097
URL: http://www.wacs.org

Wild Oceans
International House
Bank Road
Bristol BS15 2LX
T: +44 (117) 984 8040
F: +44 (117) 967 4444
E: wildinfo@wildwings.co.uk
URL: www.wildwings.co.uk

WWF-UK
Panda House
Weyside Park
Godalming
Surrey GU7 1XR
T: +44 (1483) 426 444
F: +44 (1483) 426 409
URL: www.wwf-uk.org
[Will also provide contact details for other national WWF organisations]

GREEN-MINDED ACTION OR PROJECT GROUPS AND ACTIVITY DESTINATIONS

British Executive Service Overseas
164 Vauxhall Bridge Road
London SW1 2RB
T: +44 (171) 630 0644
F: +44 (171) 630 0624

British Trust for Conservation Volunteers
36 St Mary's Street
Wallingford
Oxford OX10 0EU
T: +44 (1491) 839 766
F: +44 (1491) 839 646

Centre for Alternative Technology
Llwyngwern Quarry
Machynlleth
Powys SY20 9AZ, Wales
T: +44 (1654) 702400

Community Service Volunteers
237 Pentonville Road
London N1 9NJ
T: +44 (171) 278 6601

Conservation Volunteers Ireland
PO Box 3836
Ballsbridge
Dublin 4
Republic of Ireland
T: +353 (1) 668 1844

Earthwatch Institute
Belsyre Court
57 Woodstock Road
Oxford OX2 6HJ
T: +44 (1865) 311 600
F: +44 (1865) 311 383

Earthwatch International HQ
680 Mount Auburn Street
PO Box 403
Watertown
MA 92272-9924
USA
T: +1 (617) 926 8200
F: +1 (617) 926 8532

Farm Holiday Bureau
National Agricultural Centre
Stoneleigh Park
Warwickshire CV8 2LZ
T: +44 (1203) 696 909
F: +44 (1203) 696 630

Field Studies Council
Preston Montford Hall
Montford Bridge
Shrewsbury SY4 1HW
T: +44 (1743) 850 674
F: +44 (1743) 850 178
URL: www.field-studies-council.org

Landmark Trust
Shottesbrooke
Maidenhead
Berkshire SL6 3SW
T: +44 (1628) 825 925
F: +44 (1628) 825 417

National Centre for Volunteering
Regent's Wharf
8 All Saints Street
London N1 9RL
T: +44 (171) 520 8900
F: +44 (171) 520 8910
E: centrevol@aol.com
URL: www.volunteering.org.uk

Scottish Conservation Projects Trust
Balallan House
24 Allan Park
Stirling FK8 2QG
Scotland
T: +44 (1786) 479 697
F: +44 (1786) 465 359
E: scp@btcv.org.uk

Sustrans
35 King Street
Bristol BS1 4DZ
T: +44 (117) 929 0888
F: +44 (117) 929 4173

Vacation Work Publications
9 Park End Street
Oxford OX1 1HJ
T: +44 (1865) 241 978
F: +44 (1865) 790 885
URL: www.vacationwork.co.uk

Voluntary Service Overseas
317 Putney Bridge Road
London SW15 2PN
T: +44 (181) 780 2266
F: +44 (181) 780 3300
URL: http://oneworld.org/vso

Willing Workers on Organic Farms
PO Box 2675
Lewes
Sussex BN7 1RB
T/F: +44 (1273) 476 286

Waterway Recovery Group
c/o Inland Waterways Association
PO Box 114
Rickmansworth WD3 1ZY
T: +44 (1923) 711 114
F: +44 (1923) 897 000
E: iwa@waterway.demon.co.uk

TOURISM AWARD SCHEMES AND MAJOR PROFESSIONAL OR TRADE SECTOR ASSOCIATIONS

British Airways Tourism for Tomorrow
Waterside (HBBG)
PO Box 365
Harmondsworth
West Drayton UB7 0GB
T: +44 (181) 562 3868
F: +44 (181) 562 8604
E: environment.1.branch@british-airways.com
URL: www.british-airways.com

Ecological Tourism Europe
(Ökologischer Tourismus in Europa
(OTE) e.V.)
Am Michaelshof 8-10
D-53177 Bonn
Germany
T: +49 (228) 359 008
F: +49 (228) 359 096
[Alliance of 12 independent environment and development organisations developing

a seal of approval – Grüner Koffer or Green Suitcase – awarded to 'environmentally oriented' tourism venues, hoteliers, travel companies and tour operators.]

Federation of Tour Operators and International Federation of Tour Operators
170 High Street
Lewes
East Sussex BN7 1YE
T: +44 (1273) 477 722
F: +44 (1273) 483 746
[FTO is a group of 17 major UK-based tour operators representing over 90 per cent of the British overseas package tour market. IFTO, the international counterpart, brings together tour operators from 19 countries and aims to represent the interests of some 40 million tour passengers a year.]

International Air Transport Association
Route de l'Aéroport 33
PO Box 672
CH 1215 Geneva 15
Switzerland
T: +41 (22) 799 2060
F: +41 (22) 799 2686
E: DobbieL@iata.org

International Civil Aviation
Organization
1000 Sherbrook Street West
Suite 400
Montreal
Quebec H3A 2R2
Canada
T: +1 (514) 286 6371
F: +1 (514) 285 6744

International Hotel Association
80, rue de la Roquette
75544 Paris
France
T: +33 (1) 47 00 8457
F: +33 (1) 47 00 6455

International Hotels Environment
Initiative
5 Cleveland Place
St James's
London SW1Y 6JJ
T: +44 (171) 321 6384
F: +44 (171) 321 6418

Pacific Asia Travel Association
1 Montgomery Street,
Telesis Tower
Suite 1000
San Francisco
CA 94014-4539
USA
T: +1 (415) 986 4646
F: +1 (415) 986 3458
E: patahq@ix.netcom.com
[With over 2000 members from both
public and private sectors, PATA sets
regional standards for environmental and
cultural safeguards over sensitive environ-
ments – the Green Leaf scheme.]

SPORT, ADVENTURE, SPIRITUAL AND OTHER SPECIAL LEISURE ACTIVITY BODIES

Balloon Club of Great Britain
Montgolfier House
Fairoaks Airport
Chobham
Surrey GU24 8HU
T: +44 (1276) 858 529

British Canoe Union
John Dudderidge House
Adbolton Lane
West Bridgford
Nottingham NG2 5AS
T: +44 (115) 982 1100
F: +44 (115) 982 1797
E: info@bcu.org.uk
URL: http://www.bcu.org.uk

British Cycling Federation
National Cycling Centre
Stuart Street
Manchester M11 4DQ
T: +44 (161) 230 2301
F: +44 (161) 231 0591

British Hang-Gliding and Paragliding Association
The Old Schoolroom
Loughborough Road
Leicester LE4 5PJ
T: +44 (116) 2611322
F: +44 (116) 261 1323

British Holidays and Home Parks Association
Chichester House
6 Pullman Court
Great Western Road
Gloucester GL1 3ND
T: +44 (1452) 526 911
F: +44 (1452) 307 226

British Horse Society
Stoneleigh Deer Park
Kenilworth
Warwickshire CV8 2LR
T: +44 (1929)707 700
F: +44 (1926) 707 800
E: inquiry@bhs.org.uk
URL: http://www.bhs.org.uk

British Mountaineering Council
177–179 Burton Road
West Didsbury
Manchester M20 2BB
T: +44 (161) 445 4747
F: +44 (161) 445 4500
URL: www.thebmc.co.uk

British Orienteering Federation
Riverdale
Dale Road North
Darley Dale
Matlock
Derbyshire DE4 2HX
T: +44 (1629) 734 042

British Parachute Association
6 Wharf Way
Glen Parva
Leicester LG2 9JF
T: +44 (116) 278 5271
F: +44 (116) 247 7662
E: skydive@bpa.org.uk
URL: www.bpa.org.uk

British Sub-Aqua Club
Telfords Quay
Ellesmere Port
Cheshire L65 4FY
T: +44 (151) 350 6200
F: +44 (151) 350 6215
URL: www.bsac.com

British Waterways
Willow Grange
Church Road, Watford
Hertfordshire WD1 3QA
T: +44 (1923) 226 422
F: +44 (1923) 226 081

Camping and Caravanning Club
Greenfields House
Westwood Way
Coventry CV4 8JH
T: +44 (1203) 694 995
F: +44 (1203) 694 886

Canoe Camping Club
25 Waverley Road
South Norwood
London SE25 4HT
T: +44 (181) 654 1835

Cyclists' Touring Club
Cotterell House
69 Meadrow
Godalming
Surrey GU7 3HS
T: +44 (1483) 417 217
F: +44 (1483) 426 994

Dartington Hall Programme
Totnes
Devon TQ9 6EL
T: +44 (1803) 866 688
F: +44 (1803) 865 551
E: dart.hall.prog@dartington-hall.org.uk
URL: dartington.u-net.com

National Federation of Sea Schools
Purlins
159 Woodlands Road
Woodlands
Southampton
Hampshire SO40 7GL
T/F: +44 (1703) 293 822
URL: www.nfss.co.uk

National Retreat Association
Central Hall
256 Bermondsey Street
London SE1 3UJ
T: +44 (171) 357 7736
F: +44 (171) 357 7724

Pedestrians' Association
126 Aldersgate Street
London EC1A 4JQ
T: +44 (171) 490 0750
F: +44 (171) 608 0353

Ramblers Association
1-5 Wandsworth Road
London SW8 2XX
T: +44 (171) 359 8500
F: +44 (171) 359 8501
E: ramblers@london-ramblers.org.uk
URL: www.ramblers.org.uk

Resurgence
Ford House
Hartland
Bideford
Devon EX39 6EE
T: +44 (1237) 441 293
F: +44 (1237) 441 203

Raleigh International
Raleigh House
27 Parson's Green Lane
London SW6 4HZ
T: +44 (171) 371 8585
F: +44 (171) 371 5118
E: info@raleigh.org.uk
URL: www.raleigh.org.uk

Royal Geographical Society
1 Kensington Gore
London SW7 2AR
T: +44 (171) 591 3000
F: +44 (171) 591 3001
URL: www.rgs.org
(Expedition Advisory Service
T: +44 (171) 591 3030;
F: +44 (171) 591 3031)

Royal Scottish Geographical Society
10 Randolph Crescent
Edinburgh EG3 7TU
Scotland
T: +44 (131) 225 3330

Royal Yachting Association
RYA House
Romsey Road
Eastleigh
Hampshire SO50 9YA
T: +44 (1703) 627 400
F: +44 (1703) 629 924
URL: www.rya.org.uk

Schumacher College
The Old Postern
Dartington
Totnes
Devon TQ9 6EA
T: +44 (1803) 865 934
F: +44 (1803) 866 899
E: schumcoll@gn.apc.org
URL: www.gn.apc.org/schumacher
college/

Ski Club of Great Britain
The White House
57–63 Church Road
Wimbledon
London SW19 5SB
T: +44 (181) 410 2000
F: +44 (181) 410 2001
E: info@skiclub.co.uk
URL: www.skiclub.co.uk

Skyros
92 Prince of Wales Road
London NW5 3NE
T: +44 (171) 267 4424/284 3065
F: +44 (171) 284 3063

Youth Hostels Association
Trevelyan House
8 St Stephen's Hill
St Albans
Hertfordshire AL1 2DY
T: +44 (1727) 855 215
F: +44 (1727) 844 126

OFFICIAL NATIONAL AGENCIES, TOURISM PROMOTERS OR FRANCHISEES, BY COUNTRY

Antigua

Antigua Department of Tourism
PO Box 363
Long and Thames Streets
St John's
Antigua
T: +1809 462 0480
F: +1809 462 2483

London Office:
15 Thayer Street
London W1M 5LD
T: +44 (171) 486 7073
F: +44 (171) 486 9970

New York Office:
Suite 311
610 Fifth Avenue
New York

NY 10020
USA
T:+1 (212) 541 4117
F:+1 (212) 757 1607

Argentina

Secretaría de Turismo

Calle Suipacha 1111, 21°
1368 Buenos Aires
Argentina
T: +54 (1) 312 5621
F: +54 (1) 313 6834

New York Office:
12 West 56th Street
New York
NY 10019
USA
T: +1 (212) 603 0443
F: +1 (212) 397 3523

Australia

Australian Tourism Industry Association

Tourism House
40 Blackall Street
Barton
ACT 2600
Australia
T: +61 (6) 273 1000
F: +61 (6) 273 4999

Australian Tourist Commission

80 William Street
Woolloomooloo
Sydney
NSW 2011
Australia
T: +61 (2) 360 1111
F: +61 (2) 331 3385

Tourism New South Wales

140 George Street, Sydney
NSW 2001, Australia
T: +61 (2) 931 1525
F: +61 (2) 931 1516

London Office:
10–18 Putney Hill
London SW15 6AA
T: +44 (181) 789 1020
F: +44 (181) 789 4577

Northern Territory Tourist Commission

PO Box 1155
43 Mitchell Street
Darwin
NT 0801
Australia
T: +61 (89) 993 900
F: +61 (89) 993 888

London Office:
1st Floor, Beaumont House
Lambton Road
London SW20 0LW
T: +44 (181) 944 2992
F: +44 (181) 944 2993

Queensland Tourist and Travel Corporation

36th Floor
Riverside Centre
123 Eagle Street
Brisbane
QLD 4000
Australia
T: +61 (7) 38 33 54 00
F: +61 (7) 38 33 54 79

London Office:
Queensland House
392 The Strand
London WC2R 0LZ
T: +44 (171) 240 0525
F: +44 (171) 836 5881

South Australia Tourism Commission

170–178 North Terrace
Adelaide
SA 5000
Australia
T: +61 (8) 303 2222
F: +61 (8) 303 2231

London Office:
(as Northern Territory)
T: +44 (181) 944 5375
F: +44 (181) 944 5326

Tourism Tasmania

Argyle Street
Hobart
TAS 7001
Australia
T: +61 (02) 347 202.

Western Australia Tourism Commission

16 St George's Terrace
Perth
WA 6000
Australia
T: +61 (9) 220 1700
F: +61 (9) 220 1702

London Office:
Western Australia House
115 The Strand
London WC2R 0AJ
T: +44 (171) 240 2881
F: +44 (171) 379 9826

Bahamas

Bahamas Ministry of Tourism

PO Box N-3701
Bay Street
Nassau
The Bahamas
T: +1809 322 7500
F: +1809 328 0945

New York Office:
28th Floor North
150 East 52nd Street
New York
NY 10022
USA
T: +1 (212) 758 2777
F: +1 (212) 758 6531

Bahamas

Barbados Tourism Authority

PO Box 242
Harbour Road
Bridgetown
Barbados
T: +1809 427 2623
F: +1809 426 4080

London Office:
263 Tottenham Court Road
London W1P 0LA
T: +44 (171) 636 9448
F: +44 (171) 637 1496

New York Office:
800 Second Avenue
New York
NY 10017 USA
T: +1 (212) 986 6516
F: +1 (212) 573 9850

Belize

Belize Tourist Board
PO Box 325
83 North Front Street
Belize City
Belize
T: +501 (2) 77213
F: +501 (2) 77490

London Office:
Caribbean Tourism
Vigilant House
120 Wilton Road
London SW1V 1JZ
T: +44 (171) 233 8382
F: +44 (171) 873 8551

New York Office:
421 Seventh Avenue
New York
NY 10001
USA
T: +1 (212) 563 6011
F: +1 (212) 563 6033

Bhutan

Bhutan Tourism Corporation Ltd
PO Box 159
Thimphu
Bhutan
T: +975 (2) 24045
F: +975 (2) 23392

Bolivia

Dirección Nacional de Turismo, Bolivia
Calle Mercado 1328
Casilla 1868
La Paz
Bolivia
T: +591 (2) 367 463
F: +591 (2) 374 630

Botswana

Department of Tourism
Private Bag 0047
Gaborone
Botswana
T: +267 353024
F: +267 308675

London Office:
6 Stratford Place
London W1N NAE
T: +44 (171) 499 0031
F: +44 (171) 495 8595

Brazil

Tourist Office (CEBITUR)
Rua Mariz e Barros 13
6° andar
Praça da Bandeira,
20270-000 Rio de Janeiro
RJ
Brazil
T: +55 (21) 293 1313
F: +55 (21) 273 9290

London Office:
32 Green Street
London W1Y 4AT
T: +44 (171) 499 0877
F: +44 (171) 493 5105

Cambodia
Ministry of Tourism
3 Monivong Boulevard
Phnom Penh
Cambodia
T: +855 (23) 26107
F: +855 (23) 24607

Canada
Tourism Canada
235 Queen Street
Ottawa
Ontario K1A 0H6
Canada
T: +1 (613) 954 3851
F: +1 (613) 952 7906

London Office:
Visit Canada Centre
62–65 Trafalgar Square
London WC2N 5DT
T: +44 (171) 715 000

Supernatural British Columbia
1117 Wharf Street
Victoria
British Columbia V8W 2Z2
Canada
T: +1 (604) 663 6000
F: +1 (604) 356 8246

Maison du Tourisme
12 Ste Anne Street
Québec City
Québec
Canada

London Office:
59 Pall Mall
London SW1Y 5JH
T: +44 (171) 930 8314
F: +44 (171) 930 7938

New York Office:
Rockefeller Center
17 West 50th Street
New York 10020-2201
USA
T: +1 (212) 397 0200
F: +1 (212) 757 4753

Cape Verde
Instituto Nacional do Turismo
CP294 Chã da Areia
Praia
São Tiago
Cape Verde
T: +238 631173
F: +238 614475

Cayman Islands
Cayman Islands Department of Tourism
The Cricket Square
Elgin Avenue
PO Box 67
Grand Cayman
T: +1809 (94) 90623
F: +1809 (94) 94053

London Office:
6 Arlington Street
London SW1A 1RE
T: +44 (171) 491 7771
F: +44 (171) 409 7773

Chile
Tourism Service
Casilla 14082
Avenida Providencia 1550
Santiago, Chile
T: +56 (2) 696 0474
F: +56 (2) 236 1417

London Office:
12 Devonshire Street
London W1N 2DS
T: +44 (171) 580 6392
F: +44 (171) 436 5204

Colombia

Corporación Nacional de Turismo
Apdo Aéreo 8400
Calle 28 No 13A-15
Santa Fe de Bogotá DC
Colombia
T: +57 (1) 283 9466
F: +57 (1) 284 3818

Cook Islands

Tourist Authority
PO Box 14
Rarotonga
Cook Islands
T: +682 29435
F: +682 21435

London Office:
S Pacific Tourism Council
375 Upper Richmond Road
London SW14 7WX
T: +44 (181) 392 1838
F: +44 (181) 392 1318

Costa Rica

Instituto de Turismo
Apartado 777
Edificio Genaro Valverde
Calles 5 y 7
Avenida 4
1000 San José
Costa Rica
T: +506 223 1733
F: +506 255 4997

Cuba

Empresa de Turismo Internacional (Cubatur)
Calle 23, No 156, entre N y O
Apartado 6560
Vedado
Havana
Cuba
T: +53 (7) 324 521
F: +53 (7) 333 104

London Office:
167 High Holborn
London WC1V 6PA
T: +44 (171) 379 1706
F: +44 (171) 379 5455

Dominica

Dominica Division of Tourism (NDC)
PO Box 73
Valley Road
Roseau
Dominica
T: +1809 448 6032
F: +1809 448 5840

London Office:
Caribbean Tourism
Vigilant House
120 Wilton Road
London SW1V 1JZ
T: +44 (171) 233 8382
F: +44 (171) 873 8551

New York Office:
20 East 46th Street
New York
NY 10017
USA
T: +1 (212) 682 0435
F: +1 (212) 697 4258

Ecuador

Ecuador Tour and Travel Association (ASECUT)
Casilla 9421
Edificio Banco del Pacifico
5 Piso
Avenida Amazonas 720 y Veintimilla
Quito
Ecuador
T: +593 (2) 503 669
F: +593 (2) 285 872

Egypt

Egyptian Tourist Authority
Misr Travel Tower
Abbassia Square
Cairo
Egypt
T: +20 (2) 284 1707
F: +20 (2) 285 9551

London Office:
T: +44 (171) 493 5282

New York Office:
T: +1 (212) 332 2570

El Salvador

Instituto de Turismo
Calle Rubén Dario 619
San Salvador
El Salvador
T: +503 222 0960
F: +503 222 1208

Ethiopia

Commission for Tourism
PO Box 2183
Addis Ababa
Ethiopia
T: +251 (1) 517 470
F: +251 (1) 513 899

Falklands

Falkland Islands Tourist Board
Old Transmitting Station
Stanley
East Falkland
T: +500 22215
F: +500 22619

London Office:
Falkland House
14 Broadway
London SW1H 0BH
T: +44 (171) 222 2542
F: +44 (171) 222 2375

Fiji

Ministry of Tourism
GPO Box 2220
Suva
Fiji
T: +679 312 788
F: +679 302 060

London Office:
address as for Cook Islands

French Guiana
Bureau of Tourism
BP 801
12 rue de Lalouette
97338 Cayenne
French Guiana
T: +594 300 900
F: +594 309 315

The Gambia
Ministry of Tourism
New Administration Building
Banjul
The Gambia
T: +220 226706

London Office:
57 Kensington Court
London W8 5DG
T: +44 (171) 376 0093
F: +44 (171) 937 9095

Germany
DRV Internationale
Umweltauszeichnung
Deutscher Reisebüro-Verband e.V.
Mannheimer Strasse 15
D-6000 Frankfurt 1
Germany
T: +49 (69) 2739 0724
[Industry body for German travel and tour operators]

Ghana
Ministry of Tourism
PO Box 4386 Accra
Ghana
T: +233 (21) 666314
F: +233 (21) 666182

Guatemala
Tourist Commission
7 Avenida 1–17
Centro Cívico
Zona 4 Guatemala City
Guatemala
T: +502 (2) 311 333
F: +502 (2) 318 893

Guernsey
States of Guernsey Tourist Board
PO Box 23
St Peter Port
GY1 3AN
Guernsey
T: +44 (1481) 723 552
F: +44 (1481) 721 246

Guyana
Tourism Association of Guyana
Hotel Tower
74–75 Main Street
Georgetown
Guyana
T: +592 (2) 72011
F: +592 (2) 65691

Guyana Overland Tours
PO Box 10173
48 Prince's and Russell Streets
Charlestown
Georgetown
Guyana
T: +592 (2) 69876

Haiti

Office National du Tourisme d'Haiti
Avenue Marie-Jeanne
Port-au-Prince
Haiti
T: +509 221 729

Honduras

Instituto de Turismo
Apartado Postal 3261
Centro Guanacaste
Barrio Guanacaste
Tegucigalpa
Honduras
T: +504 383 975
F: +504 382 102

Honolulu

State Office of Tourism
PO Box 2359
Suite 1100
220 South King Street
Honolulu HI 96804
USA
T: +1 (808) 586 2550
F: +1 (808) 586 2549

India

Department of Tourism, India
Parliament Street
New Delhi 110 001
India
T: +91 (11) 371 4114
F: +91 (11) 371 0518

London Office:
7 Cork Street
London W1X 2LN
T: +44 (171) 437 3677
F: +44 (171) 494 1048

New York Office:
Suite 15
30 Rockefeller Plaza
New York
NY 10020
USA
T: +1 (212) 586 4901
F: +1 (212) 582 3274

Indonesia

Direktorat Jenderal Pariwisata Indonesia
16/19 Jalan Merdeka-Barat
Jakarta 10110
Indonesia
T: +62 (21) 386 0822
F: +62 (21) 386 7589

London Office:
3–4 Hanover Street
London W1R 9HH
T: +44 (171) 493 0030
F: +44 (171) 493 1747

Isle of Man

Department of Tourism and Leisure
Sea Terminal Buildings
Douglas
IM1 2RG
Isle of Man
T: +44 (1624) 686 801
F: +44 (1624) 686 800

Jamaica

Jamaica Tourist Board
2 St Lucia Avenue
Kingston 5
Jamaica
T: +1809 929 9200
F: +1809 929 9375

London Office:
1–2 Prince Consort Road
London SW7 2BZ
T: +44 (171) 224 0505
F: +44 (171) 224 0551

New York Office:
20th Floor
801 Second Avenue
New York
NY 10017
USA
T: +1 (212) 856 9727
F: +1 (212) 856 9655

Jersey

Jersey Tourism
Liberation Square
St Helier
JE1 1BB
Jersey
T: +44 (1534) 500 700
F: +44 (1534) 500 899

Kenya

Kenya Tourist Corporation
PO Box 42013
Utalii House
Uhuru Highway
Nairobi
Kenya
T: +254 (2) 330820
F: +254 (2) 227815

London Office:
25 Brook's Mews
London W1Y 1LF
T: +44 (171) 355 3144
F: +44 (171) 495 8656

New York Office:
424 Madison Avenue
New York
NY 10017
USA
T: +1 (212) 486 1300
F: +1 (212) 688 0911

Laos

Tourism Department
Ministry of Tourism
BP 3556
Vientiane
Laos
T: +856 (21) 217151

Lesotho

Lesotho Tourist Board
4th Floor
Christie House
Orpen Road
PO Box 1378
Maseru 100
Lesotho
T: +266 313760
F: +266 310108

Madagascar

Maison de Tourisme
BP 610
Tsimbazaza
101 Antananarivo
Madagascar
T: +261 (2) 26298
F: +261 (2) 26710

Malawi

Department of Tourism
PO Box 402
Blantyre
Malawi
T: +265 620 300
F: +265 620 947

London Office:
33 Grosvenor Street
London W1X 0DE
T: +44 (171) 491 4172
F: +44 (171) 491 9916

Malaysia

Tourism Promotion Board
17th, 24th–27th & 30th Floors
Menara Dato' Onn
Putra World Trade Centre
45 Jalan Tun Ismail
50480 Kuala Lumpur
Malaysia
T: +60 (3) 293 5188
F: +60 (3) 293 5884

London Office:
57 Trafalgar Square
London WC2N 5DU
T: +44 (171) 930 7932
F: +44 (171) 930 9015

Maldives

Ministry of Tourism, Maldives
Boduthaku/Rufaanu Magu
Malé 20-05
Maldives Republic
T: +960 323 224
F: +960 322 512

Mali

Ministry of Tourism
BP 1759
Bamako
Mali
T: +223 228058
F: +223 230261

Mauritius

Mauritius Tourism Authority
Emmanuel Anquetil Building
Port-Louis
Mauritius
T: +230 201 1703
F: +230 208 5142

Mexico

Fondo Nacional de Fomento al Turismo
17th Floor, Insurgentes Sur 800
Colonia del Valle
03100 México DF
Mexico
T: +52 (5) 687 2697

London Office:
60–61 Trafalgar Square
London WC2N 5DS
T: +44 (171) 734 1058
F: +44 (171) 930 9202

New York Office:
Suite 1401
405 Park Avenue
New York NY 10022
USA
T: +1 (212) 755 7261

Morocco

Morocco Tourism Office
31 Angle rue Oued Fes
Avenue Abtal
Agdal
Rabat
Morocco
T: +212 (7) 68 15 31
F: +212 (7) 77 74 37

London Office:
T: +44 (171) 437 0073

New York Office:
T: +1 (212) 557 2520

Namibia

Ministry of Environment and Tourism of Namibia
Private Bag 13346
Windhoek
Namibia
T: +264 (61) 284 2111
F: +264 (61) 221 930

London Office:
T: +44 (171) 636 2924

Nepal

Department of Tourism, Nepal
Patan Dhoka
Lalitpur
Kathmandu
Nepal
T: +977 (1) 523 692
F: +977 (1) 527 852

New Zealand

New Zealand Tourism Board
PO Box 95
256 Lambton Quay
Wellington
New Zealand
T: +64 (4) 472 8860
F: +64 (4) 478 1736

Nicaragua

Inturismo
Hotel Intercontinental
Nicaragua
T: +505 (2) 281 137
F: +505 (2) 281 187

Pakistan

Tourism Division, Government of Pakistan
13-T/U College Road
Commercial Area
Markaz F-7
Islamabad 44000
Pakistan
T: +92 (51) 827 024
F: +92 (51) 815 767

Panama

Instituto de Turismo
Apartado 4421
Centro de Convenciones ATLAPA
Vía Israel
Panamá 5
Republic of Panama
T: +507 226 3167
F: +507 226 3483

Papua New Guinea

Tourism Promotion Authority
PO Box 7144
Boroko
Papua New Guinea
T: +675 272 310
F: +675 259 119

Paraguay

Dirección General de Turismo
Palma 468
Asunción
Paraguay
T: +595 (21) 441 530
F: +595 (21) 491 230

Peru

Fondo de Promoción Turística
Calle Uno
s/n Urb. Corpac
Lima 27
Peru
T: +51 (1) 224 3142
F: +51 (1) 224 3133

Philippines

Philippines Department of Tourism
Teodoro Valencia Circle
T.M. Kalaw Street
Ermita
Manila 1000
Philippines
T: +632 (5) 23 84 11
F: +632 (5) 26 49 55

London Office:
17 Albemarle Street
London W1X 7HA
T: +44 (171) 499 5443
F: +44 (171) 499 5772

Senegal

Ministry of Tourism
BP 4049, 23 rue Calmette
Dakar, Senegal
T: +221 236 502
F: +221 229 413

Seychelles

*Seychelles Ministry of Tourism &
Transport*
Independence House
PO Box 92
Mahé
The Seychelles
T: +248 225 313
F: +248 224 035

London Office:
T: +44 (171) 224 1670

Singapore

Tourist Promotion Board
Raffles City Tower #32-01
250 North Bridge Road
Singapore 0617
T: +65 339 6622
F: +65 339 9423

London Office:
1st Floor, Carrington House
126–130 Regent Street
London W1R 5FE
T: +44 (171) 437 0033
F: +44 (171) 734 2191

New York Office:
NBR
12th Floor, 590 Fifth Avenue
New York NY 10036
USA
T: +1 (212) 302 4861
F: +1 (212) 302 4801

Solomon Islands

Tourist Authority
PO Box 321
Honiara
Solomon Islands
T: +677 22442
F: +677 23986

New York Office:
c/o Suite 800B
820 Second Avenue
New York NY 10017
USA
T: +1 (212) 599 6194
F: +1 (212) 661 8925

South Africa

South Africa Tourist Board
442 Rigel Avenue South
Erasmusrand 0181
(Private Bag X164)
Pretoria 0001
South Africa
T: +27 (12) 347 0600
F: +27 (12) 454 889

London Office:
T: +44 (181) 944 8080

New York Office:
T: +1 (212) 730 2929

Sri Lanka

Sri Lanka Tourist Board
PO Box 1504
78 Stewart Place
Colombo 3
Sri Lanka
T: +94 (1) 437 059
F: +94 (1) 437 953

London Office:
22 Regent Street
London SW1Y 4QD
T: +44 (171) 930 2627
F: +44 (171) 930 9070

Surinam

Suriname Tourism Company
Rudielaan 5
Paramaribo
Suriname
T: +597 492 892
F: +597 497 062

Tahiti

Tahiti Tourisme
BP 65, Fare Manihini
Boulevard Pomare
Papeete
Tahiti
T: +689 505700
F: +689 436 619

London Office:
c/o Maison de la France
178 Piccadilly
London W1V 0AL
T: +44 (171) 629 2869
F: +44 (171) 493 6594

Tanzania

Tanzania Tourist Board
PO Box 2485
Dar es Salaam
Tanzania
T: +255 (51) 27672
F: +255 (51) 46780

Thailand

Tourism Authority
372 Bamrung Muang Road
Bangkok 10100
Thailand
T: +66 (2) 226 0060
F: +66 (2) 226 6227

London Office:
49 Albemarle Street
London W1X 3FE
T: +44 (171) 499 7679
F: +44 (171) 629 5519

New York Office:
5 World Trade Center
New York NY 10048
USA
T: +1 (212) 432 0433
F: +1 (212) 912 0920

Trinidad & Tobago

Tourism Trinidad and Tobago
10–14 Philip Street
Port of Spain
Trinidad
T: +1809 624 2953
F: +1809 623 4056

Tunisia

Office National du Tourisme
1 avenue Mohamed V
1002 Tunis
Tunisia
T: +216 (1) 341 077
F: +216 (1) 350 997

London Office:
77A Wigmore Street
London W1H 9LJ
T: +44 (171) 224 5561
F: +44 (171) 224 4053

Uganda

Uganda Tourist Board
PO Box 7211
Parliament Avenue
Kampala
Uganda
T: +256 (41) 242 196
F: +256 (41) 242 188

United Kingdom

British Tourist Authority and English Tourist Board
Thames Tower
Black's Road
London W6 9EL
T: +44 (181) 846 9000
F: +44 (181) 563 0302

Tourist Board of Northern Ireland
59 North Street
Belfast BT1 1NB
Northern Ireland
T: +44 (1232) 246609
F: +44 (1232) 240960

Scottish Tourist Board
PO Box 705
Edinburgh EH4 3EU
Scotland
T: +44 (131) 332 2433
F: +44 (131) 343 1513

Wales Tourist Board
Brunel House
2 Fitzalan House
Cardiff CF1 2UY
Wales
T: +44 (1222) 499 909
F: +44 (1222) 485 031

USA

United States Travel & Tourism Administration
14th and Constitution Avenue, NW
Washington, DC 20230
USA
T: +1 (202) 482 3811
F: +1 (202) 482 2887

State Division of Tourism
524 West Fourth Avenue
Anchorage
Alaska AK 99501-2212
USA
T: +1 (907) 465 2010
F: +1 (907) 465 2287

Arizona Office of Tourism
2702 North 3rd Street
4015 Phoenix
AZ 85004
USA
T: +1 (602) 230 7733
F: +1 (602) 240 5475

Division of Tourism
PO Box 1499
801 K Street
Suite 1600
Sacramento
California CA 95812
USA
T: +1 (916) 322 2881
F: +1 (916) 322 3402

London Office:
52–54 High Holborn
London WC1V 6RB
T: +44 (171) 405 4746
F: +44 (171) 242 2838

Florida Division of Tourism
Suite 566, Collins Building
107 West Gaines Street
Tallahassee
FL 32399-2000
USA
T: +1 (904) 488 5607
F: +1 (904) 487 0134

State Division of Tourism
633 3rd Avenue
New York
NY 10017
USA
T: +1 (212) 803 2247
F: +1 (212) 803 2279

State Tourism Office
17100 North Congress
Suite 200
PO Box 12728
Austin
TX 78711-2728
USA
T: +1 (512) 462 9191
F: +1 (512) 936 0089

US Ecotourism Society
PO Box 755, North Bennington
Vermont 05257
USA
T: +1 (802) 447 2121
F: +1 (802) 447 2122

US National Wildlife Federation
Educational Outreach Department
8923 Leesburg Pike
Vienna
Virginia 22184-0001
USA
T: +1 (703) 790 4055

Vanuatu

National Tourism Office
PO Box 209
Kumul Highway
Port Vila
Vanuatu
T: +678 22515
F: +678 23889

Venezuela

Corporacion de Turismo
Av. Lecuna
Parque Central
Torre Oeste
Piso 37
Caracas
Venezuela

Vietnam

Vietnam Tourism
69–71 Ngyun Hue Blvd.
Ho Chi Minh City
Vietnam
T: +84 (8) 291276

London Office:
West-East Travel
271 King Street
London W6 9LZ
T: +44 (181) 741 1158
F: +44 (181) 563 0969

Zambia

National Tourist Board
Century House
Cairo Road
PO Box 30017
Lusaka
Zambia
T: +260 (1) 229087
F: +260 (1) 225174

London Office:
T: +44 (171) 509 6343

New York Office:
T: +1 (212) 972 7200

Zimbabwe

*Zimbabwe Tourist Development
Corporation*
PO Box CY286
Causeway
Harare
Zimbabwe
T: +263 (4) 793 666
F: +263 (4) 793 669

London Office:
T: +44 (171) 836 7755

New York Office:
T: +1 (212) 332 1090

CHAPTER 18
NOW READ ON...
RECENT SOURCES OF
INFORMATION AND FURTHER
READING

BOOKS AND MANUALS

This is not an exhaustive list, but it covers most of the bases the non-specialist Green Traveller might want to know about and a few more, concentrating on key and easy-to-get works and on recent books mentioned in the text of this Guide.

Archer, B et al (eds) (1996) *Sustainable Tourism in Islands and Small States: Issues and Policies* Pinter Publications [First of a series on tourism's impacts on the Third World]

Badger, A et al (eds) (1996) *Trading Places: Tourism as Trade Tourism Concern* [Assesses effects of macro-economic policies, introduces principles of Fair Trade in tourism]

Baird, N (1998) *The Estate We're In* Indigo [An easy-to-read assault on the excesses of car culture]

Baker, C et al (eds) (1996) *World Travel: A Guide to International Ecojourneys* Time-Life [In Nature Company Guides series, lists 68 wild venues worldwide]

Bramwell, B and B Lane (1995) *Rural Tourism and Sustainable Rural Development* Channel View Books [Proceedings of (1993) conference, mainly EU emphasis]

Briguglio, L (1996) *Sustainable Tourism in Islands and Small States: Island Case Studies* Pinter Publications

Cater, E and G Lowman (eds) (1994) *Ecotourism: A Sustainable Option?* J Wiley and Sons [Sound round-up from a wide array of viewpoints, still fairly current]

Ceballos-Lascuráin, H (ed) (1996) *Tourism, Ecotourism and Protected Areas* World Conservation Union [Relevant legal instruments and treaties]

Coccossis, H and Nijkamp, P (1995) *Sustainable Tourism Development* Avebury

Croall, J (1995) *Preserve or Destroy: Tourism and the Environment* Calouste Gulbenkian Foundation [Perceptive angles, especially on UK and Ireland situations]

Eber, S (ed) (1992) *Beyond the Green Horizon: Principles for Sustainable Tourism* Tourism Concern and WWF-UK [Guidelines and case studies, sound student text]

Elkington, J and Hailes, J (1992) *Holidays that Don't Cost the Earth* Victor Gollancz

Foehr, S (1992) *Eco-Journeys: World Travel Guide to Ecologically Aware Travel and Adventure* Noble [Lists over 100 challenging destinations, includes working holidays]

Forsyth, T (1996) *Sustainable Tourism: Moving from Theory to Practice* Tourism Concern and WWF-UK [Surveys tourism 'greening' in Britain and strongly questions worth of self-regulation]

France, L (ed) (1997) *The Earthscan Reader in Sustainable Tourism*, Earthscan, London

Geffen, A and C Berglie (1993) *Ecotours and Nature Getaways* Clarkson Potter [Already slightly dated guide to 'environmental vacations around the world']

Grotta, D and S Wiener Grotta (1992) *The Green Travel Sourcebook* J Wiley and Sons [Aimed at 'the physically active, intellectually curious and socially aware']

Harris, R and N Leiper (1995) *Sustainable Tourism: An Australian Perspective* Butterworth Architecture [Telling case studies of Australian tourism 'greening']

Hunter, C and H Green (1995) *Tourism and the Environment: A Sustainable Relationship?* Van Nostrand Reinhold

Inskeep, E (1991) *Tourism Planning: An Integrated and Sustainable Development Approach* Van Nostrand Reinhold [Sensible guidelines for disciplined planning]

Krotz, L (1997) *Tourists* Faber (USA) [Focus on what makes tourists and their hosts tick rather than tourism in general. Full of anecdotes and offbeat figures]

Lane, B and B Bramwell (1997) *Sustainable Tourism: Principles and Practice* John Wiley and Sons [Up-to-date professorial overview with good reference add-ons]

Laplanche, S (1996) *Stepping Lightly on Australia: a Traveller's Guide to Ecotourism* Globe Pequot [Nicely put together although prone to counsels of perfection]

McIntyre, G (1993) *Sustainable Tourism Development: A Guide for Local Planners* Unipub [Handy practical and policy blueprints for the planner]

McNeely, J A et al (1994) *Protecting Nature: Regional Reviews of Protected Areas* Findings from IVth World Congress on National Parks and Protected Areas, Caracas, Venezuela, World Conservation Union (IUCN) [Comprehensive horse's-mouth account of people, parks and wildlife dilemmas, issues and solutions]

Nelson, J G et al (eds) (1993) *Tourism and Sustainable Development: Monitoring, Planning, Managing* University of Waterloo

Priestly, G K et al (eds) (1996) *Sustainable Tourism? European Experiences* CAB International

Seabrook, J (1997) *Travels in the Skin Trade: Tourism and the Sex Industry* Pluto Press [Non-sensationalist but scary look at sex tourism issues and cases]

Sidu, S (1994) *Aviation and Sustainable Tourism: Emerging Trends* South Asia Books [Stodgy but informative look at air travel from a Southern viewpoint]

Strauss, R (1996) *Adventure Trekking: A Handbook for Independent Travelers* Mountaineers Books [Gung-ho but green in the right places]

Tribe, J (1996) *The Economics of Leisure and Tourism* Butterworth-Heinemann [Mainly on hardcore trade and economics concerns, some green issues]

UNEPIE (UN Environment Programme Industry and Environment Programme, Paris) (1996) *Environmental Good Practice in Hotels* UNEP/IHRA, Paris

UNEPIE (1996) *Awards for Improving the Coastal Environment: the example of Blue Flag* UNEP/WTO/ FEEE

Wahab, S and J Pigram (eds) (1997) *Tourism, Sustainability and Growth* Routledge

Whelan, T (ed) (1991) *Nature Tourism: Managing for the Environment* Island Press [Brisk and practical milestone work although by now slightly dated]

Wong, P P (ed) (1993) *Tourism vs Environment: The Case for Coastal Areas* Geojournal Library Vol 26, Kluwer Academic [Not new but still valuable]

Wood, K, J Waldren and S House (1991) *The Good Tourist Guide* Mandarin Books

JOURNALS AND NEWSLETTERS

In Focus, the newsletter of Tourism Concern, offers vivid commentaries on tourism and development in a low-budget format. Also available through Tourism Concern is *Contours*, the Bulletin of the Ecumenical Coalition on Third World Tourism. *Tourism Focus*, an irregular publication of UNEPIE, Paris, highlights case studies of better practice and outcomes of recent conferences. The Conservation Foundation's *Network 21* magazine, published twice a year, usually features tourism articles as part of a global remit 'to network information encouraged by Agenda 21' and coverage of the Ford Conservation Awards for Europe. The World Trade Organisation issues annual forecasts of tourism statistics and market trends in print and online and a quarterly *Travel and Tourism Barometer*, as well as a newsletter for local planners on sustainable tourism development. See Chapter 17, Connections, above, for contact details. For a more academic approach providing detailed research and case studies on a wide range of tourism topics, Elsevier Science publishes a regular international journal, *Annals of Tourism Research*.

ONLINE RESOURCES

Today, Internet and e-mail are the most dynamic and responsive sources of information and interactive debate on all aspects of travel and tourism. On-line facilities offer up-to-the-minute information on holiday opportunities, discussion groups on ethical issues and scope for independent research into the local realities that prevail in and around tourism destinations. In fact on-line information is such an active growth area that no list of sites can remain definitive for long. The following recommendations are handy places to start but not the only ones that you'll find. Go surfing!

A good place to start is the Eco-Source web site www.podi.com/ecosource set up by the former US travel industry executive Carolyn Hill. Eco-Source hot-links include:

- Eco-Orbit E-Zine, an online ecotourism and sustainable tourism magazine
- Adventure Travel Society Inc, an ethical corporation promoting tourism with integrity
- EarthWise Journeys, an independent resource for responsible adventure travel
- TravelSource Eco Tours, a world list of tour operators currently offering ecotours
- Tour Operators, another list of tour operators with a search niche for ecotourism
- One World Travel, a not-for-profit ethical travel agency run by Community Aid Abroad
- Ecotourism Research, a site about new ideas in ecotourism, including an online game
- Adventure Tour Directory, over 20 adventure travel catalogues, including ecotours

Environmental sites are also listed comprehensively in several crossroads sites such as www.yahoo.com http://altavista.digital.com or www.hotbot.com These are very comprehensive sites, for example if you search for ecotourism, adventure tourism or cultural tourism you are likely to get literally thousands of potential sites and hot-links to more, so you will need to refine your search down to more specific enquiries. In fact you can find almost anything from a city guide to practically any city in the world, to help on how to use the internet to plan your holiday.

If you don't have time to browse, other more specific sites for environment and tourism include:

www.traveler.net/two/	Weekly Travel Online journal
www.wtgonline.com	World Travel Guide set up by AT&T with Columbus Internet
www.ecomanage.com/ecobriefs.html	International Society for Eco-Tourism
www.unepie.org/contact.html	UN Environment Programme
www.ecouncil.ac.cr	Earth Council
www.wttc.org	ECoNETT Project Office (at World Travel and Tourism Council)
www.oneworld.org/tourconcern	Tourism Concern
www.ecotourism.org/guid.html	Ecotourism Explorer, guidelines for Nature Tour Operators
www.lonelyplanet.com	Lonely Planet site with access to country-specific information
www.cedro.ab.ca/index.html	Centre for Environmental Design Research and Outreach
www.cedro.ab.ca/culturaltourism	ICOMOS links on cultural tourism
www.international.icomos.org/icomos/e_touris.htm	ICOMOS conservation of monuments

www.atlas-euro.org/cultour.htm	ATLAS Cultural Tourism Research Programme
www.culturalawareness.com/home.html	Cultural Awareness International, training
www.british-airways.com	British Airways Tourism for Tomorrow (tourism award scheme)
www.eldertreks.com/other.html	Elder Treks worldwide adventure travel for the over 50s
www.handilinks.com.cat1/t/t189.htm	Complete Tour Operators Directory, Guide, Links
www.ran.org/info_center/ecotourism.html	Includes case studies, and how to pick a tour
www.gwu.edu/iits/journal/ecowhat.htm	Journal on tourism, hospitality and event management
www.ecole-adventures.com/freebies.html	Ecole Adventures International, online freebies
www.escapeartist.com	Escape Artist, American site, information for work and travel overseas
http://earthrise.sdsc.edu/earthrise/main.html	aerial photographs from the space shuttle
www.terraquest.com	Virtual Travel site – the utimate low-impact travel experience

A few examples of country and activity specific sites that can be found from browsing cross-roads sites include:

www.clarionmusic.com/education/education.html	Cultural awareness through the world's music
http://puravidaspa.com/ecotours3.html	Costa Rica, ecotourism, adventure and spiritual tours
www.ecoventurebrazil.com/whyeco.htm	Brazil, ecotourism/adventure trips in national parks
http://eco-america.com/	Ecotourism in Latin America and hot links to ecotourism worldwide
http://bcadventure.com/nechakolodge/index.html	British Columbia, wilderness adventures
www.dist.gov.au/tourism/publications/talktour/html/page9.html	Indigenous tourism, Australia
www.east-cape.co.za/tourism/adventure.htm	Eastern Cape Province, South Africa, official site
www.biopark.org/sprtqu3.html	International Biopark Foundation, indigenous medicine tours
www.phuket.com/conservation/	Thailand, Asian Elephant Conservation/

elephants.htm	ecotourism
www.tourism.gov.au/ecotour/ecotip.html	Ecotourism tips for travellers to Australia
www.tourism.gov.au/ecotour/ecoacred.html Australia,	National Ecotourism Accreditation
www.kingresearch.com/jk/bcp/nz.html	Scott Ellington's cycle trip in Australia/New Zealand 1994
www.thetripmaker.com/	Access to wide range of adventure travel, expeditions and outdoor sports
www.discovery1.com/	Jordan, desert adventure, excavations, conferences and conventions
www.fijifvb.gov.fj/ecotour/ecotour.htm	Fiji, official information on nature, culture and adventure
www.kiwiadv.co.nz/EcoTourism.htm	New Zealand and ecotourism/adventure holidays
www.gov.im/tourism	Official information on tourism in the Isle of Man

Other online addresses are included (where available) in Chapter 17, Connections and in the contact details accompanying the main text of Sections One and Two of this Guide.

INDEX

EARTHSCAN

Ecotourism and Sustainable Development
Martha Honey

Ecotourism is defined as responsible travel in natural areas which conserves the environment and improves the welfare of the local people. *Ecotourism and Sustainable Development* presents a vivid first hand account of ecotourism projects around the world with in-depth case studies of seven destinations (Galapagos, Costa Rica, Cuba, Zanzibar, Tanzania, Kenya and South Africa). It examines ecotourism's feasibility for economic development and environmental protection in developing countries and takes a unique and compelling look at the promise and pitfalls of ecotourism.

Pb £18.95 1 55963 582 7 *Island Press*

Not for sale in North America and Australasia

Shadows in the Sun
Travels to Landscapes of Spirit and Desire
Wade Davis

'Wade Davis is a rare combination of scientist and scholar, poet and passionate defender of all life's diversity. His writing is a joy to read, exhilarating in the scale of its vision and compelling in its urgent implications' David Suzuki

A series of enthralling and wide-ranging journeys take us from a voodoo sorcerer's den to Tibetan temples; from the depths of the Amazon to the Arctic tundra. The writing celebrates the richness of historical depth and the diversity of indigenous cultures and alerts us to the threats they face.

Hb £18.99 1 55963 354 9 *Island Press*

Not for sale in North America and Australasia

Earthscan Reader in Environmental Tourism
Edited by Lesley France

Finding environmentally sustainable forms of tourism is crucial, but establishing the criteria and guidelines for responsible tourism has proved extremely difficult. This volume brings together the most penetrating and influential contributions to this growing debate. It is the benchmark and sourcebook for the growing range of leisure and tourism studies courses and for those in the industries concerned to understand and resolve the issues.

Pb £16.95 1 85383 408 4

The Living Ocean
Second Edition
Boyce Thorne-Miller

'superbly explains marine biological diversity, shows how our protective systems are failing, and makes sound suggestions for the future' Frank Talbot, director, National Museum of Natural History, Smithsonian Institution

The importance of biodiversity to planetary health and even human survival is now undisputed, yet surprisingly little information exists about the importance of marine biodiversity. Highly praised in its first edition, this book will continue to be a vital tool for environmentalists, policy makers and all those concerned with the conservation of our marine environments.

Paperback £15.95 1 55963 678 5 *Island Press*

Not for sale in North America and Australasia

State of the World 1999
Lester R Brown, The Worldwatch Institute

'Essential reading' *The Good Book Guide*

'The environmentalist's bible' *Times Higher Education Supplement*

State of the World 1999 presents a clear and concise view of our changing world that we and our leaders cannot afford to ignore. The 16th edition of this authoritative annual review takes an insightful look at the sweeping changes of the last 100 years and the challenges we face in the next century to build a sustainable economy that reuses and recycles materials, is powered by renewable energy sources and has a stable population. It provides us with a framework for the global debate about our future in the 21st century and a guide to emerging solutions.

Pb £14.95 1 85383 594 3

Not for sale in the USA and Canada

The Natural Wealth of Nations
David M Roodman, The Worldwatch Institute

Every year, the world's governments spend over $700 billion subsidizing activities that harm the environment. This book shows how cutting these wasteful subsidies can actually boost the economy, save tax and help the environment. By raising taxes on harmful activities like air pollution whilst cutting taxes on payrolls and profits, pollution is discouraged and both work and investment boosted. This comprehensive global survey provides examples from Sweden to Spain to Malaysia of the growing number of countries that are successfully using market-based approaches to clean up their environments.

Pb £12.95 1 85383 592 7

Not for sale in the USA and Canada

Factor Four
Doubling Wealth, Halving Resource Use
Ernst von Weizsäcker, Amory B Lovins and L Hunter Lovins

'One of the 1990s' most important books' Geoff Mulgan, Head of Social Policy, Prime Minister's Office

'if you read one book this year, make it this one, it really is very clever indeed' *Social and Environmental Accounting*

'*Factor Four* made my spine tingle. This is a book which captures the moment, which crystallizes a set of seemingly conflicting trends and issues around a simple idea – that by organizing our economies around the principle of "resource productivity", as opposed to labour productivity, we can, in Lovins' words, "live twice as well – yet use half as much"' *Tomorrow* 'the message of a radical, profitable and sustainable change comes through loud and clear' *Nature*

'*Factor Four* is well-documented, punchy, and clearly written, often brilliantly incisive, full of information and original proposals' *People & the Planet*

Factor Four is about 'doing more with less', but this 'is not the same as doing worse or doing without'.

Pb £9.99   1 85383 406 8   Colour plates

Richer Futures
Fashioning a New Politics
Edited by Ken Worpole

In every area of life, traditional, centralized, party politics has been failing, and the seeds of a new form of political life are being sown. This is true in housing, in education, transport, consumption and many other areas. In all of them new forms of communication, decision-making and self-help within and between communities are emerging. This uplifting collection of essays, by many of the best known thinkers and writers on these subjects in Britain today, charts the rise of these new solutions, showing how much richer our lives can become in the process. All of the writers here acknowledge an explicit debt to the work of Colin Ward (who also contributes to the volume) over the last few decades, in finding innovative forms of self-help, cultural invigoration and sustainable living.

Pb £12.95   1 85383 539 0

Which World?
Global Destinies, Regional Choices – Scenarios for the 21st Century
Allen Hammond, World Resources Institute

'It is past time that [we] began to steer [the planet] along a course of long-term sustainability. For this we need a lot of knowledge and a bit of vision. In *Which World?* Allen Hammond offers both' Stephan Schmidheiny, Founder of the World Business Council for Sustainable Development

Allen Hammond explores several possible worlds, each embodying a different vision of the future: Market World, Fortress World and Transformed World. Present social, economic and environmental trends in the ten major continental regions are analysed to show what may happen in each. But the book does not make predictions – our destiny is not predetermined and the different worlds imply a choice: which world do we want to pass on to our children and grandchildren?

Hb £18.99   1 85383 582 X
Not for sale in the USA and Canada

The Green Web
A Union for World Conservation
Martin Holdgate

In the last 50 years, conservation and the natural environment have become matters of huge public and political concern all over the world. At the very centre of this concern is an organization which has been described as the conservation world's 'best-kept secret' – the World Conservation Union (IUCN). A unique organization in many respects, it has done more than any other single body to orchestrate action on behalf of the natural world.

In *The Green Web*, Martin Holdgate gives us a thorough and engrossing history of the IUCN and its achievements, and of the surrounding developments of conservation activity throughout the world.

Drawing fully on archives and interviews with past and present members of the Union, he reveals the often turbulent story behind its work and the success it has achieved in establishing the environment as a priority for governments and voters.

Pb £17.50 1 85383 595 1 Photographs

■■■■■■■■

Forests of Hope
Stories of Regeneration
Christian Küchli

'An extremely readable book with a hopeful message that deserves to reach a wide audience' J P Jeanrenaud, WWF International

'This book presents the experiences of a range of fascinating characters, showing how the lives of peoples and communities are becoming integrated with the preservation, use and enjoyment of forests' Ian Rowlands, *Living Earth*

'refreshing to come across a book that presents positive stories of forest conservation' *Nature*

Drawing on his intimate knowledge of forest ecosystems, Christian Küchli introduces us to many of the most remarkable achievements of individuals and communities using and enjoying the forests around them – from the Chagga tribespeople in Tanzania to the TreePeople of Los Angeles. Each chapter is set in a different country and is accompanied by stunning photography.

Pb £19.99 1 85383 505 6 180 Colour photographs

■■■■■■■■

The Work of Nature
How the Diversity of Life Sustains Us
Yvonne Baskin

'a text that carries you as strongly as a Stephen King thriller… Baskin tackles some of the most difficult questions…This is an ecology text to curl up with' *New Scientist*

'should be widely read and discussed. Indeed, it should be required reading' *BioScience*

'a well-written popular account of the recent investigations of community ecologists and ecosystem scientists whose findings are relevant to ecosystem services' *Nature*

It is the lavish array of organisms known as 'biodiversity' which makes the earth a uniquely habitable planet. Yet pressures from human activities are destroying biodiversity at an unprecedented rate. While we have begun to accept the importance of biological diversity in providing food, shelter, clothing and industrial products, most people do not appreciate that biodiversity provides us with such basics as clean air and water. *The Work of Nature* is a superbly attractive and accessible book on the practical consequences of declining biodiversity, on ecosystem health and function, and on human society.

Pb £14.95 1 55963 520 7 Illustrations *Island Press*

Not for sale in North America and Australasia

EARTHSCAN
For more details contact:
Earthscan Publications Ltd, 120 Pentonville Road, London, N1 9JN
T: +44 (171) 278 0433   F: +44 (171) 278 1142
E: earthinfo@earthscan.co.uk   URL: www.earthscan.co.uk